"*Let This Radicalize You* is part handbook, part liberatory vision, designed to inspire you to deepen your involvement in radical movements while accompanying you along the way. Holding hope amid a dystopian world, Kelly Hayes and Mariame Kaba created a book that will serve our movements for years to come." —**Ejeris Dixon**, coeditor, *Beyond Survival: Strategies and Stories from the Transformative Justice Movement*

"The compounding crises of this era can so easily drive us into paralysis and despair. This beautiful book pulls us instead toward a politics rooted in our deepest values of care, compassion, and community. Kelly Hayes and Mariame Kaba have created a visionary and urgently needed guide to cultivating hope and action in treacherous times." —**L.A. Kauffman**, author, *Direct Action: Protest and the Reinvention of American Radicalism*

"Kelly Hayes and Mariame Kaba have produced one of the most essential treatises on mutual aid ever written. It begins and ends with the reality that any movement that truly wants to remake the world has to be founded on one unshakeable principle: care. *Let This Radicalize You* is a letter addressed to our vulnerable hearts, reminding us that our love, support, and solidarity really can build a whole new world." —**Shane Burley**, author, *Why We Fight: Essays on Fascism, Resistance, and Surviving the Apocalypse*

The Abolitionist Papers Series

Edited by Naomi Murakawa

Also in this series:

Rehearsals for Living
Robyn Maynard and Leanne Betasamosake Simpson
Foreword by Ruth Wilson Gilmore
Afterword by Robin D. G. Kelley

Abolition. Feminism. Now.
Angela Y. Davis, Gina Dent, Erica R. Meiners, and Beth E. Richie

We Do This 'Til We Free Us:
Abolitionist Organizing and Transforming Justice
Mariame Kaba, edited by Tamara K. Nopper

PRAISE FOR *LET THIS RADICALIZE YOU*

"This is a prophetic work, one that will be pressed with great urgency into the palms of friends and comrades, kin and colleagues, and anyone else ready to rise up against machineries of mass death. With great clarity and generosity, Hayes and Kaba model how participants in movements can be tough on systems while being gentle with one another and themselves, nurturing a 'counterculture of care' as an integral part of building the next world." —**Naomi Klein**, author, *On Fire: The (Burning) Case for a Green New Deal*

"In this time of perpetual crisis, when too many of our movements are imploding and the work often feels soul crushing, Kelly Hayes and Mariame Kaba have turned decades of collective wisdom and experience into the text we desperately need right now. This book will radicalize even the 'radicals' by reminding us that to be radical is not to have all the answers or some special portal into transcendent knowledge. It is about seeing and moving differently in the world. It means having the courage to imagine, make mistakes, trust, listen, learn, think, and rethink; to resist punditry, pedestals, and perfection; to reject cynicism and embrace critical analysis; to plot; to hold on; to care and commune; to show up; to love. They teach us to mourn and organize, and that we who believe in freedom have to rest. And they understand better than anyone what Dr. King meant when he called on us to 'rededicate ourselves to the long and bitter, but beautiful, struggle for a new world.'" —**Robin D. G. Kelley**, author, *Freedom Dreams: The Black Radical Imagination*

"*Let This Radicalize You* is a rich treasury of practical lessons and insights from organizers and activists across many of today's most important sites of struggle. Through deeply moving storytelling, Kelly Hayes and Mariame Kaba share a stirring vision of commitment and collaboration that is rooted in love, reality, and solidarity—and one that doesn't shy away from the challenges we face inside and outside our movements or the high stakes. This book is a gift for everyone, no matter their level of political engagement, interested in building the new worlds of care and mutual flourishing that we need." —**Astra Taylor**, author, *Remake the World: Essays, Reflections, Rebellions*

"There is so much incredible goodness between these covers. How I wish I had this wisdom when I was young. Everything within fills me with hope and joy for our future. This book is about reclaiming our humanity and care for one another as we seek to heal ourselves and our world. It is an essential work that can change the course of the history we create each day!" —**Lisa Fithian**, author, *Shut It Down: Stories from a Fierce, Loving Resistance*

"*Let This Radicalize You* is geared toward helping young organizers learn to strategize, make critical analyses, and to act effectively and with integrity in the communities they work with. Perhaps most important of all, it shows the need to go beyond having a nuanced critique or organizing one-off events—it is a text that teaches us how to build a movement. The authors have more than succeeded in meeting their task: *Let This Radicalize You* should be required reading for anyone entering social movements and wishing to eradicate harm and create more liveable futures. But this book is also a movement encyclopedia for anyone who is oriented toward liberation or even slightly curious about what it might mean for us to get there. This is a necessary text for the freedom dreamers, the poets, the seasoned activists, the rebels, and the community builders from all walks of life, because it shows us what it means to be transformed in the service of liberation. Kelly Hayes and Mariame Kaba show us that freeing ourselves and freeing one another is work, but, importantly, that it is work that can and must be done together." —**Robyn Maynard**, coauthor, *Rehearsals for Living*

"*Let This Radicalize You* is a beacon of world-making potential you won't find anywhere else. In the wretched catastrophes of the racial capitalocene, this book is your guide to elsewhere, and it is brilliant." —**Leanne Betasamosake Simpson**, coauthor, *Rehearsals for Living*

LET THIS RADICALIZE YOU

ORGANIZING AND THE REVOLUTION OF RECIPROCAL CARE

Kelly Hayes and Mariame Kaba

Foreword by Maya Schenwar
Afterword by Harsha Walia

Haymarket Books
Chicago, Illinois

Published in 2023 by
Haymarket Books
P.O. Box 180165
Chicago, IL 60618
773-583-7884
www.haymarketbooks.org
info@haymarketbooks.org

ISBN: 978-1-64259-827-8

Distributed to the trade in the US through Consortium Book Sales and Distribution (www.cbsd.com) and internationally through Ingram Publisher Services International (www.ingramcontent.com).

This book was published with the generous support of Lannan Foundation and Wallace Action Fund.

Special discounts are available for bulk purchases by organizations and institutions. Please email info@haymarketbooks.org for more information.

Cover artwork by Kah Yangni.

Printed in Canada by union labor.

Library of Congress Cataloging-in-Publication data is available.

10 9 8 7 6 5 4 3

This book is dedicated to the people we have marched, wept, laughed, and planned alongside. Everything worthwhile is done with other people.

CONTENTS

Radicalization Is Vital

Maya Schenwar

On a rainy day over a decade ago, as I was doing research for a book on the impacts of incarceration, I met up with Mariame Kaba at a café in Chicago to interview her about prison abolition. I already considered myself an abolitionist—someone who thought that structures of imprisonment and policing needed to be dismantled and real ways of making "safety" needed to be uplifted and created. I'd read the books! I'd attended the protests! I'd reported on prisons for years. And as a person who had come up in the antiwar movement and devoted my life to social justice journalism, primarily as the editor-in-chief of *Truthout*, I thought I was already radicalized.

However, I exited that café three hours later feeling like my radicalization was just beginning. As Angela Davis says, "radical" means "'grasping things at the root,'"[1] and as I walked to the train station in the rain that day, I felt myself tugging at the roots of my assumptions more than ever before. I'd interviewed Mariame in search of answers—but now my brain was buzzing with questions upon questions.

"So, what do we do instead of prisons?" I had asked Mariame.

"What do you think we should do?" she'd asked me back.

"If we don't have police," I'd asked Mariame, "who do we call?"

"Who do you think we should call?" she'd asked. "What do you think we should create?"

It wasn't that Mariame didn't have a million brilliant insights in response to my queries—she spent much of the afternoon generously recounting her decades of experience building new ways of creating safety and supporting people in collectively pursuing it outside of oppressive systems. However, it was the questions that stuck with me most, because Mariame was urging me—as she urges everyone—to understand that we *all* have a role in imagining and building the world we want to live in. No one gets to simply ask, to simply write down the answers. Even journalists.

Over the years, Mariame has pushed me to transform my way of being in society, always knowing that it—the work of changing, imagining, reimagining, building, and rebuilding the world—is on me, too, because it's on all of us.

The universe has its ways, and not long after I met Mariame, I met Kelly Hayes. Kelly initially joined the *Truthout* staff to work on social media, but she is an extraordinary writer as well as an indomitable organizer, and, of course, her words soon made their way to our pages. (Now she hosts *Truthout*'s flagship podcast, *Movement Memos*.) In the beginning, Kelly mostly wrote about activism unfolding in Chicago, and I was struck by how she, like Mariame, was *doing* the things that she thought should be happening and asking herself the questions she wanted answered, even as she always sought input from others, too.

If someone was arrested at a protest, Kelly was the first to ask how we could get them out—and to motivate others to join her in taking action to free them. If someone was evicted, Kelly was going to ask how to find them housing—and to spur others to work together to make that happen. If the city was shutting down mental health clinics, closing schools, killing people with its murderous police department, Kelly was out there asking herself and others, "What should we do? What should we create?" and collaboratively organizing unforgettable actions at every turn.

Kelly was clearly a dreamer—I knew that from the first time we had drinks together and spent three hours devising our ideal universe (which, in addition to being free of borders, police, and capitalism, involved near-constant karaoke and, on Kelly's insistence, an endless stream of *Star Trek* playing in the background). But she inspired me most with her vision of organizing as fundamentally action driven. In 2014, when Kelly launched *Transformative Spaces*, her blog about organizing, she conveyed that spirit in her first entry: "The struggle for freedom and transformation is not a dream. It's a fire that's burning in real time. And the blaze is spreading."[2]

Since then, Kelly and Mariame have organized a mind-boggling number of campaigns, actions, events, fundraisers, and formations, supporting countless people's lives and a vast array of social movements. They are always fueling the blaze—not just telling you *about* the blaze, not just insisting the blaze is necessary, but helping to ignite it themselves and urging you to help gather kindling and imagine strategies to keep it going, to help it spread in generative and life-giving ways, ways that will nourish lush new growing things.

When we consider the origin of the word "radical" in relation to "roots," let's not forget what roots do: they make life possible. "Radical," in its historical definition, is synonymous with "vital"—"designating the humour or moisture once thought to be present in all living organisms as a necessary condition of their vitality."[3] I think that in a world facing ever more-urgent existential threats, growing more radical—going deeper politically, becoming more courageous in both our dreams and our daily practices—will indeed be a necessary condition for life on Earth.

Kelly and Mariame did not have time to write this book, but they did it anyway, because they sensed a necessity to share decades of organizing wisdom—their own and that of a multitude of co-strugglers whose stories grace these pages—with newer activists in this precipitous moment.

The day before Kelly and Mariame asked me to edit *Let This Radicalize You*, I had sensibly promised myself that I would "not say yes to anything else." But I said yes, because, come on.

I am so glad I did. The past few years have depleted my hope reserves. I bet they've depleted yours, too. As environmental organizer and spiritual leader Joanna Macy put it near the start of the COVID-19 pandemic, "We are in a space without a map. With the likelihood of economic collapse and climate catastrophe looming, it feels like we are on shifting ground, where old habits and old scenarios no longer apply."[4] How do we hope without a map—without being able to glimpse some identifiable point in the future where things might get better? And how do we act, if we don't know where our hope will come from?

If you're grappling with these questions, too, it's a good thing you have this book in your hands (or on your phone, or in your ears). Reading *Let This Radicalize You* recharged my ability to hope, and to act, and to understand how deeply those two verbs are connected. The book is powered by hope. And it draws that hope not from theoretical aspirations but from existing movements that—in spite of all the scary odds—are winning.

Those wins sometimes look like recognizable, celebrated victories. But usually, they don't: often, they are about supporting people's basic needs in the face of a climate-caused disaster; defending someone's right to remain in their home; administering life-saving medical care in the midst of a protest; sustaining a coalition or an activist group in the face of conflict; growing new organizing efforts out of old ones that have run their course. Often, they're about making it possible for a person, or a family, or a community, to survive another day.

Kelly and Mariame interviewed dozens of organizers and read piles of books and zines and articles and tool kits and screeds to write *Let This Radicalize You*. Each page of the book is dense with collective wisdom. By reading it, you will come to know in your marrow that every day, everywhere, people are striving to make change in their communities, and that where there is profound injustice, there is always also creative struggle.

"Hope and grief can coexist," Kelly and Mariame remind us, amid millions lost to the pandemic, amid rising fascism, amid many-sided attacks on our most basic bodily autonomies—"and if we wish to transform the world, we must learn to hold both simultaneously."

This book derives its title from the words Mariame often repeats in times of deep crisis: "Let this radicalize you rather than lead you to despair."

As you read the book, I challenge you to follow the title's suggestion: let it radicalize you. To do this, you will need to let your guard all the way down. Let your inner cynic take a nap. Tell your inner devil's advocate to take a few days off. Then let yourself be lifted by the stories of the organizers that fill these pages—people who are stubbornly practicing hope each day and taking imaginative action, in spite of doubts, losses, and heartbreak.

If you engage with the book in this way, I'm willing to bet you'll want to take action, too. After all, these days, becoming radical isn't an impulsive dalliance. It's a leap toward allowing yourself to believe in the possibility of our collective survival—and to believe that even if we don't make it, we are all still worth fighting for, to the last breath.

If you are up for the challenge, keep turning these pages.

Remaking the World

Kelly Hayes

If You find Your imagination cannot stop itself from churning out the scripts of the Death Machines, pull its plug. Dismantle it. Reprogram it. Dream Daylight. Manufacture Daylight. We are the Magicians.

Make Magic.

—Krista Franklin, "Call"[1]

When I learned about the death of the radical poet Diane di Prima in late October 2020, I was immersed in community safety planning, as organizers braced for the political uncertainties of the 2020 election. In organizing meetings, we mapped out possible scenarios: If Donald Trump were victorious, would we see emboldened state action against dissidents and accelerations of state violence? If Trump were defeated, would his followers escalate their attacks? We discussed safety plans and ways we could mobilize. My body and mind had been screaming for a break since a two-month bout of COVID, but I had made commitments around the election that I felt the need to see through.

1

Then I learned that di Prima had died, and I sat down to grieve the best way I know how—by stringing words together until they tell me something about myself, the moment, or what needs to happen next. The resulting essay was a rant against despair and a meditation on the poetics of organizing. I still return to that rant, just as I return to di Prima's work, to ground myself and to remind myself that organizing is the work of dreaming new worlds into being. As Robin D. G. Kelley writes in *Freedom Dreams: The Black Radical Imagination*, "In the poetics of struggle and lived experience, in the utterances of ordinary folk, in the cultural products of social movements, in the reflections of activists, we discover the many different cognitive maps of the future, of the world not yet born."[2]

I first shared a version of the words that follow in *Truthout*, on October 28, 2020. I offer them here as a call to engage deeply with your own imagination as you read this book, and to envision the construction of a world that has not yet been born.

¶

A professor I was friendly with introduced me to di Prima's poem "Rant" when I was a freshman in college. Its value didn't register at first. But later, particular lines were echoing in my mind, late at night, while I was trying to write. Sometimes, I would close my eyes and repeat di Prima's words as I tried to find my own. She said, "The war that matters is the war against the imagination / all other wars are subsumed in it."[3]

Over a decade later, I reached a place in my organizing work where people would frequently invite me to speak at protests. I would not write speeches in advance, but I would sometimes read aloud beforehand, to stretch my voice and center myself. Over the years, friends have lovingly tolerated my back-seat readings of "Rant" on the way to marches and rallies. One friend especially enjoyed the words "you are an appendage of the work, the work stems from / hangs from the heaven you create."[4]

I have been returning to that poem, as I puzzle over my own words, since the age of nineteen. I return because it reminds me that we are world builders. Just as great writers construct vivid, fictional realms that we as readers can actively envision, our minds create vast landscapes that fill in the gaps in our understandings of the past, present, and future. Our mental maps of the world, and of history itself, are the products of our own world-building process. We fill in the empty spaces with theory, prediction, and possibility. Sometimes the filler is gray, pessimistic and cynical, and we assume the worst of every detail. This does not demand much of us, in terms of learning or creativity.

Some people color in the blank spaces with optimistic assumptions. Some are true detectives, seeking every concrete detail they can, as forensically as possible. Some seek to reinvent everything. We do the same to the present. We do the same to the future.

But, as di Prima said,

> the ultimate claustrophobia is the syllogism
> the ultimate claustrophobia is "it all adds up"[5]

I know that claustrophobia too well—the belief that you've come to understand something awful and inescapable. It's a feeling I have confronted many times. But I eventually learned that the answer is always the same: when you feel trapped by an oppressive inevitability, you never stop trying to escape, because every jailbreak begins with a decision to reject the inevitable. It is the courage to pick up a pen, every time, knowing you may not finish the story, but knowing full well that you will reject the ending you've been given, every step of the way.

Reality is malleable. As di Prima said,

> history is a living weapon in yr hand
> & you have imagined it, it is thus that you
> "find out for yourself"
> history is the dream of what can be, it is
> the relation between things in a continuum[6]

To understand the past, we must investigate the stories we were not told, because those stories were withheld for a reason. We must search out all the pieces we weren't meant to find, the things that disrupt the narratives we've been given. How did people survive desolate times? How did they find the joy and humor that sustained them in long stretches of siege and survival? How did they build relationships that allowed people who disagreed to collaborate and achieve convergence? What did those uneasy alliances look like? What helped them succeed, and what caused them to fail?

History is, as di Prima said, "a living weapon."[7]

As an organizer, I like to think of history as a map of the world, cut like cardboard into a jigsaw puzzle. Its pieces have been scattered and cast in all directions. They are tucked inside books in libraries. They are buried in the stories of people we don't know. They are tucked into memories that we ought to write down but often let drift away, unpreserved. They are embedded in photographs and paintings and pencil marks. They are buried in graves and amalgamated with the dirt, water, and wind of this world—because the elements carry fractions of history, too. Stories of nuclear fallout and contaminated oceans. Stories about what lived and died and grew in a place, long before our feet touched the soil.

It's important to both ground ourselves in the here and now and also remember that the world is much bigger than this moment, bigger than us and our experience of it, and much bigger than we imagine when we are afraid.

Organizers seek to impact all of these things—the way people reconstruct the past, the way we understand the present, and ultimately the way we envision what could be. Creating against the grain.

What stories are we telling ourselves? What are we sowing into the world when we speak?

Our politics are the product of this world-building process. And storytelling is a fight for the future. That fight is inescapable in a world on fire. The only questions are how the fight and the fire will shape us, and how we will shape the fight and the fire.

I believe we write the meaning of life as we live it. I believe it is up to us to write a story worth living. I do not believe in the surrender of hope or imagination any more than I believe it is acceptable to give up on the survival of others, or of all life on Earth. There are some things we never surrender, and some things we never surrender to. When we try to change the world, when we create containers for work, initiate relationships, or chart strategic paths forward, we are always battling assumptions. What myths underlie those assumptions? How can those myths be ripped out from under the lies they prop up? How can inevitability—a construct of the wicked—be ripped apart?

The restoration of possibility amid despair is an act of destruction paired with a call to imagine—which is a call to arms. The armament of knowing you have not been defeated. The armament of knowing that the present and the future will have histories that have not been written yet. Possibility is the hope we wear when we charge into battle. It is stronger than assumption or reaction because it is intentional. It is an awareness that cannot be snatched away. The knowledge that there is always another ending in play, even if we don't know what it is. So we charge into the breach if that is the only way forward, because possibility is worth it. As di Prima wrote,

> There is no way you can not have a poetics
> no matter what you do: plumber, baker, teacher
>
> you do it in the consciousness of making
> or not making yr world
> you have a poetics: you step into the world[8]

We all have politics, too. But poetics and politics can be reshaped. Organizers are aspiring authors and artists, creating elements of stories, in constellations we are often unaware of, with pockets of unseen work happening far and wide. Creating connection, potential, and possibility is creative work. We are in a moment when we must hold prediction and possibility all at once. It is a time to act together, with vision and with hope. As di Prima told us,

> There is no way out of the spiritual battle
> the war is the war against the imagination
> you can't sign up as a conscientious objector
> the war of the worlds hangs here, right now, in the balance
> it is a war for this world, to keep it[9]

¶

In many ways, this book is an invitation. An invitation to dream, an invitation to consider, an invitation to build, to experiment, and to act. As organizers, we extend many invitations, and we hope that people will join us in the streets, on the picket line, at a meeting, or to learn together and share ideas. We invite, we hope, and we try to extend something worthwhile. This is true whether we are planning a protest, holding a meeting or teach-in, or writing a book.

This book is intended for organizers who are young in their work, though we hope it will be beneficial to others as well. In thinking about what to include in a book for people who are newer to movement work, I thought about how I had learned and grown as an organizer, and what had been most helpful to me. One answer seemed particularly relevant: long talks with mentors on the way home from protests.

When Mariame and I first began co-organizing events together, we lived in the same part of Chicago. So after a long night of marching, or rallying outside police headquarters, we would often wind up in the same car on the way home. Sometimes Mariame would be driving, but she would always be talking. She would talk about the action and its relationship to the moment. She would share histories and personal anecdotes, ask questions, and recommend books. We would not always agree, but our dialogues were so constructive that I enjoyed being challenged by Mariame. In a world that often shames us for what we do not know, I found those conversations enlivening and at times life changing. By the time I got out of the car, I would feel curious, creative, and ready to learn or do more. I have experienced similar moments with other organizers, on road trips to protests, in coffee shops, or sitting on sidewalks at jail support, during the hours-long wait for the release of other protesters. I came to think of those conversations as "rides home," too, even if they did not take place in a vehicle, because there was something about that descriptor that I liked—the idea of an important conversation that helped bring me home.

Those talks helped to shape my perspective as an organizer, and they have also helped me grapple with tough questions about myself and about movement work. Some of the people I was lucky enough to have those conversations with, in addition to Mariame, are featured in this book. Because, while this book is a mash-up of manifesto, anecdotes, and advice, my greatest hope for this project is to create a book full of rides home. We know that many of you will be taking action in the days ahead and that some of you are already hard at work, trying to remake the world. We are so grateful for you. We know what you are up against, in the form of state repression, and that you have inherited a world on fire. We share your fears and your fury, and we trust your creativity.

If you are completely new to the work of movements, welcome. Please know that you are needed and that while your journey will be messy, possibility is worth it.

We talk a lot about possibility and hope in this book, and we are by no means attempting to minimize the stakes or the obstacles you will face in your work. I know these are frightening and even soul-shaking times. I cannot tell you that the tumult will relent, because it will not. But I can tell you that here, on the edge of everything, we are each other's best hope. As organizers, we are builders in an era of collapse. Our work is set against all probability—and it is in that space of cherished improbability where our art will be made, where our joy will be found, and where our ingenuity will fashion ways of living and caring for each other, even as the ground shifts beneath our feet. Life will be a scramble, but we will not scramble alone.

Together, we will fight for this world, to keep it.

Although we hope to cross paths with many of you in the streets, or wherever we hold our ground collectively against injustice, the limits of time and space mean that we probably won't see you at your next protest. But it is my sincere hope that, through this book, we still might be able to offer you a ride home.

INTRODUCTION

We Can Only Survive Together

Mariame Kaba

> If we can recognize that change and uncertainty
> are basic principles, we can greet the future and the
> transformation we are undergoing with the under-
> standing that *we do not know enough to be pessimistic.*
>
> —**Hazel Henderson**[1]

I came of age in New York City in the 1980s. I was incredibly lucky to find some wonderful touchstones. These people were patient with me, sometimes hard on me, but most important, they listened to my ideas. They were role models who taught me about the limits and possibilities of lifelong activism and organizing. Yet, I must admit that I write these words with retrospective admiration. When I was fourteen and fifteen years old, I didn't appreciate these people in the way I do now. As a teenager, I thought that they were too cautious and lacked revolutionary zeal.

The truth is that I was being seduced by another group of people—I'll call them the butterflies. These were the people who always had a ready quote by Fanon, Malcolm, Che, or Marx. Only

8

men, of course. They carried around tattered books that I had not yet read. This would send me scurrying to the library or to Liberation Bookstore to find those exact tomes. These were the people in my life who spent the most time talking about revolution. In retrospect, I know that the reason I was so enthralled was because it was exciting to imagine myself as a revolutionary. My untested ideas were always brilliant around them. They were fun to be around because they rarely participated in the actual hard work of building organization, and they had a lot of criticisms of those who did that work.

While others were going door to door in Harlem to talk with community members about affordable housing, the butterflies were lamenting the fact that "the people" were not being sufficiently engaged in "our" struggles. None of them ever went door to door. We talked a lot about "new" models of engagement, even though the old ones would have served us just as well. We were not getting out there and talking to people. We weren't putting ourselves on the line or risking being told to F off.

Early on in my activism, these people dazzled me. They were shiny, analytically brilliant, and looked the part of committed organizers for social change. I was a major brat to people who I proudly proclaimed were sellouts because they had to be accountable to private funders and to "the man." Those were heady days.

Then, one afternoon I won't soon forget, as I spouted off about someone or other being "a sellout," one of my mentors asked me a question that helped shape the trajectory of my activism and organizing.

"What have you built?" he asked. I must have looked perplexed. So he asked me again, "What have you built?"

"I don't know what you mean," I answered.

"Come back and talk with me when you've figured it out," he told me.

I was so pissed off by that exchange that I left the office where I was working as a volunteer in a huff. I didn't have an answer for him for another two or three years. It turned out that I hadn't "built" anything. He was asking me, *Who are the people to whom you're accountable?* When had I been brave enough to actualize and execute the ideas and theories that I was always so quick to offer to others? What was I actually doing?

My mentor had been passionate about the issue of affordable housing and had built something significant—a community-based organization (where I was volunteering) to implement his ideas, to test them against his theories. Once I understood his question, he became one of my greatest teachers. The butterflies began to lose their appeal.

¶

From the mid-1980s to the present, I have been part of cocreating a number of projects, formations, and organizations. I've also co-organized issue-based campaigns. This work had mainly taken place outside of my paying jobs. It wasn't until I was in my late thirties that some of my organizing work would actually overlap with my employment. For over thirty-five years I have devoted myself to working with others to transform our conditions to be more just.

In 2011, I became aware of the criminal case against Marissa Alexander, a Black mother of three who tried to protect herself from an abusive husband by firing a warning shot into the ceiling after he had threatened her again. Marissa's attorney tried to use Florida's "Stand Your Ground" law, made infamous after George Zimmerman's 2012 killing of Trayvon Martin, as Marissa's defense—but a judge prohibited him from doing so.

Historian Danielle McGuire has written in her excellent book *At the Dark End of the Street* that there was a time in this country when it was presumed that Black women could not be raped. The idea, enforced by police and courts and structural white supremacy and patriarchy, was that Black women were naturally promiscuous and that their bodies were inviolable. In other words, *no* never meant *no* for Black and brown women (and some poor white women). This idea has carried over, I think, to the concept of "self-defense" as applied to Black and brown women. If Black women's bodies can always be violated and if Black women are easily killable, then the notion of self-defense can never apply. Black women do not have a "self" worth defending.

I was deeply engaged with other organizing projects at the time, but in the summer of 2013 I decided that I would organize a teach-in on Marissa's case. I hosted it on her birthday in September in response to a national call to action by the Free Marissa Now campaign, which was mobilizing people around the world to get Marissa free and organize more broadly against incarceration and gender-based violence. I reasoned that if local participants in Chicago were exposed to the injustice of the case and provided with an opportunity to organize on Marissa's behalf, then they would. That's exactly what happened. While I initially warned that I would only be able to serve as a sporadic adviser to the local defense committee, I ended up getting drawn into a co-organizer role fairly early. Working with my fellow Chicago Alliance to Free Marissa Alexander (CAFMA) organizers was one of the best organizing experiences that I've had.

One of the important lessons that I've learned in my years of organizing with defense committees—groups that focus on supporting and working to free a criminalized person—is how isolating and lonely the criminal legal process is. This is particularly true for detainees who find themselves jailed while awaiting trial or a plea deal and are dealing with both the loss of their freedom and the anxiety of not knowing whether they'll be convicted. Letters and other communications are lifelines for those who find themselves trapped behind bars. Many of the people we've supported with defense committee work have shared that receiving letters made them realize people on the outside cared about them, remembered them, and supported them. Often, they've said, it makes the difference between giving up and staying hopeful.

In spite of her husband threatening to kill her and the State of Florida relentlessly pursuing her social death, Marissa walked out of a Duval County jail on January 27, 2015. She would spend two years electronically shackled under house arrest, but collective action had prevented the state of Florida from stealing decades of Marissa's life. CAFMA would ultimately transition into a new organization, Love

& Protect, with the broader mission of supporting women, trans, and gender nonconforming/nonbinary people of color who are criminalized or harmed by state and interpersonal violence. Love & Protect is a founding member organization of Survived & Punished, a national organizing project to end the criminalization of survivors of domestic and sexual violence.

I no longer live in Chicago, but my co-organizers who grew Love & Protect have continued that work in concert with Survived & Punished California, California Coalition for Women Prisoners, and Survived & Punished NYC, which I cofounded and currently organize with.

I highlight this particular struggle to point out that a great deal of advocacy, care, resistance, and support arose from the struggle to free Marissa—work that reverberates to this day. Rather than simply expressing my feelings about the case or the organizing around it, as the butterflies might have, I took action by offering a way for others to mobilize to support Marissa. When others did volunteer to help, we created an organizing container for that action. When Marissa's case had been resolved, the care and resistance that her struggle had fostered inspired people to keep building and working to free others.

Mutual aid, of which defense committees are good examples, has the power to change our social relationships, to galvanize us into groups and communities that confront specific crises—and then move on to fight much broader battles. We saw that kind of reconfiguration happen around Marissa's case, as people moved from concern to collective action, and from collective action to the building of an enduring organization.

I have learned to take the construction work of organizing as it comes, creating things that I believe have to exist, and working with others to build containers, organizations, and projects that I believe the world needs. I am always dreaming up new ideas and making things, because the world is not transformed primarily by what we think of it. Transformative change happens when we are willing to build the things that we know must exist.

¶

This book that you are reading is one that I wish I had as a young activist. It's our attempt to distill some of the lessons we've learned about organizing over the past few decades and to include some lessons from other organizers. We wrote it with new activists and organizers in mind. We also wrote it as a love letter to the many organizers we've been privileged to work with over the years.

This book is not intended to be a manual about how to do community organizing or how to run issue-based organizing campaigns. There are many excellent books and manuals that already do that. Instead, it is a book of stories, reflections, and guidance designed to inform, inspire, and encourage your movement work.

I don't remember when Kelly Hayes and I first met, but it feels like we've always known each other. For at least ten years, we've been comrades and friends. We've coconspired and co-organized together to shut down prisons, to win reparations for police torture survivors, to free people from prison through defense campaigns, and more generally to help uproot oppression. Some of the most meaningful work Kelly and I have done together has involved working to free incarcerated people, from migrants in immigration detention to criminalized survivors, like Marissa Alexander, Naomi Freeman, and Bresha Meadows.[2] I have learned a lot from Kelly and learned even more through the writing of this book.

Kelly and I are often asked to define what it means to be an activist and an organizer. For us, there is a distinction, however tenuous, between activism and organizing—though the terms are not mutually exclusive. We would argue that every organizer is an activist, but not every activist is an organizer.

Activism encompasses all the ways we show up for justice. It can take a multitude of shapes, depending on a person's skills, interests, and capacity. An activist might conduct research, canvass, fundraise, or attend marches or meetings regularly, or they may simply practice a skill in their own home, such as art making, in the service of a cause or campaign they support. Activism can be done on our own, in which case we are accountable to ourselves. Activists are essential, whether or not they are also organizers.

Organizing, on the other hand, is a more specific set of practices. It is a craft that requires us to cultivate a variety of skills, such as intentional relationship building and power analysis. As we were preparing to write this book, historian and organizer Barbara Ransby told us, "There are people who are in motion, who may be the people who go to demonstrations, who go to rallies, who go to vigils or advocate or write or express their solidarity with a movement in various kinds of ways, but they're not necessarily the people who are, in a strategic methodical way, trying to move other people in terms of campaigns or in terms of movement building." Those protest attendees are activists, while the movement builders are organizers. "I think of organizers," Ransby told us, "as people who really are trying to move other people, [and] create collective movement in a very conscious, deliberate and strategic way, informed by a larger social change agenda."

Abolitionist scholar and longtime organizer Ruth Wilson Gilmore points out that organizing centers on the cooperative pursuit of a particular end. "Being an organizer, to me, means seeing the kinds of things that people either are doing or might be able to do, given what their energy and excitement or vulnerability is, and helping people achieve a goal that undoes some aspect of what makes life too difficult or makes it not precious," says Gilmore. "So that can be anything from organizing with organized labor, to helping loved ones who have people going to trial, sit through the proceedings and listen with them, to anything in between, but it's achieving something other than notoriety for the problem."

This book is intended for activists and for organizers. We hope that what we've shared will be of use to you, whether you are working to take action in limited, specific ways or looking to strategically co-organize mass movements.

No matter how we choose to take action, we are usually working toward a future that we will be unlikely to see. It's a future built on the hopes and the sacrifices of our ancestors upon whose labor and love we stand. Mary-Wynne Ashford writes, "Since you cannot see into the future, you simply proceed to put one stone on top of another, and another on top of that. If the stones get knocked down, you begin again, because if you don't nothing will get built."[3] Making positive change is difficult. Uprooting oppression is the work of many lifetimes. There are some terrific highs, but they are mixed with many setbacks.

Yet, I have learned over these many years of organizing that the most important thing you can do to transform the world is to act. Taking action is a practice of hope. Experience and meaning are derived from doing. To transform the conditions of our oppression(s), we can only do what we can today, where we are, in the best way that we know. We can only survive together. This book is your invitation to act in the best way that you know and to survive together.

CHAPTER 1

Beyond Alarm, toward Action

In order for the oppressed to be able to wage the struggle for their liberation, they must perceive the reality of oppression not as a closed world from which there is no exit, but as a limiting situation which they can transform.

—Paulo Freire, *Pedagogy of the Oppressed*[1]

On a cold night in February 2015, fifteen people were huddled in parked cars or unassumingly loitering on foot outside Chicago mayor Rahm Emanuel's home. Then, an organizer gave them a signal to move, and at once, over a dozen activists sprung out of the cars and from around corners to spell out a message in lights outside of Emanuel's home. Each person held a large sign of a letter, illuminated with LED lights, spelling out a larger message that read "REPARATIONS NOW."

Emanuel knew that survivors of police torture in Chicago were demanding justice, but now we were bringing that message to his doorstep in lights. When a light inside the house went off, we knew we had been seen. As expected, the police descended upon us quickly, but our attorney, Jerry Boyle, ran interference long enough for Kelly to take a picture, capturing the image we were after, to help spread our narrative online. That image helped us tell the story of a campaign that made history in Chicago.

This was not a new campaign—the fight had already been waged for decades before our action outside the Emanuel house took place. Between 1972 and 1991, Jon Burge, a Vietnam vet turned police commander in Chicago, tortured or supervised the torture of more than 120 people[2]; all except one were African American. The torture was perpetrated by a group of white detectives who called themselves the "A-team" and was always verbally laced with racist insults. The methods of torture were diverse, systematic, and brutal. The cops' techniques included Russian roulette, electric shock, beatings, suffocation, burning, and more. They systematically tortured "suspects" for decades with impunity.

Burge torture survivor Darrell Cannon has spoken out about his experience, which echoes the stories of so many others. It was 1983 and the police wanted a confession. Cannon was terrorized with Russian roulette while being called a "nigger." Officers attached cattle prods to his genitals and electrically shocked him. After hours of torture, he confessed to murder and spent over twenty years in prison, fourteen of those caged inside a torture chamber called Tamms Supermax, a maximum-security prison. Many other men shared Darrell's experience, caged for decades due to "confessions" obtained through torture.

Beginning in the mid-1980s, survivors of Burge's torture started to organize behind bars while their families began to organize on the outside. It took years of litigation, agitation, investigative reporting, mobilizations, and organizing for Burge to eventually be fired in 1993. Many more years of organizing would lead to his federal prosecution for lying about torture and his conviction and sentencing to four years in prison. What became clear through the years, though, was the real inadequacy of traditional legal remedies to make individuals and communities whole in the wake of systemic harm.

Something else was needed. So, in 2010, a group of artists, lawyers, torture survivors, and organizers came together to form the Chicago Torture Justice Memorials (CTJM). This grassroots group asked police torture survivors and the larger community to imagine how they would publicly memorialize these cases of torture and imprisonment, recognizing the difficulty and immensity of depicting the harms perpetrated, while also recognizing the decades-long struggle for justice.

Through visioning sessions, teach-ins, creative outreach, and community dialogue, CTJM sought to spark the collective imagination of communities to conceptualize what was necessary for the city to provide in order for individuals and communities to begin to heal from torture. This call served to redirect everyone's attention beyond the usual cries for "accountability" for police violence and to focus on holistic means of meeting the material needs of all members of impacted communities, and offering positive visions for healing and repair.

Out of these brainstorms, dreams inspired by a call made in 2008 by civil rights attorney Standish Willis, cofounder of Black People against Police Torture, came an expansive Chicago Reparations Ordinance and Resolution.

In addition to the establishment of a $5.5 million reparations fund for Burge torture survivors, the ordinance called for the city to provide survivors and their families with specialized counseling services at a new center on the South Side; free enrollment in city colleges; and priority access to job training, housing, and other city services. Additionally, it called for a history lesson about the Burge torture cases to be taught in Chicago Public Schools in the eighth and tenth grades and a permanent public memorial to be erected to commemorate those who were tortured—as well as the resistance.

The action at Emanuel's home in February 2015 was one component of an intense and successful six-month Reparations NOW campaign, after which the ordinance passed and Chicago became the first municipality in the United States to offer reparations to those violated by racist law enforcement. The reparations law represented the first time the Chicago City Council formally acknowledged and took responsibility for the police torture that occurred and recognized its obligation to provide concrete redress to the survivors and family members.

The reparations ordinance is a memorial for the living. The ordinance's stubborn insistence that people—no matter what they have done—should be compensated for torture was a little earthquake. It shook up and reconfigured the normalization of punishment. Few believed that the Reparations NOW campaign would succeed when we officially launched it in December 2014. This included some of the key organizers of the campaign. As we sat in a coffee shop in fall 2014, Mariame said that she'd been talking with members of CTJM and other organizers about how the power of the protests after the killing of Mike Brown in Ferguson, and others in our own community, could be harnessed to push for local victories. Kelly thought this sounded really exciting. As she bit into a muffin, Mariame said that we were going to organize to make the police torture reparations ordinance law. Kelly kept munching and said nothing. Mariame didn't know it at the time, but Kelly didn't believe that it was a winnable campaign. It wasn't until many years later that Kelly disclosed that she had worked on the campaign fully convinced that it wouldn't succeed.

Why did Kelly agree to join in that Reparations NOW campaign even though she did not believe the battle could be won? It's simple: Mariame and Kelly had an established relationship and had built trust over the years. While Kelly's skepticism about the political system kept her from initially believing in the possibility that we might win, her belief in Mariame and other organizers convinced her the fight would be meaningful, generative, and worth waging, even if the measure did not pass. She later said that she learned a powerful lesson about what is and isn't possible in organizing.

Kelly understood and knew the facts about Burge's torture. But those facts alone would not have been enough to convince her that a campaign for police torture reparations would succeed. And they would not have been enough to convince her to launch herself fully for months, without any compensation, into an organizing campaign. Facts are not enough to mobilize people into action.

It's Not Just about Facts

Where do we begin, as we attempt to mobilize people around a major issue? Often, we assume our jumping-off points should be facts and fear. This is understandable. From the climate crisis to the COVID-19 pandemic to the horrors of the prison-industrial complex, organizers often raise the alarm about present or future catastrophes. Our work is usually informed by a daunting awareness of the crises we face. Becoming well versed, or even immersed, in the realities of these crises is crucial but can sometimes lead to a near constant state of alarm. Since we did not always have this knowledge and now feel motivated by it, it's easy to assume that if others knew how bad things were, they, too, would want to take action. This assumption can sometimes lead activists to become walking, talking encyclopedias of doom.

However, as organizers, our job is to help move people to action, and no fact is so shocking or profound that its utterance will spontaneously spark a movement. Our work is full of truths that should be unthinkable—yet, the mere recitation of these facts does not move people into the streets or lead them to join movements. Indeed, in some cases, it prompts people to turn off the television. In 2018, Chris Hayes, host of MSNBC's *All In with Chris*, tweeted, "Every single time we've covered [climate change] it's been a palpable ratings killer."[3] This does not absolve the media of moral responsibility by any means, as they have a duty to inform the public about these threats, but it is useful information for us as organizers: fear alone doesn't usually hold people's attention, let alone inspire them to action. Similarly, social media bombards us with flashes of tragedy and injustice throughout our waking hours, but most of these stories do not widely reconfigure worldviews or provoke new action; they often prompt people to retweet and move on.

As organizers, we're repeatedly disappointed by others' lack of response to urgent crises. In cases like these, it's tempting to impose moral binaries—to deem people good or bad based on whether the facts moved them to act. An activist who informs someone of the severity of the climate crisis and is met with complacency or fatalism, for example, might assume the person does not care about the natural world or other people. If someone is unmoved by the facts, we might conclude we simply don't share the same values. But things are rarely this simple.

Our personal realities are patchworks of things we've seen, been exposed to, and potentially come to understand, bound together by belief. Our interpretation of the information and stimuli we are given is the product of many influences. Remove any one of those influences, or add another, and one's worldview may change drastically. Or it may not. We interpret new information on the basis of how it compares to what we have already seen, experienced, or contemplated. For many, new and conflicting information is simply measured against experience, their current worldview, and input from influential sources. If the information does not fit their sense of reality, people will often let it go or even forcefully reject it.

It can be easy to deem people who reject crucial facts as "bad people." Some may, indeed, be doing terrible things. But many are just laboring through life, making sense of it as best they can. We have to strive to receive people on these terms.

When a fact or set of facts prompts people to change course, it's usually because someone or something has interrupted the narrative they knew and told a story that feels more true—one worth making changes over.

During the Reparations NOW campaign, participants actively worked against any sensationalizing of the horrors torture victims endured. While traumatic details were part of the campaign's storytelling, those details were handled respectfully and presented in the context of transformative demands and a different vision of the future. Rather than simply asking people to absorb terrible facts, organizers were inviting people to imagine the reparations ordinance as a step toward a world without the violence it sought to address, and to fight for that world.

When these narrative shifts occur among communities and groups of people, new potentials arise. People are capable of taking actions that defy systems of oppression and popular expectations.

But to ready people for such moments, we must do more than raise the alarm about injustice.

Telling Stories, Sharing Visions

When we were writing this book, our friend Ruth Wilson Gilmore told us a story about facts, engagement, and action. Gilmore was invited to speak to a large group of students at Berkeley High School, in Berkeley, California, which Gilmore describes as "one of the most segregated places on Earth." Affluent white students at Berkeley High School often have bright futures, Gilmore told us, and are prepared to attend colleges like Yale, Cornell, and UC Berkeley, while Black, brown, and poor white students are largely subject to what Gilmore calls "organized abandonment."[4]

When Gilmore entered the auditorium, she was met with a large crowd of Black and brown students, along with some likely impoverished white students. Looking back, Gilmore says, "I should have realized how reluctant they were to be in the room."

Gilmore was introduced to the students by the white high school teacher who had organized the event. The teacher opened with the words, "One in three Black men will go to prison." This statistic did not incite a sense of shared outrage or solidarity among the students, as the teacher had likely hoped, but seemed to deflate the crowd.

"I sat there and I watched all these kids lose whatever strength, confidence, and hope they had," Gilmore told us. "And they just kind of folded into themselves, and clearly without even talking to each other—and there were no smartphones then—made the determination to endure this and get back to their lives. There was not one thing we could say that was going to interest them."

The young people Gilmore encountered did not need another voice shouting about how bleak their futures were. They had no interest in a conversation that began on such terms. Of course, any meaningful conversation about prisons would have to acknowledge what those young people were up against, but opening with talk of their inevitable doom simply caused them to shut down.

Decades later, Gilmore still thinks about how that event should have begun. She says that if she had it to do over again, "I would have asked them questions about their lives, and why they thought their teachers thought they should listen to the people presenting the assembly. I would have asked them why I should want them to trust me, and told a story about not trusting myself—not, I hope, some 'I used to be young, too' story—and then tried to get people enthusiastic about challenging the situation that brought us all together."

The kind of engagement Gilmore describes is key to creating a sustainable flow of communication, education, and potential inspiration. Everything is a story, and people need to understand themselves as having a meaningful role within the story you, as an organizer, are telling. If their role in your story feels like "doom appreciator," most people will recoil, retreat to their own smaller story, and keep the focus there. This is not to say that we should not dramatize the size or severity of this system's death-making. Given the state of the natural world and the existential threat this system poses to most life on Earth, it makes sense that some protests visually dramatize the global catastrophes of climate change, for example. Such imagery can be heartrending and devastating. But not every action, speech, or conversation about climate should be an apocalyptic snapshot, for the same reason that not every protest against police brutality should be a die-in. Death and devastation are only one part of the story organizers are trying to tell. They are an essential part of that story, and people should be moved to appreciate the stakes, but appreciating the stakes is not enough.

If spitting horrifying facts at people changed minds and built movements, we would have overthrown the capitalist system long ago, because the facts have always been on our side.

To move past the expectation that facts alone will transform people's politics, we have to sit with our discomfort that oftentimes *people know*. When it comes to many of the issues around which we're organizing, most people are aware of the problem, even if they are not acquainted with all the horrid particulars. In fact, some might be quite familiar with the problem and still choose not to act.

Occasionally, you may encounter a situation where the public has virtually no awareness of the issue—such as a corporate cover-up of a toxic chemical leak or an emerging pandemic—but, in many cases, people have heard the facts before or at least know how to access them.

Consider that nowadays, in spite of the mainstream media's failings, there is a profusion of sources of facts out there. While some information is withheld from the public, on most topics there is no shortage of journalistic reports, academic and scientific studies, government reports, viral videos, or anecdotal testimony that should shock and alarm the public. And millions upon millions of people voraciously consume this information daily.

Why don't more people *act*? Some people believe the problems are insurmountable, or they may believe that most people are too selfish or lousy at working together to do anything about them. Others conclude some problems are unfortunate but "necessary evils." For example, when confronted with facts about prison conditions, people will often respond that "people wind up in prison for a reason." We have encountered similar attitudes around the treatment of unhoused people and people who use substances. While many people will acknowledge that conditions are not ideal, they also often believe that certain people bring negative experiences upon themselves. These beliefs did not emerge organically, as the powerful have always generated stories that excuse their own violence. Beliefs about the inferiority of Black and Native people, for example, did not precede chattel slavery and colonial genocide but emerged to justify violence that was already in motion.

These assumptions create not only justifications for violence but also a basis for cooperating with violence. Until those assumptions are undermined or dismantled, facts alone will not motivate a person whose inaction is buttressed by them.

What works when facts fail?

Over the course of our movement work, we have learned that people understand the world in stories. This means organizers must be effective storytellers. We are not suggesting that you should withhold information, but it's important to understand that how we convey that information is central to our success. As Patrick Reinsborough and Doyle Canning write in *Re:Imagining Change*, "Narrative power analysis starts with the recognition that the currency of story is not necessarily truth, but rather meaning. In other words, we often believe in a story not necessarily because it is factually true; we accept a story as true because it connects with our values, or is relevant to our experiences in a way that is compelling."[5]

The COVID-19 pandemic imparts valuable lessons in this respect. In 2020, public health guidance around slowing the spread of COVID-19 was at its most stringent. Some of us marveled at the obliviousness of people who did not seem cognizant of how harmful their defiance of COVID safety protocols was. Many people have similarly been shocked by vaccine hesitancy in the United States. We have often seen people divided into moral categories over these matters. It would be easy, in fact, to dismiss everyone who acts against the collective good as "selfish" or "bad." But would such characterizations help us alter the terrain? As organizers, we must always pose the question, "Why is this happening?"

Steven Taylor's 2019 book *The Psychology of Pandemics* describes the range of individual responses to major health threats. Some people react to a public health crisis with what scientists call "monitoring" behavior. To cope with uncertainty, monitors seek all available information, such as reading as many news updates as possible or checking for new information on government websites. However, monitors with a low tolerance for uncertainty may eagerly search for answers in unreliable places, which can lead to the embrace of hoaxes or conspiracy theories. Meanwhile, others are prone to what's known as "blunting" behavior, which involves "the distraction from, and minimizing of threatening information." Still others exhibit what's known as "unrealistic optimism bias," characterized by the belief that they are more likely than others to evade harm and experience positive outcomes. Research has shown that monitors are responsive to emotional appeals as well as detailed information about risk factors and harm reduction strategies, whereas blunters are likely to avoid such messaging; for them, simple, logical messaging is likely most effective.[6] Understanding these different reactions is essential to effective messaging and highlights the importance of taking multiple approaches in our organizing.

One activist who tackled the issue of vaccine hesitancy constructively is a young social worker in Seattle named Jenni Martinez-Lorenzo. Martinez-Lorenzo comes from a family of immigrants, and her work as a social worker primarily involves connecting immigrant families with financial resources. COVID-19 hit the communities Martinez-Lorenzo works with especially hard. When she learned that vaccines would soon be available, she hoped the nonprofit she worked for would be a resource, in terms of educating the community and perhaps even hosting a vaccine clinic. But she soon found her coworkers were hesitant to raise the matter. "Everyone was too afraid of seeming pushy," Martinez-Lorenzo told us. "No one wanted to bring it up."

Some of the nonprofit's employees had their own hesitations about vaccination, which made them even less eager to raise the subject with community members. Martinez-Lorenzo pointed out that educational materials and information about the vaccine were not being made widely available in Spanish, which meant many community members were not getting the chance to decide for themselves if they thought the vaccine was worth taking. The local registration process for appointments was likewise fraught for non-English speakers, and she hoped her workplace could be a resource in that regard as well, perhaps hosting its own vaccine clinic.

Dissatisfied with her employer's response, Martinez-Lorenzo began to gently raise the topic at a women's group that she had begun for community members the nonprofit served. She shared information after she got her own vaccination appointment and after her first dose. But Martinez-Lorenzo knew that merely sharing some facts, in her capacity as a social worker, was unlikely to change anyone's minds and that if she pushed for vaccination in those meetings, she might alienate people. "I think there is this power dynamic between me coming in as the social worker of the group," she told us. Martinez-Lorenzo knew some people would not want to question her in front of the group, so as not to be rude, and that others might take offense if she pushed the matter, "like I know better and I'm telling them, 'You have to get it.'"

From her experience as an activist, Martinez-Lorenzo knew that the matter would come down to persistent, patient, and curious conversations and story sharing. She knew that people had anxieties about the vaccine, some of which were rooted in personal, historical, and systemic trauma, and she wanted to offer them a place to voice those anxieties, beyond the internet, where hesitant people were largely being met with misinformation or with scorn for their perceived selfishness. She made phone calls and had one-on-one conversations with mothers from the group, asking what they thought of the information about the vaccine that she had shared. She also told the story of her own parents getting vaccinated and what it was like for them.

Martinez-Lorenzo took the same approach outside of work in her relationships and community, in recurring conversations that, in most cases, went on for months. Rather than speaking from a place of authority, or lecturing people, Martinez-Lorenzo explored the topic with people, searching out answers to any new questions that arose and sharing her family stories of vaccination. By the time Martinez-Lorenzo's employer agreed to arrange a Q&A session with Spanish-speaking public-health experts, interest in the vaccine had risen among the families Martinez-Lorenzo worked with, and by the time the organization was ready to host a vaccine clinic, many people were eager to sign up.

Martinez-Lorenzo told us in April 2021, "I started doing those types of phone calls back in January and it's taken up until this past weekend, where we got most of our families vaccinated at a clinic that we did." Martinez-Lorenzo noted that even after people signed up, some would call her later and say, "Can you tell me again about the vaccine?" Patience was key. Contrary to popular characterizations, the people Martinez-Lorenzo helped to get vaccinated were not unthoughtful or selfish. They needed information, and they needed to be heard and reassured, repeatedly, but their participation in a larger action, aimed at protecting large numbers of people, was wholly attainable.

So why are people so hard to reach, particularly when the threats at hand seem so blatantly obvious? Human consciousness can be overwhelming, even in the absence of an existential threat, but when we add something like a pandemic, or the climate crisis, or other extreme threats to the mix, people cope in a spectrum of ways, some of which are helpful, and some of which are not. We have seen some of the ugliness that fear and uncertainty can generate, as antimask and antivaccine movements have become increasingly widespread and aggressive. By the time such ideas are entrenched, it can be very hard to reach people, which is yet another reason why we cannot yield the terrain of crisis to reactionaries, who are organizing avidly in these times. Leveraging fear gets great results for people who want to bring out the worst in others, but it garners lesser returns for those who want to bring out the best.

But, Taylor writes, people can also react in positive and healthy ways amid crisis. While pandemics can result in antisocial behaviors, he says, "affiliative, supportive, prosocial behaviors are more common, where widespread sickness and debility evoke acts of mutual aid among members of a community in crisis."[7]

We saw many of these "supportive, prosocial behaviors" emerge early in the pandemic as hundreds of mutual aid projects sprung up around the country, seemingly overnight. The Seattle-area resource Big Door Brigade defines mutual aid as "when people get together to meet each other's basic survival needs with a shared understanding that the systems we live under are not going to meet our needs and we can do it together RIGHT NOW!"[8] In spring 2020, as people around the country grappled with economic free fall and mass illness and death, many people identified needs within their communities and leveraged social media and other resources to create local response teams. We saw new and old formations organize themselves to deliver groceries and medicine for high-risk individuals, who could not risk shopping in person. Many people with sewing machines mass-produced cloth masks, some of which were sent to medical facilities, as health-care workers grappled with a devastating shortage of personal protective equipment. Some people made masks on their own, as a solo effort, while others teamed up in formations like the Auntie Sewing Squad, created by performance artist Kristina Wong. Within the "Auntie" network, in one year, volunteers between the ages of eight and ninety-three donated more than three hundred thousand masks to people in need.[9] On Kelly's reservation, Maeqtekuahkihkiw Metaemohsak (Woodland Women's Group)—a group of Menominee women who, prior to the pandemic, gathered weekly for crafting, cultural education, and mutual support—organized grocery deliveries for elders and others who could not safely run their own errands.

To inspire constructive behaviors like these, we must embrace storytelling that centers support and inspiration not just fear.

We spoke with Shana McDavis-Conway, the codirector of the Center for Story-Based Strategy, about how to build a different kind of political messaging. Story-based strategy, a participatory approach that links movement building with an analysis of narrative power, positions storytelling at the center of social change.

McDavis-Conway points to climate activism as an area that overwhelmingly relies upon fear-based communication, and she gestures toward a different path.

"We do need to tell stories that evoke emotion," she says, "and fear is an emotion, but it is not the only emotion available to us. There are many other emotions we can tap into."

How can we move or provoke people to take action around the climate crisis without emphasizing fear? "We can use admiration," says McDavis-Conway, "like admiration for Indigenous activists who are fighting pipelines. We can tap into nostalgia for coastal cultures. They're impacted by rising sea levels. We can tap into love and sadness and excitement, outrage, even disgust." McDavis-Conway notes that "anyone who has a child who loves slimy creatures knows how disgust and fascination can inspire someone to spend hours on an activity." Ultimately, she says, when we ask people to process a fearful message that they are not prepared for, we risk losing them altogether. But when we tap into the diverse spectrum of human emotion, we have an opportunity to inspire people to view themselves as part of a larger story—and to make moral decisions about who they are in relation to other human beings.

Eco-philosopher and educator Joanna Macy has come to a similar conclusion about the role of fear in activist messaging and the opportunities that emerge when we access a broader range of emotions. In 2017, she talked with environmental journalist Dahr Jamail about how activism for the environment, for peace, and justice had been hampered by "this difficulty people have in sustaining the gaze," which she once chalked up to apathy. But Macy came to realize it was not "apathy" that caused people to turn away from injustice:

> Back then we were trying to scare people to pay attention. You don't [know] how bad it is with climate change, you don't know how many nuclear warheads are on high alert. Get roused. And it wasn't working. People thought the public was apathetic. But I realized . . . it was not that people didn't care or didn't know, but that people were afraid to suffer. It was the refusal or the incapacity to suffer.
>
> So this has been a lot of my work. To help people open to and become enamored of the idea that they'd really like to see what was going on. And to open the eyes and open the heart to discover, again and again, universally in the work, that acceptance of that discomfort and pain actually reflected the depths of your caring and commitment to life.[10]

What we offer as organizers is not simply alarming information, nor is it the guarantee of success in a particular campaign. We must offer people a vision of how things could be and the opportunity to connect with the people, projects, and movements that can bring this vision to fruition. That is the organizer's unique gift: an invitation to participate in a transformation worth experiencing and fighting for. Organizing welcomes people into a different way of thinking and living in relation to one another and allows people to cultivate—and dwell in—hope, collectively.

Rejecting Our Fear of Each Other

When people comply with an action or tolerate a situation they know is harmful or wrong, fear is often a factor. Fear—of punishment, of the unknown, of one another—often prevents us from protecting and connecting with each other. Powerful actors must keep us convinced that it's the people around us—everyday folks whose struggles overlap with our own—who pose the greatest threat to our safety, well-being, and happiness. It is the grandest illusion ever created: in a world where corporations and governments worldwide are poised to annihilate most life on Earth, we are made to believe that other disempowered people are the greatest danger we face.

Of course, many of us know this is not true, at least intellectually. We know that the military and corporations are the primary drivers of climate chaos. We know that governments maintain conditions that generate despair and therefore produce interpersonal violence. And we know that under changed conditions, we would have far less to fear in the world, both from the system and from other people. We know that in a society where everyone's needs are met, we would no longer need to fear being unable to pay for our health care, or losing our jobs and going hungry, or being hurt by desperate, disillusioned people. Yet many of us accept the violence, limitations, and boundaries imposed by the system as though they are natural laws—inalterable, inevitable, and final—and view everyday people as an existential threat to control, contain, and manage.

Obviously, other people can and do harm us, regardless of how much we share. But the conditions that alienate us and enable harm are wholly alterable. People are capable of generating social mechanisms and relations that foster safety and understanding within communities. People are capable of overcoming, or at least negotiating, difference for the sake of their common interests, *especially* in moments of crisis. As the unprecedented flourishing of mutual aid projects during the pandemic has demonstrated, many people respond to communal crisis with generosity and shared concern. The idea that disasters autogenerate panicked, aimlessly violent hordes of people who must be controlled with an iron fist is an authoritarian fever dream. While the powerful would have us believe that frightened people are always selfish and hypervigilant, cooperation and collaborative care are common human responses to disaster.

People across history have largely turned to one another for comfort, sustenance, and protection in moments of crisis. Acknowledging this truth threatens a social order built on the myth that we need authority to protect us from our own chaotic impulses in times of crisis. The state sees communal care as an ideological threat. This is why mutual aid movements are routinely targeted and undermined by the US government. Mutual aid projects are a manifestation of power that contradicts the state's primary narrative about what it is, who we are, and whose purpose it ultimately serves.

Capitalism requires an ever-broadening disposable class of people in order to maintain itself, which in turn requires us to believe that there are people whose fates are not linked to our own: people who must be abandoned or eliminated. Absent that terrible belief, we would not tolerate the horrors that unfold around us each day. We would be collectively enraged that people live unsheltered and hungry or die of treatable illnesses because they lack money. We would be horrified that millions of people live in the bondage of the prison system and that people die in the process of struggling to reach unwelcoming borders in the hopes of salvation. Many of us are deeply upset about these things, but this manufactured politics of disposability and the fears that enable it prevent people from taking action against these harms. There are many layers of fear associated with this abandonment: fear of what would happen if the system no longer managed our lives, fear of being devoured by the system ourselves, fear that we cannot win, and perhaps most dauntingly, the fear that we cannot do any better than this, that our hopes to the contrary are the utopian dreams of childish idealists. These fears create a psychic fortress around the death-making forces that are killing us in real time.

Fortunately, the death-makers of this system have never gone unopposed. There have always been dissenters and freedom fighters organizing against the violence and avarice of capitalism and white supremacy. From prison-industrial-complex abolitionists organizing to free people from cages to Indigenous people defending their ancestral lands around the world, these battles have powerful lineages. Joining the ranks of such struggles may come naturally to some. For many people, though, choosing to believe that change is possible and that it can only come from working in concert with other people requires tremendous courage. Challenging the mythologies of this system, reordering our fears, and investing ourselves in collective struggle are huge steps, and they are not steps most people will take merely because conditions are deteriorating.

Organizing gives us the opportunity to do more than map out the monstrosity that is the system; it allows us to build bonds between people in unique and powerful ways. By expanding our relationships and embracing interdependence, we can leverage power against the threats we face and extend care amid crisis. We can courageously reach out and connect with other people, even if we feel like we don't have much in common with them. When we experience a taste of collective power, our courage will grow, as we recognize that we are stronger together and that we are not alone.

When we are no longer ruled by a manufactured fear of one another, we experience a form of liberation. It is not a total liberation, as the structures that oppress us are, for now, very much intact, but we experience a kind of unshackling that allows us to begin the process of dismantling individualism—a violent ideology that has siloed us and stifled our collective potential. When we challenge our anxieties about "other people" and begin to see unlikely points of connection as points of potential stability and strength, we become more powerful.

Unraveling our fear of one another is a multilayered cultural project. After all, it's undeniable that people sometimes hurt one another, and many people are accustomed to following certain rituals of order when harm happens—even when those rituals do nothing to ameliorate their suffering. For example, many people know no recourse for violence besides calling the police, even if they do not believe that doing so will lead to any form of resolution. We have been taught to imagine that "the alternative" to policing is nothing less than brutal chaos. Then, in addition to building relationships that foster collective power, interdependence, and care, we must educate people about alternative interventions that actually address the needs of people affected by violence, poverty, and climate collapse. We must also continue to create our own works of visual art, fiction, and poetry that drive people to envision cooperation and mutual aid as our primary responses to crisis.

And we must help people imagine a world in which we can rely on one another. As author and organizer Shane Burley told us, "Solving a problem collectively takes a great deal of faith in others. We have been trained to see our survival in opposition to the community, something we do by putting ourselves and our families first. So it is a big leap to start trusting that collective liberation will actually care for us."

The mutual aid efforts of groups like the Auntie Sewing Squad and Maeqtekuahkihkiw Metaemohsak can help build that net, Burley says. To have faith that "a liberatory approach" is their best option, some people want to see evidence that we have helped one another survive and that we can do it again. "That's what building up projects of solidarity and mutual aid does: it creates a belief in what is possible, so that when even larger crises form, we have shown that by fighting the oppression of another we really do have the ability to target our own oppression as well," Burley told us.

In order to invest in a new vision, and a new way of living, we have to believe in each other and our capacity to create something better. Our belief in human potential must outweigh our fear of human failure. Our imaginations must be courageous.

Antidotes to Fear: Anchoring Ourselves and Belonging

In March 2022, activist and professor Dean Spade was having a conversation with his class about the climate crisis. Some of Spade's students expressed that the topic was painful for them because they had relatives in prison, and imprisoned people are routinely abandoned by authorities during climate catastrophes. Rather than simply acknowledging their feelings and pushing forward with the conversation, Spade chose to make room for what the students were experiencing. When describing the moment to Kelly on the *Movement Memos* podcast, Spade indicated that he wanted to honor "how deep that abandonment is" and "how heartbreaking and wrong that is."[11] So, Spade led his class in a thought exercise, saying, "What if we just sat down and just imagined in the most complex way we can, a plan for breaking people out of prison?" Spade asked students to consider catastrophic scenarios: "If the lights go out, if the earthquake comes, if the fire comes . . . what would we have to research that we don't know now?" Spade asked students to consider what skills they would need to develop, what conditions at the prison might be like, and how the staff might respond to their actions. Spade encouraged them to be bold in their imaginations. "How else would that plan ever happen if a lot of people didn't take time to try to dream it and try to imagine it? Which is true of every bold plan."

Regardless of whether Spade's students ever participate in a prison break, the activity of imagining what a refusal to abandon imprisoned people might look like is generative. As a teacher, Spade was asking his students to discuss a difficult subject, and when that topic caused some of his students pain, Spade suggested an activity that helped ground the students in their values. This also reminded them of their power and encouraged them to imagine how they might express that power collectively in order to rescue people whom society might otherwise leave behind. It was an anchoring moment that allowed students to inhabit a difficult reality together, rather than retreating or despairing.

In a world where we are steadily being splintered apart, where so much of our social lives have been reduced to commercial interactions, and where fellowship and belonging are desperately lacking, we must relearn how to hold space and belief together in ways that anchor us to each other and to our collective moral commitments.

This is not simply a task of educating ourselves but the ongoing work of charting and experiencing reality together and sharing our joy and grief over the wonders and tragedies of our times. Our atomized and alienated society leaves little organic space for political communion or even shared compassion. And in the spaces between us, fear grows.

In order to overcome these impediments, organizers must work to construct anchors that can provide a coherent understanding of the world in catastrophic times and help people maintain their values and commitments. If we do not take the work of anchoring seriously, we may find that our ships scatter or even sink with every strong gust of wind.

Anchors can take numerous shapes: a story, a community space, a sense of fellowship, a memorial—anything that helps ground people in a shared sense of history, compassion, and purpose. Projects and actions that anchor us awaken compassion, enliven our connectedness, reinforce our values, and, when necessary, reorient our political focus. We will need many such efforts in the coming years, as people's values are increasingly imperiled by the further normalization of mass suffering and death, and collective memory is continuously whitewashed by the powerful. Fundamentally, people who have been conditioned, out of fear, to view their own interests in isolation, rather than to find strength in collectivity, must learn to anchor themselves to one another for the sake of survival.

Commitment itself is an important anchor. Normalization is an insidious process, and it can warp people, reshaping the views and actions of people who have made no conscious decision to abandon their beliefs or other people. When it comes to resisting the propagation of harmful ideas or cooperation with harmful actions, an existing, declared commitment that runs counter to the harmful idea or action at hand is one of the best defenses we have against persuasion.[12] This is why commitments and affirmations should play important roles in the development of spaces and practices that anchor people. We must be concrete in our commitments to one another, to humanity, and to the Earth, and we must reaffirm those commitments regularly.

This can look like saying or singing our commitments in unison, creating artistic representations of those commitments, or asking people to join us in making public pledges. At some of the protests we have organized, we have invited members of the crowd to engage in dialogue with someone close by and to name what commitments they are making in the cause or campaign. We can also participate in symbolic acts that affirm our commitments. In Chicago, we co-organized many protests that ended at or took place entirely outside Cook County's Juvenile Temporary Detention Center. Such protests facilitate a moment of connection between protesters and the imprisoned children inside the building, some of whom can see the assembled activists from their rooms. At some events, attendees sing to the youth and carry a lighted message that reads, "WE LOVE YOU." The children inside often respond by pounding on their windows, making gestures of love and solidarity with their hands or writing messages in soap on their windows. Attendees at these protests experience a moment of political communion—one that helps anchor them in their values and the reality of what must be fought.

But even heartfelt commitments will often falter if people cannot develop a sustained sense of fellowship. Many people enter movement spaces wounded, traumatized, and hurting. Even in the absence of such feelings, entering a new space can be intimidating. We may wonder if we will be accepted or understood. Will people be kind? Will they judge us and decide we aren't knowledgeable enough to speak? Amid all of this uncertainty, people are also moved by the anxiousness of hope when entering a new space—the hope of a worthwhile experience, of a new journey or purpose, of finding friendship or solidarity. People come into movement spaces for a variety of reasons, but one that we rarely name or recognize is that we have a basic human desire to belong, and our competitive, commercial, individualistic society does not foster belonging. The disconnection of modern capitalist society has left many people hurting in ways they cannot make sense of, with injuries that cannot heal in isolation.

The remedy to alienation, a state that often keeps people cooperative and docile in the face of injustice, is belonging. As longtime organizer and nonviolent direct action trainer Lisa Fithian told us, "We have to intentionally build a culture of belonging that embraces the time and space for healing work as part of that culture." Some common organizing models are transactional and extractive, often replicating the oppressive dynamics of capitalism, where organizers function like managers, treating volunteers as workhorse employees. Frameworks that treat activists as mere unpaid labor, or as bodies to arrange for photo ops, without cultivating hope, purpose, or belonging for those individuals—or granting them any power in the entity they work within—can lead to frustration and burnout and cause many people to drop out of movements. We cannot win by replicating the dynamics of the dominant society. There is no "beating them at their own game." We are not managers or CEOs. We can only win by building something entirely different that offers people something that the oppressor cannot.

Effective organizing, therefore, does not begin with having the most compelling argument or the most dazzling direct action, but with developing the capacity to bring people into relationship with one another, such that they might begin to overcome alienation and fear.

We are told by the powerful that, in times of instability, our fears will bring out the worst in us. In reality, it is the stability of this system that best demonstrates the awesomely destructive power of our fears. Governed by fear, people are largely cooperative with systems that produce torture, mass death, and annihilation. That is the greatest danger that fear poses: not panic amid disorder, but cooperation with an order that we ought to find unspeakable—one that is actually poised to bring about our own extinction. But by building community and cultivating a sense of belonging between alienated people, we can begin a courageous process of dreaming new possibilities into being. We can also invite people to imagine what's possible by modeling and rehearsing the world as it should be in real time, in the spaces, groups, and relationships that we build.

Many people have no real sense or experience of community. They may think of communities in purely geographic terms—their town, their neighborhood, their school. But to build community in a relational sense we must overcome the isolation imposed by this society—an isolation that stifles our problem-solving abilities and leaves us dependent upon structures that in times of crisis are inadequate at best and, at worst, plainly destructive.

Concretely, what does it mean to build community? In simple terms, a community is a group of three or more people with whom we share similar values and interests and with whom we experience a sense of belonging. Establishing a community around mutual aims, such as the collective well-being of people living in proximity to each other, requires us to cultivate a sense of shared belonging. Radha Agarwal writes that belonging is "a feeling of deep relatedness and acceptance; a feeling of 'I would rather be here than anywhere else.'" Agarwal tells us that "belonging is the opposite of loneliness. It's a feeling of home, of 'I can exhale here and be fully myself with no judgment or insecurity.' Belonging is about shared values and responsibility, and the desire to participate in making your community better. It's about taking pride, showing up, and offering your unique gifts to others. *You can't belong if you only take.*"[13]

There is no substitute under capitalism for the sense of shared potential and understanding that exists when our work embodies our values and how we believe people should relate to one another. Yes, there will be breakdowns in that order, because we are all coming from this society, and we have its destructive muck all over us. But if we begin with that understanding and process harms with care as they arise, organizing spaces can offer a pause button for the atomization of the dominant culture. This feeling is part of what helps bring people back, however often a group meets.

What becomes increasingly possible in spaces where people experience belonging, imagine new ways of living, and practice those kinder, more just beliefs in relation to each other, is the cultivation of hope. Because if we can experience other people as co-strugglers—not as competitors or fearful enemies—we can act on the values of the world we want to build. We can experience moments of justice, peace, and liberation and in so doing realize that these concepts are not fantasies but realities that can be constructed.

Another crucial anchor for organizing is carefully constructed political education. This element is especially important as we work to confront our fears. Creating space for people to come to grips with disturbing truths and grapple with them in collectivity helps us build braver communities, where people find strength and inspiration in one another.

As activists, we sometimes poke holes in people's worldviews, perhaps damaging assumptions or allegiances, and this can feel satisfying. But a deeper kind of education is needed to uproot fear and spur action. The more difficult work begins when a person must reconfigure or replace their damaged or delegitimized worldview. If you leave them to it, they may find ways to patch over the holes you poked in their old point of view and rebuild something similar.

Anyone can tell someone who is wrong that they are mistaken. Organizers go farther, welcoming people into the practice of envisioning and enacting change. As old worldviews fall away, new worlds must be built. Part of our work is helping people understand the world on a new set of terms—a framework in which the social dynamics of capitalism are spelled out in gritty, honest terms but also understood as malleable, impermanent, and breakable. Imagining how the world ought to be, and then fighting and rehearsing for that world, demands a great deal of the human psyche. People need new, transformative stories to embrace in place of the false narratives they must let go—or that are being ripped out from under them. They may need to reimagine what the fulfillment of their values looks like—or even reimagine their values.

Organizers must help people reimagine the world, commit to rehearsing for and building that world, and develop creative ways to remain grounded in an increasingly chaotic and fractious environment, together.

CHAPTER 2

Refusing to Abandon

Monica Cosby is an organizer, mother, grandmother, writer, and prison abolitionist. In November 2020, Kelly spoke with Cosby on *Movement Memos* about her experiences organizing collective care as an incarcerated person.[1] Prisons are notoriously fascistic, and women in prison are punished at higher rates than men and for smaller infractions. In Illinois prisons, women are frequently ticketed for "insolence" and can wind up in solitary confinement over their verbal tone or a goofy facial expression. Cosby said she came to a realization when she first learned of Ruth Wilson Gilmore's theorization of "organized abandonment." She noted that the care work she experienced in prison functioned in opposition to abandonment and that imprisoned people often defy the system by "refusing to abandon each other." Cosby explained, "We've already been thrown away. We've been thrown away by the system." She added that, to some extent, many imprisoned people have also been "thrown away" by their families and people they knew before entering prison, who no longer stay in contact with them. Even imprisoned people with loving families can feel abandoned, as loved ones struggle to balance costly visits and phone calls with other financial strains and responsibilities. According to Cosby, that shared sense of having been discarded creates a solidarity among some imprisoned people that's about "refusing to throw each other away." Put simply, Cosby explains, "We refuse to abandon."

In prison, visible acts of care or bonds of solidarity can be punishable offenses. Alan Mills, the executive director of Uptown People's Law Center, has sued the state of Illinois on behalf of imprisoned people who have endured the abuse the state characterizes as "mental health care." When Mills spoke with Kelly for *Truthout*, he laid out the stakes for people who might practice mutual aid in prison. Mills explained that "one of the most important things that people who have a mental illness can do [in prison] is find a supportive community to be in," but prison rules are engineered in opposition to such support systems. Mills said, "Generally in prison, any sort of group like that is considered an unauthorized organization, and prisons view it the same way that they would view a gang." According to Mills, creating mutual aid formations, or even forming close bonds with others, can land imprisoned people in solitary confinement.[2]

In a torturous, spirit-breaking environment where solidarity can have punitive consequences, Cosby explained how some imprisoned women create their own social life support system—one that she credits with saving her own life. Cosby explained that, given her initial sentence of eighty-three years, she did not see any "light at the end of the tunnel." But other women, who were also serving lengthy sentences, offered Cosby support and guidance when she arrived. "They were the light in my tunnel," Cosby said. "We were all in the tunnel together just making light."

There were multiple occasions during Cosby's incarceration when she considered taking her own life. "I just didn't want to be in prison anymore," she said. Cosby's family had moved out of state shortly after she began serving time in prison. While at Cook County Jail, Cosby had weekly visits with her family. But in prison, she was unable to visit with relatives or use the phone. She missed her children. "I just was fucked up," Cosby said of the experience.

Amid her despair, Cosby became suicidal. She made a plan to wait until other women had left her cell block for dinner and then hang herself from a rail. She tore a sheet to create a noose and began giving her personal belongings away. That night, Cosby sat on some steps, near the spot where she planned to tie her noose to the rail, watching as people exited the area for dinner. She watched "just waiting for the door to close" behind them, so she could enact her plan. But to Cosby's surprise, not everyone had left for dinner. "Kimmy Keller, who is out here now, and Tammy Evans, who is still locked up . . . they didn't go to chow that night," she said. The two women were among the people Cosby had given her belongings to. Recognizing what this behavior likely indicated, they resolved to keep an eye on Cosby. When Keller and Evans found Cosby sitting alone on the stairs, waiting for an opportunity to die by suicide, they sat with her. Cosby explained, "They knew because they had either been there before or they had seen other people in that space before, but they knew what it was and they didn't let me go. They just refused to abandon me."

Cosby has paid this kindness forward on many occasions, at times sitting with people who were grappling with untreated mental health issues who might not be "present in our particular reality that we're living in" but who still required the support, care, and companionship of another human being. "I have sat with other women because I remember when somebody sat with me," Cosby said.

The social life support system that Cosby described also involved the cultivation of joy as a form of sustenance and a means of rebellion. To lift each other's spirits and imbue life with a more joyous energy, some of the people Cosby was imprisoned with would sing until they got in trouble—and then keep singing. While working shifts in the kitchen, Cosby was among those who would sing. "Every so often, whatever COO or kitchen supervisor or whatever come by and be like, 'Shut that shit up, cut that shit out.' And we'd be like, 'Alright.' And sing any motherfucking way," Cosby said. When the women were issued a disciplinary ticket for singing, they would respond by making up a song about the ticket. This rebellion of song created space for joy in a brutally oppressive environment. Despite the fascistic nature of prison life and the surveillance that dominated their lives, amid playful bouts of song, Cosby and the other women were able to "smile and laugh and dance."

Cosby also noted that imprisoned women regularly made gifts for one another, even though such items were regularly confiscated as contraband. Imprisoned women would often commission artwork from one another. "Some of the best artists I've ever seen in life are in the fucking prison," Cosby noted.

In addition to rebelliously singing and commissioning artwork that would likely be destroyed, the imprisoned women also made up holidays in order to create more cause for celebration. In addition to celebrating holidays like Christmas and Mother's Day, Cosby said, "we also just make up holidays just because. And we feed each other. We make these fantastic, fantastic meals out of nothing."

Cosby said that few accomplishments—from finishing a GED class to simply waking up for another day—went unappreciated amid the imprisoned women's intentional cultivation of joy. "We celebrate every little fucking accomplishment because it's not a little accomplishment. . . . It's the constant celebration of just us. We're celebrating the fact that we done did some shit. We woke up this morning. We celebrate."

These practices of cultivating hope and joy as a matter of survival, under extremely oppressive conditions, are instructive in these times. We must throw our energy into building active relationships with other people whom we refuse to abandon and who refuse to abandon us. To resist the erosion of empathy, we must invite people to participate in acts of care, defense, aid, and rescue. We must normalize acts of mutual aid amid the everyday crisis of capitalism and build these mechanisms into our organizing work at the ground level.

Against Misanthropy

We have heard it many times, often from exasperated activists: "I give up on people!" We sometimes hear these words in the wake of electoral outcomes, or when the public has been unresponsive to a crisis. It is the voice of exhaustion. We empathize with that exhaustion. The natural world is being killed by corporations and the military-industrial complex, while millions of people languish in prisons and disabled people are treated as disposable the world over. Indigenous people are murdered for defending the land and water while anti-Black racism, homophobia, and transphobia drive violence daily. When people fail to act against these forces, or fail to even denounce them, our frustration is valid. People should be moved by injustice, and they should take action. When they don't, it is easy to judge them for their failures and release ourselves from any further obligations toward them.

But when we assess the conditions that precipitate our struggles, we can see that they are not being orchestrated by most people. Most people are merely cooperating with the world as they understand it, either under the threat of violence or because they are navigating the illusions that were constructed around them. The people driving those conditions are a relative minority whose greed and violence does not define all of humanity, no matter how much they would like us to suppose it does. Amid a landscape of catastrophe and extraction draped in bright plastic product displays and endless streams of escapism, most people are simply being herded along. They do as they are told and try to replicate the same set of relations that defined life before. As things deteriorate, they keep trying. They do not know what else to do. Nothing in their experience or imagination has prepared them to conceptualize the realities of the capitalist system, their real relationship to it, or any fathomable escape.

As humans on Earth in these times, we are raised into a rigged game, traumatized by its violence, and coached to replicate its dynamics. We are surrounded by lies, illusions, and coercion. We are sold punishment as justice and annihilation as progress, and many people cannot imagine anything else. But just as we do not abandon people we love who are in crisis, we have not given up on humanity. We have witnessed transformation too often to dismiss its possibility, and we have an obligation to that possibility in individual lives and in larger groups of people.

Whether caring for people, or caring for communities, we must draw some boundaries to preserve ourselves, but we must also live in opposition to abandonment, following Cosby's example. Struggling people need resources they are being denied and an opportunity to heal and reorient their lives. As organizers, we work to connect other people with the resources, relationships, information, and understanding they need to change their lives and the world. We organize opportunities for discovery, exploration, and the pursuit of justice. Some who take these journeys with us are transformed by their experiences and through their own labor and healing, just as we have been transformed by our own journeys. Political evolution is a lifelong process, and it is messy. Being present for people will always mean being there for the mess created by human conflict and trauma.

Organizers do not have the luxury of misanthropy. We have to believe in people, and we have to believe in ourselves.

Building Relationships

As organizers, beyond believing in people, we have to build with them. That means prioritizing relationships within movement work.

Our friend Ejeris Dixon is an organizer and political strategist with twenty years of experience working in racial justice, transformative justice, LGBTQ liberation, antiviolence, and economic justice movements. She is also the founding director of Vision Change Win Consulting, where she partners with organizations to build capacity and deepen the impact of their organizing strategies.

In a conversation about relationship building, Dixon told us, "For me, relationship building is as much of a politic as my commitment to abolition is, or my commitment to anticapitalism. Some people see building relationships as a chore, but I actually feel like you've got to believe in it. You have to believe that it matters."

Dixon considers herself an introvert. However, building relationships is not about being the life of the party. Instead, Dixon said, it revolves around a key principle: "If you show up for people, they show up for you." She engages with people accordingly, whether she is interacting with neighbors in her apartment building or working with organizations. In practice, showing up for people can look like bringing someone food when they are ill, cop-watching (observing and documenting police activity in order to discourage or bear witness to police violence) if a neighbor has to deal with police, listening and extending comfort to someone experiencing an emotional crisis, or offering to lighten someone's load if they are overworked. There are structured ways groups and communities can agree to show up for each other— such as neighbors making a collective agreement to cop-watch if they observe police activity.

Dixon talks about relationship building as a skill that needs to be sharpened and maintained. For her, that sharpening came through years of daily canvassing. At one point, Dixon was organizing Work Experience Program workers in New York City parks. The city's Work Experience Program was created as a "workfare" program to extract labor from people seeking public benefits. Worker advocates have described the program as "New York City's Public Sector Sweat Shop Economy."[3] When canvassing around the issue, Dixon would walk around city parks waiting for workers to take breaks so she could chat with them about their working conditions and whether they would want to a join a community organization "where folks were fighting to not have to work for the city for their public assistance benefits, and instead could get job training or go to school."

Dixon worked for that base-building organization for two years, which required her to do four to six hours of outreach work per day, every day, "and I'm grateful for that," she told us. "I am grateful because I realized that relationship building had to be an everyday, every-minute commitment, because movements are based on oppressed people coming together, because we have people power. So we need people for the people power."

However, building people power is not simply about adding people to fill in gaps in our work. Rather than recruiting people to fulfill the roles that we envision for them, Dixon stresses the importance of learning what people are passionate about and "finding an intersection" between someone's interests and the work at hand. "Relationship building is also a process of hearing what people's needs and dreams are and creating space for people to collaboratively or collectively take care of each other," Dixon said. "So I think a lot about starting with asking, 'What do you want? What do you need? How can I help? Here's what we're working on. How does that sound to you? What are we missing? What else is needed?' Not 'Do you want to get involved?' or 'You should get involved.'"

While not everyone will be as immersed in direct outreach as Dixon was during her canvassing days, canvassing and outreach are powerful opportunities to broaden our practice of communication and to learn how to relate to people we would not ordinarily speak with. She encourages would-be organizers to try engaging with activities like door knocking, if they're able, because such activities bring us into contact with people we may never have encountered otherwise.

"You don't know what's on the other side of that door, which means that you don't get to pick and choose who you're building with," Dixon said. "And sometimes that's good."

Canvassing work, such as door knocking, requires us to speak to and engage with people from a variety of backgrounds and offers us the opportunity to practice listening, sharing stories, and—perhaps surprisingly—asserting boundaries. Authentic communication with strangers often requires us to share stories that reveal some of our vulnerability, while also drawing lines about what remains personal.

Dixon warned against lecturing people or pontificating as we work to build organizing relationships.

"This idea that we know better than a community [about] what they need, without asking and being in conversation, isn't relationship building. It's more like political imposition," she said. "And so I think when you start with a politic of asking people what they need, or if what you're working on resonates for them, or what is missing, then you build stronger relationships than when you just say 'Come to the rally' or 'Come to the meeting' or 'Come to the event.'"

When eliciting people's concerns, interests, and vulnerabilities, Dixon cautioned that the goal is not to "prey on people's fears" or "push their buttons." She warned, "There's a fine line between what people can call agitation and manipulation."

Manipulation is not a sound basis for participation, and it does not build strong relationships. Rather, Dixon suggested, an organizer should acknowledge what an individual has shared and extend options or requests that may resonate with the person they're approaching. An organizer can also ask, "'What would make this more interesting and appealing for you? What would make this more interesting for the people that you know? Are there other people that you know that want to get involved?'" We build better relationships, Dixon said, "when we build projects where people honestly have a stake in the project, not because we told them they have to, but because we've asked them what they need and we are responsive to the needs of multiple people."

Examples of this kind of responsive organizing include campaigns that are grounded in demands and input that come directly from those who are being encouraged to get involved. Young organizers with #NoCopAcademy in Chicago, for example, canvassed Garfield Park, the neighborhood where a proposed police training complex was slated to be built, and got input from residents on how they would prefer to see the money spent and what investments they would rather see made in their communities. Those demands and visions were foundational to the campaign to stop the complex. While the campaign did not ultimately halt the project, young organizers did a tremendous amount of relationship building, engaging community members in discussions about what they wanted for their neighborhood. Those relationships could prove crucial in future organizing endeavors.

Sometimes good outreach is not about extending an ask or even eliciting ideas. As Dixon told us, "There was a time when I was working at a community-based organization [and] we did a lot of work around violence. Whenever there was an incident within somebody's area, we'd make calls. And we'd be like, 'There was this issue, we're calling to check on you.'" During such outreach, Dixon and her co-organizers would inquire about people's well-being and needs, "and that's not the time to say, 'We know you care about violence, so clearly you should come and make calls too.' They were literally just check-ins. We were checking in with people, and sometimes connected to that, people were interested in getting more involved, and I think those are real relationships. And it also created different relationships."

The centrality of relationship building to organizing means that, within an organization, everyone should be doing it. It shouldn't be one person's job, Dixon said; everyone should see it as part of their organizing role to bring in more people.

That doesn't mean outreach and relationship building are easy. But placing relationships at the core of our work is key to building sustainable movements. As Carlos Saavedra, founder of the Ayni Institute,[4] told us,

> The journey of community organizing is not an easy one, as it involves bringing people together with many different perspectives to build something new and do something that feels impossible to do. In the first year, what determines whether the project or the leadership can continue is the quality and depth of their relationships with one another. This brings organizers to the realization that they must spend most of their waking hours listening to others, building trust, and taking small actions that give people a glimpse of their true power.

Building strong relationships can also help organizations and groups survive conflicts, which are inevitable in all organizing spaces. Dixon said that "when folks are building projects based on their shared dreams and needs, there is a bond that solidifies with politics in a way that helps people navigate conflict or fissures, because you start with the practice of showing up for each other, and you start from the practice of getting to know each other in a way that we can actually show up for each other."

Sometimes We Save Each Other

In a 2017 piece written in the wake of Hurricane Harvey, climate writer Dahr Jamail used texts from his loved ones who lived in the Houston area to frame his reporting on how anthropogenic climate disruption had intensified the storm.[5] According to the National Weather Service, Houston had experienced "epic and catastrophic flooding." Jamail explained that "sea-surface temperatures near Texas were between 2.7° and 7.2°F above average, making them some of the warmest ocean temperatures on Earth."[6] Those warm surface level temperatures turned a tropical depression into a catastrophic Category 4 hurricane within two days. Harvey was also the first storm on record in the Gulf of Mexico to have ever intensified in the twelve hours prior to making landfall.

The piece began with a text from Jamail's mother that concluded with "We are okay. Tired. Love you, Mom." Jamail ended the piece with a text from a friend who lived near downtown Houston. The text read,

> It will take years to recover.
> We are all rescuing each other.
> Odd to think that our future can be summed up like that.[7]

When Jamail's friend said, "We are all rescuing each other," he could have been referring to community-led rescue missions, where anarchists, antifascists, and other volunteer rescuers coordinated with stranded neighbors on social media in order to rescue people by boat. He could have been referring to the distributions of food, diapers, and other essentials—or to the emotional support people were extending to one another as they endured a world-crushing experience. He could have been talking about all of those things and more, because there are many ways that we rescue one another in a crisis, and, as Jamail's friend observed, we will be rescuing each other for years.

As fires rage and sea levels rise in the coming years, we will be called upon to rescue one another again and again. That impulse—to find our boats after a storm and to pull each other from the water on unauthorized, community-led rescue missions—will be key to surviving these times and to the creation of a new future. It is not saviorism, but collectivity and solidarity, that will fuel our best efforts. One of the greatest struggles of our time will be to cultivate a life-affirming political culture that can be enacted in the everyday, a counterculture of rebellious care.

The act of showing up for each other can be as simple as checking in on a friend who is sick or grieving to see what they might need, or it can be as dramatic as saving someone's life. In this society, the idea of "saving" people is a troubled one. Often, when people talk about saving others, they are talking about something coercive, like criminalization. Laws that criminalize sex workers and people who use illicit substances, for example, are often depicted as "saving" those people from harmful, depraved forces. In reality, the enforcement of such laws plunges people into a system that inflicts physical and sexual violence upon them, while also robbing them of our most finite resource—time. Some people view themselves as saving others by attempting to convert them to Christianity. For these reasons, many have come to associate the idea of saving with glory-seeking and a lack of respect for the agency of others. Some people state definitively that we cannot save others—that we can only help them save themselves. But the truth is, we sometimes save each other, and that's a good thing.

If your neighborhood floods, for example, and you have access to a boat, you may wind up pulling people from the water. While officials often discourage DIY rescue efforts, we know that many people would be left behind in the absence of such efforts. Now, if your neighborhood floods regularly, and you are the only one trying to help people, that is a problem. Or if you were to become egotistical about your role as rescuer and sought fame or adulation for your efforts, that would likewise prove problematic. But the importance of saving others should not be dismissed—and we should recognize that, in these tumultuous times, none of us are far from needing saving ourselves. Our goal should be interdependence: to be part of a community where rescue is viewed not as exceptional but as something that we owe each other.

We do not need heroes. We need people who are committed to one another's survival, who are willing to act on the basis of that commitment. Unfortunately, we are living in an era where refusing to abandon people can be a revolutionary act. It could also be the key to our collective survival.

As Chris Begley, who is a wilderness survival instructor, anthropology professor, and author of *The Next Apocalypse: The Art and Science of Survival*, has argued, many people who worry about catastrophe and collapse are preparing for "the wrong apocalypse."[8] Begley argues that while the survival skills he teaches, such as how to build a fire or purify water, can be important in a crisis, "social and political skills, and more immediately, how you treat people, will be most important in ensuring survival in the end."[9]

Having studied apocalyptic events across the course of human history, as well as the likely disaster scenarios of our time, Begley quashes notions of rugged individualism, insisting that "basic traits like kindness, fairness, and empathy" will be the basis of any sustainable, meaningful effort at collective survival—and as Begley stresses, we cannot survive alone.[10]

We know that some people, such as displaced Black people, are more likely to be targeted for violence in the wake of catastrophe, as reactionaries double down on their bigotry and a mentality of scarcity—the idea that they must protect what is theirs from people whom they would sooner shoot dead than assist. We saw this kind of violence in New Orleans after Hurricane Katrina, when some white residents armed themselves and hunted displaced Black people amid the flooding. While some defensive action may be necessary in such moments, Begley emphasizes the need to build community, rather than brave violent onslaughts alone or in small groups.

"I am not suggesting that you should not protect yourself or your stuff," Begley writes. "I am saying that if you are in a situation where your continued well-being depends on you having frequent high-risk violent encounters, you are bound to lose eventually, and that is not a viable strategy."[11] While many people fantasize about forming small teams of skilled people who would somehow brave the perils of an apocalypse together, perhaps fighting off zombies or right-wingers, Begley argues that an insular approach cannot facilitate long-term survival. We must instead learn from the failures of this society, including inequities in health care, education, food, and housing. "I keep coming back to community as the solution," he writes.[12] To brave shifting conditions, we will have to strive to create communities "in which everyone's basic needs are met," because "leaving people out eventually costs everybody." Interdependence and the social skills that facilitate that connectedness or cooperation are at the heart of Begley's theory of survival.[13]

Begley stresses that while most people, once motivated, can acquire basic survival skills like fire building quickly, social skills often take much longer to develop. We need to prioritize them, starting now.

As organizers, we have experienced the power of interdependence on many occasions. For example, in the realm of direct action, we have protected and been protected by others in the face of police violence. On March 11, 2016, then presidential candidate Donald Trump attempted to hold a campaign rally in Chicago. The event was shut down by protesters. Anti-Trump protesters maintained a major presence inside the University of Illinois at Chicago pavilion, where the event was being held, and outside on the surrounding streets. At an intersection near the rally's venue, Trump supporters and police attacked a Black-led area of protest. Kelly, who was playing a supportive role at the protest, was part of a dense crowd that police were attacking with batons. Young Black organizers were brutalized, and one protester was ultimately hospitalized after being struck in the head with a police baton.

Some protesters collided as the crowd was forced backward by police, and Kelly was knocked to the ground. Kelly has back problems, and after the fall, she needed help getting to her feet, but she was not sure if anyone had seen her fall. The crowd was dense and under attack. She was absorbing accidental kicks from people being shoved backward by police, as people stumbled and attempted to stay on their feet. She felt someone begin to step on her lower body before they, too, stumbled backward. Unable to get to her feet, Kelly attempted to shield her head with her hands and arms. Suddenly, she could feel herself being lifted off the ground. In what seemed like one swift motion, she was pulled from the street and deposited on the sidewalk. She was also face to face with a friend, Philip DeVon, an attorney with the National Lawyers Guild. He had seen Kelly slip below the crowd and moved quickly to get her off the street. DeVon was talking, but Kelly was dazed and unsure if he was saying, "You're OK" or "Are you OK?," so she simply thanked him for his help. Within moments, they had both returned to their support roles at the action.

DeVon may have saved Kelly from incurring serious injuries that night, but most of their co-strugglers remained unaware of these events. Why? Because for them, this anecdote was just one example among countless others of the ways people protect and defend each other in moments of protest. DeVon's actions prevented Kelly from being trampled, just as, earlier in the night, the actions of people in direct support roles had halted cars that might have struck protesters and just as many other people in the streets took defensive action to ward off white supremacist attacks or provided care to those who were brutalized or frightened. In such circumstances, acts of rescue are essential but not extraordinary. They are interdependence at work. In the community of protest that Kelly and Philip move in, helping an injured person to the sidewalk amid police violence is not an act of heroism but what many activists believe they owe to each other. Acts of rescue and assistance are part of the natural rhythm of solidarity, love, and action that can take hold in the streets when people choose to hold their ground collectively.

Migrant justice organizer and author Harsha Walia told us that she views the bonds that can form between protesters in the streets as an underappreciated "form of mutual aid." She explained that some acts of assistance are obvious and overt, such as de-arresting fellow protesters who are being seized by police, but less noticeable actions, such as slowing the pace of a march so that no one is left behind and the group can move as one, reflect an awareness and a level of regard for one another that are at odds with the norms of this society. Walia dismissed the popular tendency to view direct action and mutual aid as separate approaches. "Sometimes mutual aid is pitted against being on the street. One is seen as more militant and one is seen as more care-based," she said. "Well, they're not mutually exclusive."

Protest, like catastrophe, can enliven our connectivity as human beings. We should not think of our protective instincts as "selflessness," rather as a connectedness that facilitates reciprocal care. By not abandoning people, we contribute to a culture where we, ourselves, are less likely to be abandoned. By defending one another, or even rescuing each other, in times of danger, we are reclaiming our capacity to help each other survive.

CHAPTER 3

Care Is Fundamental

Six days after Hurricane Maria devastated Puerto Rico in 2017, many cities were still without power, and supermarket shelves were empty. Daniel Orsini, a mutual aid organizer in Puerto Rico, was working with others to distribute free meals to people in Caguas, a city south of San Juan. Since most people in Puerto Rico had no telephone access after the storm, Orsini and his co-organizers drove around Caguas, announcing through a loudspeaker that the next day, from 6:00 to 8:00 a.m., they would be serving breakfast, and that lunch would be available between 2:00 and 3:00 p.m. "We were expecting, I don't know, maybe thirty persons in the morning, fifty in the afternoon," Orsini told us. To Orsini's surprise, one hundred people showed up for breakfast and three hundred for lunch. Orsini and his co-organizers had experience running mutual aid kitchens, so they were well positioned to round up available pots, pans, and food and coordinate meals. When people assembled to await their meals, Orsini noted the diversity of class backgrounds the crowd represented. Some of the people in line were impoverished, but others were clearly middle class and probably not accustomed to standing in long lines.

The organizers announced to people waiting in line that no one would be turned away, but they did invite people who were willing and able to contribute something in exchange for the food they would receive: money, food items, or volunteer hours. Orsini explained that some people had money but could not find food to purchase, while others might have food in their homes but no way to cook it, due to the power outage or a lack of running water. Some people had nothing but might want to contribute their time to an effort to keep everyone fed.

The organizers' project, dubbed Centro de Apoyo Mutuo Caguas (Center of Mutual Support of Caguas), was one of fourteen Centros de Apoyo Mutuo that emerged throughout Puerto Rico's mainland and archipelago as residents struggled to survive the mass neglect that ramped up the storm's death toll.[1]

While the United States federal government initially maintained that only sixty-seven people were killed by Hurricane Maria, funeral homes in Puerto Rico were overwhelmed by a massive influx of bodies in the weeks following the storm. Subsequent figures released by Puerto Rican officials established that 2,975 people died in the storm and its aftermath. Many of those deaths were preventable, had the US government funded adequate rescue and recovery efforts. Many people who required dialysis, oxygen, ventilators, and other electric medical devices died in the days following the storm. Most islands had no running water. The growth of mold in flooded homes also led to sometimes deadly respiratory infections. As the Trump administration denied the crisis and refused to extend meaningful assistance, mutual aid centers were sites of solidarity and survival.

Organizers of the Centro de Apoyo Mutuo Caguas were working out of a borrowed space, but according to Orsini, the infrastructure of the space was "not very good," so organizers set out to reclaim a more appropriate space in downtown Caguas. "We found this huge building, we opened the gates, and we started to work on it, painting it, et cetera," he said. The group prepared and served meals in the space, offered acupuncture services, and planted a community garden.

As often happens during and after moments of mass activation, some of Puerto Rico's mutual aid formations eventually splintered or disbanded. Orsini explained that the number of active Centros de Apoyo Mutuo diminished as the norms of capitalism were restored in Puerto Rico. As electricity was slowly restored across the mainland and archipelago and grocery stores and restaurants made their resurgence, fewer people sought food from community kitchens, and some groups debated where to focus their energies. Orsini left the Centro de Apoyo Mutuo Caguas in order to pursue an acupuncture-focused healing justice project.[2] But despite the impermanence or changing shape of some projects, the rise of mutual aid in Puerto Rico is a powerful example of what people are capable of when they realize that the powerful have deemed them disposable, and that solidarity with one another is their best hope.

Like an electrical current that reactivates a stopped heart, crisis can create a social defibrillation that re-enlivens our connectedness to other human beings and allows our compassion, imaginations, and political will to flow more freely. This is why protests, mutual aid projects, and innovative new modes of connection and support emerge rapidly in the most perilous times. As organizers, we must learn to conjure that social electricity even in relatively "normal" times.

We believe in caring for each other as a form of cultural rebellion. We believe in the need to foster a counterculture of care—a politics larger than any siloed issue, one that can challenge dehumanization and the erasure of atrocity while allowing us to hold on to each other and our humanity amid disasters daily and acute. The state has the capacity to help us all survive—and even thrive—but in its current form, it is actively opposed to doing so. We must have the will to survive in collectivity, as people who are willing to seize, defy, and upend whatever they must for the sake of life, dignity, and decency—and for the sake of each other.

In this moment, it is crucial that we consider the lessons of the COVID-19 pandemic, a crisis that foreshadows what is possible in the face of collapse, for better and for worse.

In the early months of the pandemic in the United States, many people were experiencing the devastating financial impacts of workplace closures, overindulging in alcohol or other intoxicants, and voicing their despair publicly on social media. Loneliness, already epidemic in our consumer-driven culture, became an overwhelming force. Substance use, already on the rise in the United States, intensified. For millions of people, the pandemic was their first experience of collapse—their first realization that the world they were taught to see as fixed and immovable could indeed collapse and that the bottom could fall out completely. But amid the suffering and unraveling of those early days, we also saw a side of humanity that is rarely featured in postapocalyptic films, which often depict an "every man for himself" response to catastrophe. In spring 2020, unprecedented numbers of people organized mutual aid efforts to help their neighbors survive. Using technology to overcome the physical barriers imposed by the pandemic, tens of thousands of people started new groups and built new mechanisms within existing organizations to meet the needs of people who were struggling. From delivering groceries and medicine to helping people access remote therapy after the loss of loved ones, people across the country devised ways to care for one another. Contrary to fictitious, popular depictions of people in dire straits, many people coping with the grief, uncertainty, and isolation of the pandemic longed to connect through acts of aid and care, and they did. Grassroots groups redistributed millions of dollars to people who were struggling. Empty refrigerators were stocked. Countless people in crisis were met with compassion and assistance. In a society where we are taught to fear each other, many were moved by the realization that we were and are each other's best hope amid catastrophe.

That realization was bolstered by the failure of the US government to respond to the crisis with any amount of decency or competence. Our austerity-worn health-care system was already unprepared for such an onslaught before the Trump presidency, but as our own government hijacked planes full of personal protective equipment meant for health-care workers and spread rampant misinformation about the virus,[3] it became clear that no government agency was going to adequately support people in their daily survival. So, everyday people, some experienced and others newly activated, toiled and organized, both according to time-tested models and with ingenuity in the absence of experience or instruction. People experimented, muddled through, and endeavored to hold each other in whatever ways they could, even at a distance. As journalist Shane Burley told Kelly during an interview for *Truthout* in late March 2020,

> I have been interviewing mutual aid networks all across the country, and dozens of them popped up within days. I mean, just days, and almost every major city has more than one. Small towns [have them]. Some of these groups have existed for a long time. You know, they come out of larger support centers, community centers, other people that are doing kind of mutual aid work, or people doing things like needle exchange or sex worker solidarity work, or some of them just popped up out of nowhere as some of them are from folks that never done anything and just decided to get chat threads together to check in with all their neighbors and compile resources and started doing runs to help each other.[4]

As Burley would tell us in August 2021, "The scale of the mutual aid groups that emerged during the pandemic was staggering, with thousands of people coming together to support each other. What was so remarkable is that much of this did not come out of radical or political communities; they were just people looking to survive by caring for one another." Burley finds hope in these efforts, arguing that such mobilizations can fundamentally alter a community's sense of what's possible. "Mutual aid is the story of this century," Burley said. "We have to be there for each other."

Care Lessons from the Rebellion

In late May 2020, as COVID-related mutual aid efforts flourished, the rebellions against structural anti-Blackness and policing began: after the murder of George Floyd was captured on film by Darnella Frazier and the world bore witness online, millions of people took to the streets in protest, despite great uncertainty about the risk that COVID-19 might pose to their health. They were certain that intervention was needed, that justice could not wait. While public gatherings were generally discouraged, 1,200 doctors signed a public letter expressing support for the protests, describing them as "vital to the national public health and to the threatened health specifically of Black people in the United States."[5] Doctors and other clinicians suggested best practices for safer demonstrations, and a culture of care sprung up at protests; the distribution of masks and hand sanitizer became standard features of marches and rallies. Through signage, outreach, rhetoric, and artwork, protesters reminded each other that masking and preventing the spread of COVID-19 were manifestations of their larger concern for their communities and each other. The phrase "we keep us safe" became both a mantra and a call to action. Protesters' safety efforts were successful: a study conducted by the National Bureau of Economic Research in the summer of 2020 ultimately found "no evidence that urban protests reignited COVID-19 case growth during the more than three weeks following protest onset." The study further indicated that "cities which had protests saw an *increase* in social distancing behavior for the overall population relative to cities that did not."[6]

Asha AE is a Black visual artist, community organizer, and undergraduate at University of Illinois–Chicago. She has engaged in campaigns with Assata's Daughters—a queer, Black, woman-led, and youth-focused organization rooted in the Black radical tradition—and with Dissenters, an antiwar, antimilitarism, and anti-imperialism organization for young people. When Chicagoans protested the murder of George Floyd on May 30, Asha was in the streets with friends, distributing kits of "essentials" that included gloves, masks, water, juice, Gatorade, crackers, and chips. "People were so delighted and surprised that we were giving away these things for free," she told us. Asha's crew, led by her friend Eva Marie, was well organized, and while unrest had yet to erupt in Chicago, they knew Chicago police were routinely violent toward protesters. "We were strapped with our own bags that included fancy wound cleaning liquids, gauze, first aid kits, clean towels, and other things," she said.

Thousands of people rallied against police violence that afternoon in Daley Plaza, in downtown Chicago. "I've never seen a more diverse crowd of people," Asha told us. "I felt like people were finally starting to get it—what Black queer women and BIPOC folk have been saying for decades, finally started to click. I even ran into people from grade school and high school who rarely went to protests."

When the rally ended, hours of intense marching began. Asha and her friends were there to offer supplies and aid to protesters, many of whom carried signs bearing messages like "Defund the Police" and "Justice for George Floyd." Asha noted that she was surprised by "the amount of explicitly abolitionist signs there were." One sign bore a list of names of people murdered by police, including trans women. Chants ranged from liberal standbys like "This is what democracy looks like" to cries of "Fuck 12." There were no clear leaders on the ground and the scene felt "rather organic."

Asha and her crew wore thick gloves, masks, and yellow vests as they wove through the crowds. Mindful of the risk of COVID-19 and the potential use of chemical weapons by police, the crew also wore goggles. "Eventually, the scene got wild and I lost my people," she told us. After backing away from a bridge and being threatened by police, Asha saw a police car on fire and realized that the protest had become an uprising. She saw a 7-Eleven store overrun by people who carried away food and other supplies. In a short time, multiple stores on downtown Chicago's State Street were overrun by rebellious young protesters. Downtown Chicago is the heart of Chicago's wealth, from skyscrapers to upscale hotels and department stores, the area sees steady investment, while Black and brown neighborhoods are starved by austerity.

"I've never felt so free at an action," Asha told us, adding, "I believe 'rioting and looting' downtown are resistance to capitalism."[7]

While Asha found the energy of the moment inspiring, she was disciplined about maintaining her role as a source of care and aid to protesters in need, even as police violence intensified. "We tried our best," Asha told us. "There were a lot of injuries that I for one was not trained to handle. I'm talking about deep wounds and gashes from the police. We had our cleaning stuff, kept our gloves on, and got to work." There were experienced street medics—trained in dealing with more complex injuries—at the protests, but an overwhelming number of people were in need of assistance. "I was horrified to learn my friend received a concussion and needed stitches on her head," Asha told us. "She was [beaten while] helping to de-arrest someone."

In response to the protests, Chicago mayor Lori Lightfoot declared a 9:00 p.m. curfew to be enforced by police, only thirty-five minutes before it would go into effect. Many residents did not receive text alerts about the curfew until after 9:00 p.m., if they were notified at all. Public transit was cut off in the downtown area, and bridges across the Chicago River were raised, effectively trapping protesters whose very presence had now been criminalized. Among other acts of brutality, police blasted the trapped protesters with chemical weapons. Eventually, after significant public outcry on social media, police opened a path to allow protesters a way out, though they continued to wage attacks and arrests. "We didn't know a curfew was called until later, but we didn't care," Asha told us. She and her friends continued to distribute supplies and care for wounded protesters well into the night, shouting, "'Free water, free snacks' and 'Masks,' and asking what people needed when we saw people injured."

Asha's experience of providing care amid rebellion was formative. In the days and weeks that followed, she continued to participate in acts of aid and care at protests. "Nearly every action I attended, folk were in need of something. I loved that we, primarily Cops out CPS and the Defund CPD squad, were able to provide.[8] We don't just do this to demonstrate what care can look like, we do this for our people to ensure their wellness despite all the forces stacked against us. Abolition can't wait."

Care as Refuge

On May 30, 2020, while Asha and other protesters experienced unrest and brutality in the streets, the Chicago Freedom School (CFS) became a crucial space of refuge and care for young people in a moment of rebellion. Cofounded by Mariame in 2007, CFS is best known for its work providing organizing and movement education for young people of color. Tony Alvarado-Rivera, the school's executive director, calls CFS "a hub for radical imagination and organizing rooted in movement history," as well as "a practice space for youth-led liberation." On that May afternoon, Alvarado-Rivera was outside Chicago police headquarters at Eighteenth and State streets, doing jail support work for protesters arrested the previous day, when a flood of police cars headed downtown. "I saw hundreds of cars pass through the precinct and thought, 'This is going to be huge,'" Tony told us. While the police mobilization was worrisome, Alvarado-Rivera had not yet imagined the extent of the violence that would unfold or the essential role CFS would play in offering care and protection to young people.

Alvarado-Rivera is a queer gender-nonconforming organizer who joined CFS a decade ago as the coordinator of youth programs. When the pandemic struck, Alvarado-Rivera was transitioning into their new role as executive director. In response to the spread of COVID-19, CFS had adopted a remote work model, but as the protests downtown intensified on May 30, a pair of young organizers contacted Alvarado-Rivera asking if CFS was open. "We're out downtown and we have nowhere else to go," the young people told them. Opening the school as a healing space and a place for young people to regroup or debrief during protests was a common practice for CFS but one Alvarado-Rivera had not anticipated that day. Yet, seeing young people in need, Alvarado-Rivera and CFS director of wellness, culture, and action Jacqulyn (Jaxx) Hamilton made their way to the school to receive young people who might need refuge, rest, or assistance.

Alvarado-Rivera and Hamilton understood that CFS would be a crucial point of retreat for young people who were being brutalized or simply trapped amid the chaos. "In organizing, especially with young people of color, it's about making sure that they have a space where they know that they are protected, where they are cared for and loved no matter what." Alvarado-Rivera said it was imperative on May 30 that the youth have a safe, judgment-free space to take refuge, whether they had been marching, extending care, or engaging in more rebellious activity. There were no questions asked as young people sought shelter. "Obviously, we welcomed all young people," Alvarado-Rivera told us, "even some adults, but focused on young folks of color, who were out in the streets mobilizing, protesting, raising their voices."

After the bridges were raised and public transit in the area was shut down, stranding and trapping protesters who were criminalized by the mayor's spontaneous curfew, organizers began spreading the word, online and in person, that youth could seek shelter at CFS. "Young people were coming in bruised up, bloodied, and just shocked," Alvarado-Rivera told us.

CFS youth organizer Essence-Jade Gatheright tweeted that young people could take shelter and access food and water at CFS, and the message quickly went viral. "That drew in more young people," Alvarado-Rivera told us. "We were seeing seventeen-year-olds, sixteen-year-olds, fourteen-year-olds—some coming from deep in the front lines, and some who were just caught up and didn't know where to go, or what was happening, as folks were either being kettled or pushed into different areas, being siloed."

Dozens of young people moved through the space. Some youth just needed food, a power outlet, or a ride, and allies and community members pitched in to get young people home safely. Trusted adults from the community were contacted to provide rides, but so many youth were stranded that community members in communication with Alvarado-Rivera or watching the situation unfold on social media eagerly offered to pay for rideshares.

Other young people required care for their police-inflicted injuries, including those who had been exposed to pepper spray and tear gas. "We would have to help some of them up the stairs," Alvarado-Rivera said. "They were crying because they couldn't see." CFS has shower stalls in its space, but they're not usually used; on May 30, Alvarado-Rivera and others quickly cleared out the supplies and files they'd piled up in the showers so that people could wash chemicals off their bodies.

Alvarado-Rivera looked up information that local organizers and street medics had shared about how to address injuries and chemical exposure. Fortunately, there were some youth from the UMedics street medic collective present "who were on the floor with other young people, just using their skills to calm young people down, to wash their eyes." Moving quickly, CFS organizers scrambled to assemble fresh clothes for young people who were soaked in pepper spray "because young people were literally coming in just burning."

At CFS that day, young people were "bleeding and crying and sobbing," Alvarado-Rivera said. Young people who had never been associated with CFS or considered abolitionist politics were voicing their horror that the police could turn on them so brutally, realizing that law enforcement was a threat to their safety.

Amid the hectic scene, Alvarado-Rivera was struck by the courage of the young people who had taken the streets and were now caring for one another: "I thought about the civil rights movement, during the Children's March, when the dogs were being set on people, when hoses were being used."

Meanwhile, amid COVID concerns, organizers worked to spread out the young people at CFS. An area was established for people who were moving through the school quickly, to charge a phone, get food, or access a ride, and a separate area was designated for young people who were "injured, gassed, pepper sprayed, and seeking medical attention," according to Alvarado-Rivera.

"We also had different dark spaces and quiet spaces," Alvarado-Rivera said, for young people who needed sensory relief.

CFS is located in Chicago's downtown area, but "we're in the South Loop, so we're in a pocket where we're usually a little hidden from actions and marches happening downtown," Alvarado-Rivera explained. "So usually it's a pretty calm space here." But on May 30, 2020, the protests and the militarized police response spilled into the school's immediate area.

Alvarado-Rivera was upstairs assisting young people when police arrived and demanded to enter the building. About twenty of the dozens of youth who had come through the building for help were still inside. Hamilton called Alvarado-Rivera and they ran down to the first floor—and saw a crowd of police in riot gear, along with a city inspector, at the building's entrance. "There were seven or eight cops, crowded around the door, and you could see a mess of squad cars parked in front."

The city inspector claimed the city had received complaints about CFS preparing food and housing young people without a license. Alvarado-Rivera told the inspector, "No, we're receiving young people because they were being attacked by the police and we're giving them pizza because some of them are hungry."

Alvarado-Rivera explained that "there was a lot of pushing back and forth" as they and Hamilton tried to hold back the police, who were attempting to gain entry. Alvarado-Rivera and Hamilton asserted their rights and said they would not allow the police inside. The officers persisted, saying that if they were not allowed to enter, they would shut down the school and arrest Alvarado-Rivera and Hamilton for obstructing them.

Alvarado-Rivera and Hamilton tried to record the situation, but by then, both of their phones had died. They sensed that they were running out of time and that the police were going to force their way into CFS and potentially arrest them both, leaving the young people inside at the mercy of riot police. The two organizers quietly agreed that Hamilton would go upstairs and lead the youth to safety.

"I stalled," said Alvarado-Rivera. After agreeing that they would ultimately allow police to enter, Alvarado-Rivera began a negotiation about how many police would be allowed inside. "I was like, 'Okay, we'll let you in. But who's coming? Because this is too many people. We feel uncomfortable and unsafe.'" The police insisted that they should all be admitted. "They said, 'We don't know who's up there. Someone might be up there with a gun. Someone might want to attack us.'" Alvarado-Rivera insisted, "'There's nobody here. It's just us now,'" in the hopes that everyone had been moved.

While Alvarado-Rivera continued their dialogue with the police, Hamilton led young people through the building's back exit, either to cars that were waiting to drive them home or to an alternate space the organizers had access to where youth could safely await their rides. Once Alvarado-Rivera received Hamilton's signal that the youth had been relocated, they agreed to let four police enter the building.

When the police entered the Freedom School's offices, they began taking photos of leftover pizza and Post-it notes from recent workshops about misogyny and misogynoir. "They were taking pictures as if everything was evidence. I told them, 'Yeah, we run a youth program.'"

Alvarado-Rivera said police were aggressive and that the inspector claimed the school was not licensed to "prepare and serve food on the premises." Alvarado-Rivera noted that the food was clearly prepared at a pizzeria and merely distributed to visitors. The inspector issued a cease-and-desist order and warned of fines between $500 and $1,000 for every day the school continued the alleged violation. The police maintained "that they would shut us down and arrest us if they heard we were 'housing and feeding young people again.'"

Alvarado-Rivera, who was still adjusting to their leadership role at CFS, was now faced with the prospect of the school being shut down unless they refused to extend care and safety to young people in jeopardy. "We had to take them to court and fight this," Alvarado-Rivera told us, "because, one, we knew that this was bigger than us. We needed a win, for us and our community, to say, 'You know what? Fuck you. We're going to continue to do our work, try to be as radical as we can, knowing that ultimately—it may not be tomorrow, it may not be in ten years, in fifty years—you will no longer exist. That, for us, will be a larger win. But right now, we will care for each other and we will defend ourselves.'"

The school filed a lawsuit against the city, demanding the cease-and-desist order be rescinded. Ultimately, the city yielded and rescinded the order without going to court. As Hamilton told the press at the time, "[City officials] know that this is an abuse of a city office. They were weaponizing a city office in order to try and intimidate Black and brown people who were organizing." City officials claimed they had tried to engage in dialogue with the school about the cease-and-desist order and were disappointed that the school filed a lawsuit. Alvarado-Rivera told reporters that if the city wanted to work with the school, "they need to defund the police and they need to start caring for Black and brown people instead of putting them in cages."[9]

The events of May 30 raised CFS's profile and brought in an influx of donations, some of which the school redistributed to other local mutual aid efforts. With young people taking action almost daily in the streets, the school became a hub for organizing and mutual aid projects in 2020 and continued to provide refuge for young people during protests, including moments of spontaneous police violence, which Alvarado-Rivera says occurred frequently that summer. CFS's healing justice approach has proven crucial in the wake of so much police violence, as well as the interpersonal friction and traumas that inevitably emerge in movement work. In the summer of 2021, CFS held a weekend-long retreat about conflict and transformative justice for youth organizers.

During the pandemic, CFS has also collaborated with other groups that work with Chicago's young people—Assata's Daughters, Circles and Ciphers, Street Youth Rise UP!, and Youth Empowerment Performance Project—to create Chicago Youth Mutual Aid (CYMA). From grocery gift cards to gas money, cleaning supplies, electronics, and other monetary assistance, CYMA has addressed a wide array of the needs faced by young people and their families during the pandemic. In collaboration with Kelly's collective Lifted Voices, CFS also distributed free bullhorns to young people in summer 2020 and tens of thousands of KN95 masks and other safety supplies in the winters of 2020 and 2021.

"I think with this mutual aid, it's allowing us to see that our organizing work is care work," Alvarado-Rivera told us. The pandemic and the 2020 rebellions pushed Alvarado-Rivera and others to consider, "How do we not just survive, but extend love and care and also have joy in that survival?" For Alvarado-Rivera, that care and joy is found in youth organizing. "When I would see young people laughing, or going into actions downtown, late at night, and they would just start dancing. . . . Knowing that in those same streets, they were beat up, gassed, with cops flipping them off and talking shit. . . . I would think, 'Yes, this is our city, and you deserve to claim all of it.'"

The Cross-Mobilization of Care and Protest

In 2020, we witnessed an unprecedented cross-mobilization of mutual aid and mass protest: many groups that organized pandemic-related mutual aid in their communities pivoted to extend aid and care to protesters as well by distributing masks, food, and water to protesters.

One popular method of organization that people engaging in mutual aid practiced during the pandemic was the formation of mutual aid "pods." Pods are a model for community care and collaboration developed by disability activist Mia Mingus in which small, autonomous groups of people practice various forms of mutual aid and collaborative support.

Mutual aid formations can also create political possibilities beyond the bounds of what people generally associate with community care. In Chicago's Edgewater neighborhood, for example, a mutual aid network that sprung up during the pandemic escalated its activities to include direct action when one of its members, Rico, reported racist behavior on the part of his building's management.

As Edgewater Mutual Aid organizer Marissa Fenley told us, "We were using a pod system to organize our food distro program. Rico was a member of my pod, so I would text him regularly to see if he needed groceries for our weekly distro and see whether or not he could pick up for his neighbors." Fenley and Rico began chatting about the Black Lives Matter protests that were unfolding. Rico shared that his building's management had been racist toward him and made him feel unwelcome. Rico owns his home, so he was not faced with the threat of eviction, but after management called the police on multiple occasions, he felt unsafe and at a loss. "I told him that he could call on his neighbors to support him, in any way we could," Fenley said. "He was very eager to pull together support from his community."

Several members of Edgewater Mutual Aid met with Rico to discuss what could be done. Rico said that he would like to protest the building's management. "His main goal was to publicize their [anti-Black] behavior and to alert them that people were watching how they treated him," Fenley explained. Rico also demanded that the building's management change their policies to explicitly include a clause prohibiting discrimination.

In a turnout that exceeded the organizers' expectations, around fifty people showed up for the protest. "I built a giant puppet and we hired a band," Fenley told us. "We stood outside the building and handed out pamphlets detailing Rico's story." With chants, music, and a "speakout," the group put the building's management on notice that Rico's neighbors were aware of the situation and would be monitoring his treatment. Thanks to the protest, Rico was able to connect with another resident who had experienced discrimination in the building. Fenley notes that the group was inexperienced and that "there are a lot of things we could have done differently," but she felt the group succeeded in laying the groundwork for neighborly defense, if the building's management harmed residents in the future.

Through building relationships and engaging in political education together, the members of Edgewater Mutual Aid expanded their understanding of what care demanded of them as a group— everything from simple acts of assistance like providing groceries and making medication runs to defensive direct action. This kind of evolution does not occur in all mutual aid projects, but it will become increasingly necessary as environmental catastrophes broaden human suffering and the carceral system, which manages problems through criminalization and the disposal of people, expands its reach.

Just as some COVID-era mutual aid efforts evolved to include direct action and support for protesters, some efforts that emerged in support of the protests ultimately pivoted into the realm of ongoing community-based mutual aid. In Chicago, for example, jail support efforts for protesters who had been arrested in spring 2020 led to the creation of Chicago Community Jail Support (CCJS), which has continued to provide mutual aid in the form of jail support on a nightly basis.

Chicago Community Jail Support was a product of the protests and mass arrests of May 28, 2020, following the murder of

George Floyd, CCJS organizer Amalia told us. Originally organized through an encrypted group chat, the jail support site was one of several locations where Chicago activists maintained a twenty-four-hour presence to await protesters who were being released. Once jail support was no longer needed outside individual precincts, support efforts were focused on Cook County Jail, where the majority of those arrested were being held. People were being released throughout the day and night, so a steady volunteer presence outside the jail was necessary in order to extend assistance.

The ongoing, daily effort now known as Chicago Community Jail Support arose organically, according to Amalia, as volunteers who were waiting for protesters to be released found common ground in their belief in abolition, decarceration, and mutual aid work. "It became clear that jail support was needed for everyone being released from Cook County Jail—one of the largest and worst jails in the country—not just protesters."

Amalia acknowledged that the practice of jail support and mutual aid work directly outside jails long predates CCJS but noted that "our daily, unrelenting presence is what sets us apart from those traditions." The group is all-volunteer and community funded, with no plans to join the "nonprofit-industrial complex."

Though CCJS no longer maintains a twenty-four-hour presence outside the jail, the group organizes its daily schedule around the hours when the majority of people are being released from the jail, which means 5:00 p.m. to 10:00 p.m. on weekdays and 5:00 p.m. to 11:00 p.m. on weekends. The group offers people who have been released from the jail access to phones, water, snacks, personal protective equipment, clothing, hygiene supplies, emergency housing assistance, rides home, and shelter from the elements under the group's tent or inside their van. CCJS also distributes naloxone, a rescue medication that can rapidly reverse opioid overdoses, with directions for its use, "and much more" to those being released, their loved ones, and "any community member who approaches us." Since the property of people arrested by Chicago police is held at precincts or in the Chicago Police Department's infamous Homan Square facility, most people are released from Cook County Jail without their belongings, rendering them stranded. "The area outside the jail is dangerous for many people being released, as gangs have often targeted those coming out as they try to make their way home," said Amalia. The group's presence offers immediate aid for people who have experienced the violence and alienation of incarceration. Volunteers also "manage case work" for people who need more long-term support. "We are always finding new ways to help," Amalia told us.

CCJS's mission is specific and aid-based but exists within the framework of broader abolitionist principles. "We believe no one should be held in a cage, especially Cook County Jail, and we make it our mission to work against the daily, unrelenting harm of incarceration by providing care when and where it is needed most," Amalia said.

Community jail support efforts were not unique to Chicago in 2020. Portland Community Jail Support, which evolved in a similar manner to CCJS, is still up and running.[10] In Charlotte, North Carolina, the group Charlotte Uprising launched its own round-the-clock jail support effort in June 2020, operating twenty-four hours a day to assist protesters and other community members until repeated police raids and organizer arrests broke the effort down. (This, and the cease-and-desist order CFS faced are clear examples of how the system reacts to powerful expressions of communal support and care amid crisis.)

Shane Burley believes that the mass activation of pandemic mutual aid and the mass mobilization of the protests collided in moments and formations that were both generative and instructive. "The pandemic was an involuntary crisis—and organizing around any issue is a mix of voluntary and involuntary—but a crisis nonetheless," Burley told us. "So what I think happened is that there was a mass orientation of mutual aid to one crisis, the pandemic, which then made the structures logical and accessible for the next crisis, the mass action in the streets against white supremacy."

In 2020, the radicalizing potential of mutual aid collided with the radicalizing potential of mass protest. The resulting moments of care, cooperation, and community defense offered a glimpse of our future in struggle. This system will continue to fail people en masse and continue its attempts to legitimate itself through violence, which will make further uprisings and mass protest inevitable. The fragile normalcy people in the United States cling to will continue to fracture, creating more opportunities for people to either retreat or rise to the moment by building new relationships and creating new formations to sustain life.

Care versus State Warfare

The forms of care and struggle described by Orsini, Alvarado-Rivera, Burley, Fenley, and others are innovative and unique to their moments, but they are also part of a long tradition. People around the world and across history have always mobilized and deployed their creativity to create modes of rescue, deliver medical care, and provide nourishment to each other on massive scales during disasters. Yet these histories are often erased in favor of popular narratives about authority or individual acts of heroism, because those authority-driven and masculinist narratives reinforce the necessity of hierarchies that mutual aid undermines. As Rebecca Solnit describes in *A Paradise Built in Hell*, everyday people and workers in the Twin Towers devised and implemented inspiring rescue and evacuation efforts on 9/11. Without any meaningful direction from authority—and in some cases, in defiance of instructions from 911 operators to shelter in place, which led to more deaths—people organized themselves to navigate dark stairwells, and some devised methods of assistance for disabled coworkers who otherwise would have been stranded as their coworkers fled. There was a mass exodus that day, not simply from the towers but also from the entire surrounding area, as clouds of ash enveloped Lower Manhattan. That exodus was enabled by people stepping up to assist one another in a moment of chaos, rather than simply focusing on their own survival. It was their natural desire and inclination to reach out for one another and to ensure that as many people survived and made their way to safety as possible.

Yet popular narratives about 9/11, as Solnit points out, almost exclusively focus on the heroic actions of official first responders. While city employees who helped people that day certainly deserve an accurate retelling of their participation, so too do the people who acted spontaneously, in tremendous numbers, to rescue, shelter, and aid one another as a catastrophe unfolded.

Why aren't these narratives of spontaneous mutual aid more widely shared in mainstream culture? Perhaps it's because a recognition of our collective capacity for care during a moment of chaos does not reinforce state hierarchy. It does not reinforce individualism or what the government ultimately wanted most out of the aftermath of 9/11: a greater allegiance to US militarism.

Care-driven organizing confounds the logics that are deployed to perpetuate wars, whether against a nation-state, against terrorism, or against "crime." All movements that offer aid and comfort to criminalized and illegalized people are antiwar movements, because they exist in opposition to the war-making of targeted criminalization, scapegoating, and escalations in militarism that accompany those efforts. Like antiwar movements that oppose wars waged in and against foreign nations, movements that counter wars of criminalization highlight the number of casualties, the systemic abuses, and the dishonest framing of the system's "warfare." They are movements against dehumanization.

As we write this book, the pandemic continues, and the supposed light at the end of the tunnel is a "return to normalcy" concocted by a government eager to restore the status quo that delivered us to this moment. In the interest of capital, we are being sold a narrative of recovery that ignores the structural failings that have magnified the impacts of this catastrophe, as well as the new era of mounting disasters that face us. There is also little focus on commemoration or memorialization, because the primary objective of the powerful is the restoration of economic stability, which means we should be shopping, dining out, and investing, rather than mourning and contemplating how we can prevent a tragedy of this scale from ever happening again. But shifts in political consciousness are not lost on the powerful. The National Intelligence Council, a center in the Office of the Director of National Intelligence that "creates strategic forecasts and estimates, often based on material gathered by U.S. spy agencies," stated in its 2021 *Global Trends* report:

> The ongoing COVID-19 pandemic marks the most significant, singular global disruption since World War II, with health, economic, political, and security implications that will ripple for years to come. The effects of climate change and environmental degradation are likely to exacerbate food and water insecurity for poor countries, increase migration, precipitate new health challenges, and contribute to biodiversity losses. Novel technologies will appear and diffuse faster and faster, disrupting jobs, industries, communities, the nature of power, and what it means to be human.[11]

The report includes projections for five possible global scenarios in the year 2040. Only two foresee a 2040 where climate change is being meaningfully addressed. In scenarios entitled "A World Adrift," "Competitive Coexistence," and "Separate Silos," world powers do not muster the will or cohesion to tackle climate change. But in the scenario titled "Tragedy and Mobilization," a vastly different vision of the world in 2040 emerges:

> Across the world, younger generations, shaped by the COVID-19 pandemic and traumatized by the threat of running out of food, joined together across borders to overcome resistance to reform, blaming older generations for destroying their planet. They threw their support behind NGOs and civil society organizations that were involved in relief efforts and developed a larger global following than those governments that were perceived to have failed their populations. As the movement grew, it took on other issues including global health and poverty.[12]

In this scenario, the National Intelligence Council projects a world where "activist groups have unprecedented ability to influence standards, marshal resources, hold violators accountable, and prod states to act. In some cases, global priorities take precedence over national interests."[13] In the "Tragedy and Mobilization" scenario, cooperating world powers are forced to take "verifiable actions to improve food, health, and environmental security, even if these were perceived as painful for wealthier states and groups."[14]

While we certainly do not view the projections of an intelligence report as a blueprint for liberation, we do find it notable that even intelligence agencies determined to maintain US global dominance at any price—agencies that have historically crushed the democratic hopes of entire nations in order to maintain the current world order— can imagine a world where activists and organizers win.

If the death-makers who manufacture our oppression can imagine us remaking the world, surely our own visions of change can far exceed what is written in such reports—and can ultimately be realized. The creative power of the oppressed will always exceed that of the oppressor, because it is the oppressed who must exercise creativity to navigate and survive a world that is set against them. It is the oppressed who create art and poetry and revolutionary ideas to cultivate hope in bleak places, so that people might galvanize and make change. It is the oppressed who, upon experiencing the defibrillation of disaster, have demonstrated what the bonds of solidarity can accomplish for the common good.

One aspect of the *Global Trends* report that we agree with is that transformative change will require global cooperation from activists and organizers and shared demands around collective survival as we respond to the disasters we have experienced and the disasters to come. For this to occur, we will have to break free from the shackles of individualism and commit to building a culture of care, in which everyone's well-being and survival are significant.

This is not the outcome the powerful are hoping for. They are relying on our cynicism, our divisions, and our despair, in addition to their mass apparatus of repression, to prevent us from cultivating a new way of living in relation to each other. To defy and defeat them, we must cultivate hope, belonging, care, and action.

A counterculture of care exists in opposition to all manner of state warfare and to the very nature of empire. It requires the undoing of individualism and siloed politics and harbors the potential for new life-giving frameworks. Care-driven organizing compels us to ask, What would it take to provide for people's needs and address the root causes of a problem? How do we care for each other as crises unfold? At what cost are we willing to offer shelter and protection to people who are under attack? These basic questions pose a challenge to the status quo, to the normalization of suffering and mass death, and to capitalism itself. To undermine or upend the violence of this system, we must free ourselves from the strictures of individualism and unite in acts of solidarity and collective care. It is in that spirit, and with that energy, that we can confront the death-making forces that would leverage cynicism and despair to keep us idle as our world burns.

CHAPTER 4

Think Like a Geographer

Life-giving organizing in this catastrophic era will require us to chart new political and social maps of the world. Our movements are already practicing and shaping new visions of how we might better relate to one another and to the Earth itself. While some people engage in politics for the sake of debate or to defend their sense of moral identity, radical organizers are attempting to create something new.

In addition to being an organizer who's been working toward prison-industrial complex abolition for decades, Ruth Wilson Gilmore is also a professor of geography and directs the Center for Place, Culture, and Politics at the City University of New York. Geography is a discipline that focuses on demystifying "relationships between people, places, and things," as Gilmore put it in a conversation with us. It is, therefore, an especially useful discipline to engage with as organizers, as we pursue new landscapes, new maps, and new formations.

While most organizers are not scholars of geography, we can, as Gilmore explains, enrich our work by thinking like geographers. "One of the things that thinking like a geographer can do is help people see, pull back the veil that makes something that's social seem natural, and something that sometimes is natural, seem social," Gilmore told us. Geography, she said, helps people ask the question, "Why is this place the way it is? Why is it like it is?" And the answer generally has got to be more detailed than "racism" or "colonialism," although those two categories and sets of relationships matter. So we can talk, for example, about how Chicago came to become the city that it is, and then think about all of the relationships that people have, or have had, as long-distance migrants, as people who've worked through the various rise and fall of industrial sectors in Chicago and Cook County, why the built environment there looks as it does, and the kind of movements of capital across territory. So when people rightly denounce gentrification, a geographer will say, "Well, what do you think that means? How does it work?" Because when we think about how it works, then that gives us some opportunity to think about what the remedy for this organized abandonment might be.

This call to understand the relationships and dynamics that inform our experience of oppression is an urgent one, because our ultimate goal is not simply to label or identify our oppression, but to upend and dismantle it. If one hopes to sabotage a machine, being able to identify the machine is a start, but understanding how the machine functions, what its various parts do, and what blows could actually disable it, are also essential. To take dynamic action against a system, we must have a dynamic understanding of how it functions. To create something new, we must likewise understand how the people of a place relate to the land and to each other and what developments have driven their current condition. Any reimagining of a community that does not take these factors into account is speculative fiction.

"What I find the most exciting about being a geographer is thinking about how we make the world, and make the world, and make the world," Gilmore told Kelly on *Movement Memos*. "The concept of place, which for many people, understandably enough, seems only to mean location, has actually a dynamic, expansive fullness to it that I love to think about." Gilmore explained that geographers examine how people are making the world, or making place, as geographers say. "It occurred to me, I don't know, twenty, twenty-five years ago, to realize that freedom is a place. That it's not like a destination, it's the place that we make."[1]

According to Gilmore, by doing this liberatory work of making place, we can "share that freedom by sharing space that every embodied consciousness who joins together in that struggle is then joining together, at least provisionally, in being free there." Whether that space is the Republic of New Afrika, a camp of water protectors, a co-op, or a mutual aid outpost, Gilmore explained that "a place need not be geometrically unbroken" and that a shared place "could be an archipelago in which people at each of the . . . same [metaphorical] elevations are doing the same thing."[2]

To think of freedom as a place we create, share, and inhabit is instructive. We live on a planet in the throes of climate chaos, where powerful actors will use borders and captivity to maintain the norms of capitalism for as long as possible. To think of our organizing efforts as the work of making place helps ground us in the larger reality of what we are fighting for: not mere words or ideas, but transformed lives in transformed places. In working toward liberation, we are making place in opposition to those who would rob us of time, space, togetherness, and possibility itself.

What are the ways that people make the places they inhabit, daily, through their participation, cooperation, and interdependence? What would those dynamics look like if those people were truly free? How can we manifest those ideas, values, and visions in the spaces we create together?

Learning as Rebellion and Rehearsal

Reading can play an important role in the exploratory work Gilmore describes. For some activists, a regular practice of reading—particularly in discussion groups and book clubs with co-strugglers—helps advance their work. Before the Caucus of Rank and File Educators

(CORE) took control of the Chicago Teachers Union and saw the union through two strikes, the group began as an informal reading group.[3] Staten Island organizers with the Amazon Labor Union, the first group to successfully unionize an Amazon warehouse, read and discussed William Z. Foster's *Organizing Methods in the Steel Industry* and distributed copies to workers.[4] And in Pennsylvania, behind prison walls, imprisoned organizer Stevie Wilson hosts abolitionist reading, study, and discussion groups.[5]

In a prison where official education programs have been gutted, Wilson facilitates group discussions of books like *Are Prisons Obsolete?* and *Captive Genders*. Due to people's varying academic backgrounds, Wilson said he found it "easier to copy out chapters of books and to work through them together." Wilson also uplifted the importance of zines (self-published print work, usually created for small-scale circulation) in a 2019 interview with Rustbelt Abolition Radio. He explained, "Zines were really big for us because it was more intimidating to give someone a book that's two hundred to three hundred pages long . . . they probably wouldn't pick it up. But if I gave someone a zine and it was three or four pages long, they could take a week and read that and we'll come back and we discuss it. So I tell you, the zines play a major role in the work inside the prison also because even for me to disseminate zines and books, it's less costly and the administration doesn't see it."[6]

Wilson also stressed that reading is a subversive act in prison, and passing around large numbers of books might result in the confiscation of those texts, in addition to harassment or punishment of those circulating them. Zines can also be shared in a more clandestine manner. "If I went to the yard and tried to give out ten books, I wouldn't make it. But if I have ten zines there, I can give them out, you see? So part of it also is knowing the inside of here because, remember this much: learned prisoners are an affront to the [prison-industrial complex]."[7]

Activists often quietly feel embarrassed about the important books they have not read. We have news for them: most people in movement spaces have not read the books everyone seems to quote. There are many reasons for this. Capitalism robs us of our time, exhausting our bodies and minds, while pollution, stress, and shifting media patterns shorten our attention spans, and other mediums offer effortless modes of escapism. The gutting of public education was geared toward the prevention of an "educated proletariat"—as a Reagan adviser once put it while denouncing free college[8]—and has robbed many young people of the opportunity to explore a great deal of history and literature and to develop a personal practice around that exploration. Consequently, most people do not read as much as they would like to. Of course, reading is not the only way to learn, and for some people, it is not the means best suited to them. But capitalism also makes it difficult for people to access information in other ways. How many times have you planned to check out a museum exhibit, a lecture, a podcast, an art installation, or any other opportunity to learn and expand your analysis, and found that you simply do not have the time or energy? Some people will call themselves "lazy" for missing such opportunities without recognizing who or what seized the time or energy they might have devoted to such tasks. We are not simply "missing out" on knowledge; we are being robbed of it. To succeed in our movements, we must resist this theft and reclaim what has been stolen from us.

Many of the histories that delivered us to this movement, the science and data of our struggles, the poetry and stories that have propelled struggle, are hidden in plain sight: in books, in documents, in films, in recordings. The ruling class is going to great lengths to obstruct the journey of discovering those lessons and tools. As the conservative movement to ban books that discuss anti-Black racism, Indigenous genocide, trans identities, and more builds momentum, organizers must fight the erasure of knowledge with the collective expansion of knowledge. Histories of the oppressions our communities have faced, as well as the struggles they have waged, have been largely suppressed in the mainstream. Learning and reclaiming those histories and ideas are essential to our movements. In addition to reading groups where entire books are discussed, zines, podcasts, teach-ins, and webinars can also create opportunities to deconsolidate crucial ideas.

For some people, making time to read and learn can be difficult. If you have a habit you are trying to cut down on, like doomscrolling, you might start by intentionally swapping out some scrolling time for an audiobook or an ebook on your phone. We urge organizers to spend more time with books and other modes of learning, not as an admonition (after all, you are reading right now) but to encourage you to claim an inheritance of knowledge your oppressors hope you never discover, embrace, or build from—the stories, wisdom, hope, and imaginings of organizers who came before us.

If you are unsure where to begin, we recommend you begin with the words or ideas that have already had an impact on you. As an exercise, pick out a quotation that has had a deep impact on your politics. Write it down. Now let's elaborate upon its context. What injustice was being challenged? What did the speaker want most immediately? Was the quote part of a statement to the press, a line from a speech or book, or a comment to a friend? Was it in a letter from a jailhouse? Who was president of the United States when these words were spoken? What was the economy like? Who might have disagreed with this quote at the time it was spoken, both within and outside of social movements? If the quote is from a book, have you read it? If not, is it possible these words are calling you on a journey?

One way to enrich our practice of reading is to rehearse, rather than recite. Ruth Wilson Gilmore has drawn the distinction between "recital" and "rehearsal" in political education. Information, Gilmore notes, does not automatically translate into knowledge that makes organizers more effective. "What is it about information that becomes knowledge that becomes useful for shaping action?" Gilmore asked in a conversation with us. To explore this question further, Gilmore examined her own reading habits.

She noted that when reading novels and poetry, she found she was pursuing the experience of joy or pleasure or "finding a thrill." Gilmore said that while reading fiction or poetry, she is searching for a recognizable pattern and enjoys the anticipation of wondering whether she's "wily enough to outsmart the wiliness of the writer, or the narrator, or the character, or whoever." Gilmore says that even as she reads poetry, that anticipation exists: "Am I catching the rhythms and the rhymes or the shape of the poem in such a way that I might be able to anticipate a feeling? Which is really thrilling. Not to know what the poet's going to say, but to kind of almost be prepared in my feelings to receive the shape that the poem puts to me."

When Gilmore assesses her manner of reading for knowledge, she sees a different picture:

> I realized that a good deal of the practice of reading that I brought to my work, my work as a scholar, my work as an activist, my work as a reader, was kind of extractivist in its character. I was reading things in order to pull something out that I could then use. . . . I was reading political economy and social theory and so forth in order to extract certain bits of knowledge that I could then hold up, like, I pulled this chunk of copper ore from the ground, see it? I pulled this other thing from the ground, see it? This extraction then left me with something I could show to people, "See, I have this copper ore, see, I have this sentence from Karl Marx," or sentence from Claudia Jones, or even an entire paragraph from C. L. R. James that I could recite. And people would just look and say, "Wow, that's really nice copper ore."

This extractive approach to reading is something many people can relate to, especially those who have mostly read for academic purposes. When doing school work, we might search for and extract whatever information helps us complete our assignments. In some cases, we might read or learn in an extractive manner because we are only seeking to confirm or reinforce our position, rather than exploring the complexities of the text, its context, or the author's perspective.

Gilmore explained how she began to counteract that extractivist tendency in reading:

> That's where I got to thinking that maybe what we should do, in thinking about reading social theory, reading history,

reading this kind of work, is to approach it as though we were actors. . . . Not ones who were going to stand up and present the pages to an audience with a dramatic reading, but rather to approach the writing in such a way that actors approach the scripts that they study, in order to act from, to say, "What makes this sentence become something in the human world?" What makes this sentence or this paragraph, or this way of thinking, or this combination of thinkers, or this particular rhythmic timeline through the colonial struggle, whatever it is we're reading—what makes this something that I can sort of put my body/mind to, in order to rehearse the revolution I'm part of now, or rehearse the preparation for the revolution I'm part of now?

When we pursue information in an extractive manner, diving for facts rather than immersing ourselves in histories and ideas and engaging with them imaginatively, we often miss the larger stories, undercurrents, and motivations that give history its context. Those larger contexts contain many precious lessons that the powerful have worked hard to erase. As Diane di Prima told us, "history is a living weapon in yr hand."[9]

Charting Your Own Terrain: "Why Not Chicago? And Why Not Us?"

During the pandemic, a group of activist researchers in Chicago saw their work deployed by a rising movement against policing in their city. Lucy Parsons Labs (LPL) describes itself as "a charitable Chicago-based collaboration between data scientists, transparency activists, artists, and technologists that sheds light on the intersection of digital rights and on-the-streets issues." Freddy Martinez, one of the cofounders of LPL, told us the project emerged in 2015 after a late-night conversation between friends in a hotel hallway. "You can imagine, that's where great decisions get made," Martinez joked. The effort was partly inspired, according to Martinez, by "some personal experiences of one of our founders being under intense police surveillance during Occupy" and also a desire to "engage in activism outside of going to protests." Martinez and his cofounders wanted to explore new ways of organizing against police surveillance, and they saw that opportunity in research. "Really, we were looking at some places doing stuff like researching and writing about surveillance in other parts of the country and we thought, why not Chicago? And why not us?"

Today, LPL offers digital security trainings for activists and at-risk communities and maintains a secure system for whistleblowers to report misconduct. The group is also developing an open-source police misconduct reporting tool, OpenOversight, and regularly fact-checks police and city officials by filing public records requests under the Freedom of Information Act and local equivalents. The group has exposed numerous city government deceptions, provided activists with data for their campaigns, and collaborated with journalists to inform the public about practices like civil asset forfeiture (in which police keep valuables they seize during arrests and investigations) and the use of Stingray technology for surveillance.

LPL's years of research on surveillance was of great help to activists during the pandemic, as opposition to police practices of brutality and surveillance escalated. People who wanted to highlight the abuses perpetrated by the Chicago Police Department had a treasure trove of organized data to work with. Then, in late March 2021, a Chicago police officer gunned down thirteen-year-old Adam Toledo in Little Village on Chicago's West Side. Body cam footage of Adam's death revealed he had followed the police officer's commands and that his hands were in the air when he was killed. The killing was the result of a foot chase instigated by the city's ShotSpotter surveillance apparatus. ShotSpotter is an AI surveillance system that uses miles of microphones to generate gunshot alerts for police. But as LPL has revealed, claims about the technology's accuracy are highly suspect.

As Martinez told Kelly on *Movement Memos*, "ShotSpotter claims that it's something like 97 percent accurate. And the way that they get to that number is quite clever. What they do is that they classify basically every sound that they pick up as either one, a gunshot, a single gunshot, multiple gunshots, or what they designate as a probable gunshot. And that's included in their accuracy number."[10] According to a report from the MacArthur Justice Center at Northwestern University School of Law, for example, 89 percent of ShotSpotter deployments in Chicago turned up no gun-related crime. Eighty-six percent led to no report of any crime at all. The report indicated that, over the 21.5 months researchers studied, there were more than forty thousand dead-end ShotSpotter deployments in Chicago.

Even if ShotSpotter were accurate in its alerts, the deployment of police does not undo, prevent, or heal violence in our communities but serves to compound it. However, LPL's research into the particulars of the technology helps reveal broader systemic injustices.

"We're abolitionists, and have long pointed out that surveillance technologies lead to further criminalizing people along racial and economic and religious lines," Martinez explained.

LPL's long-term research has put the group in a position to help propel movement work during heated moments. As Martinez explained to Kelly on *Movement Memos* in December 2021, "I remember at one point there was a journalist on Twitter who had said that weekend that Adam Toledo got murdered was like, 'I think I'm going to spend this weekend looking into everything I can about ShotSpotter.' And I said, 'Hey, don't worry about it. Go to our website, chicagopolicesurveillance.com. It's all on there.' And having those resources ready to go is really critical for just organizing work."

Following the murder of Adam Toledo, LPL joined a coalition to end the ShotSpotter contract in Chicago. As the campaign moved forward, the need for political education around the issue quickly became apparent. Martinez acknowledges that the educational process takes time, even when information has already been assembled, but he notes, "It would have taken much longer had we not spent years doing documentation and writing, trying to fully understand surveillance systems at a time when nobody else was. We anticipated the moment. As organizers, it's important to plan for the future we are creating and then actively create it."

Some people find research intimidating and are afraid they will miss key information and make mistakes. "My advice to younger people is to not overthink it," says Martinez. "Asking questions and looking for answers is basically what every journalist starts out doing. I remember one time someone told me at a public records training they were worried about getting their request for records thrown out on some technicality. Who cares? Give it a shot."

Martinez had another crucial piece of advice to offer organizers venturing into research: "Our number one piece of advice is to be obnoxious. Yes, actually obnoxious. People will do anything to get away from answering your questions. I've emailed people ten times until they responded to me." Persistence, says Martinez, is key to the process. "So much of research is just not giving up until you get answers."

A final lesson for organizers, from LPL: deep and thorough research is worth the time. In fact, it is essential when going toe to toe with powerful forces, Martinez says. The information wars are stacked against dissenters.

"The police and the mayor's office know how to defuse social pressure with misleading information," Martinez notes. "Our research has to be fifteen to twenty times better than theirs."

Learn More Than One Way to Solve a Problem

As organizers, we have seen technology evolve over the course of our work. Some of these changes have been groundbreaking, making activism more accessible and creating opportunities for collaboration and public exposure of the work, which had been extremely difficult or impossible under previous constraints. These innovations have also brought about less welcome developments for organizers, such as enhanced surveillance. We have also noticed that the popularization of digital methods of mobilization has led to a reliance on social media event pages and online announcements to spark mobilization.

Activists who experience success using online tools sometimes undervalue or neglect the kind of on-the-ground work organizers practiced before social media, and which many still practice today.

But online mobilization born out of interest in event pages or the hot political topic of the moment can be fleeting, and organizers who rely on their ability to summon large numbers of people for protests and actions via social media, without developing any fabric of community between participants, often find themselves adrift as high-intensity political moments ebb. The bonded energy of protesters in the streets can help sustain the momentum of a protest, but it does not, in and of itself, create a sustained capacity for organized political action.

It's also important to remember that social media platforms are corporate products governed by algorithms and human beings who have repeatedly stifled leftist voices, obscured state violence, and facilitated right-wing radicalization. As important as these platforms are, overdependence on them weakens our movements. We need to practice a diverse spectrum of outreach methods in digital spaces and in physical spaces, and we need to do skill-building work in our movements around those methods. Sometimes, we need to be literal about meeting people where they are at. Think about all of the places people congregate in person and remotely where conversation is possible, from restaurants to schools, parks, porches, places of worship, street fairs, text message threads—and so many more.

We also have to prepare for the eventualities of becoming a threat to the status quo. The more successfully our work challenges the status quo, the more likely social media platforms and other digital services are to blacklist us or otherwise impede our efforts. For example, we have created many effective social media kits that provided participants with sample tweets to use during moments of concentrated activity on Twitter—digital efforts that are often called "Twitter storms." These tweets have allowed us and other organizers to get hashtags trending, which in turn has allowed us to raise millions of dollars to free incarcerated people and to educate people about how they can help fight injustices. In 2022, Twitter created user guidelines prohibiting the use of replicated content (copy/pasting), which puts users who use sample tweets from social media tool kits at risk of having their accounts suspended. By deprioritizing political content,

Facebook has severely undermined groups who came to rely on the platform to publicize their issues and events.

Given how revocable and alterable these corporate-owned mediums are, we must consider, *What would we do in the case of a major political event if social media were no longer at our disposal?* And what about all the people we're not connecting with in our own communities due to some people's lack of social media use or the invisible constraints of corporate algorithms?

More than four decades before the advent of social media, when Rosa Parks was arrested, the Women's Political Council spread news of the Montgomery bus boycott throughout the city's Black community overnight. These organizers swiftly made a compelling and unifying case for a collective refusal, on the part of Black people, to use public transportation that would last thirteen months—until the Supreme Court ruled that segregation on public buses was unconstitutional. Today, most groups and organizations lack this capacity, outside of corporate-controlled technology. While it makes sense to use tools to save time and maximize our reach, we must also remember that we live in an ever-changing world and that our work must be adaptable. Work that can only occur within corporate confines can be eliminated according to corporate whims. We need to strategize around alternative modes of digital outreach and use in-person outreach methods, such as canvassing, flyering, in-person mutual aid, and other community events. Today's organizers need to use new and old methods to motivate people toward spaces where work is happening and where relationships are being built.

Many of the technologies that presently strengthen our work are fully revocable, either by the state or by corporate entities themselves. What will we do if our revocation nightmares come true? We will need to train up and familiarize ourselves with time-tested tools. Many young people, for example, have never used a paper map. In an age when we can verbally ask our phones how to get somewhere and receive verbal instructions as we move, the idea of carrying and reading a paper map seems antiquated. But what if we suddenly had to get by without GPS navigation because an internet outage or state interference prevented us from relying on the apps we are used to? What if we had to not only read maps but also draw up simple maps for our comrades to help them navigate a changing protest or police landscape, or to direct mutual aid? When we become wholly reliant on a shortcut that disappears, we are left with a knowledge deficit that can become a roadblock.

If you are a young person, you will surely see evolutions in technology that will both aid and impede your work in the coming decades. While utilizing that technology, it's important to be suspicious and observant of the forces that control and profit from it. It's also important to be aware of the precarity of its usefulness. We are not saying that you should take the time to learn every skill that technology has spared you the trouble of acquiring, but we do advise you to think critically about what services and platforms you rely on, what could be taken away, and what you would do in their absence. Many of our movements happen in public online, but our movements would still exist if every activist's social media account were purged tomorrow. What tools would we have amassed to meet that moment?

Change the Landscape

Sometimes we may find ourselves without the tools we need in a crisis. In 2018, Halle Quezada was on a Lake Michigan beach near her home in the neighborhood of Rogers Park, in Chicago, when she and others spotted two teenage girls who were drowning. The girls had fallen off a pier into an area that is known among lifeguards as a danger zone, due to a particularly dangerous current. Quezada and her family were among those who helped one of the girls out of the water, but the other girl was pulled under by the current. Six people entered the water in a desperate effort to recover the teen, but the waves were so violent that each of the would-be rescuers wound up in need of rescue. Quezada told us the fire department first went to the wrong beach, then, upon arriving at the correct beach, found the entrance blocked by a police car. Quezada says thirty minutes passed between the onset of the emergency and the arrival of firefighters. During those thirty minutes, Quezada's husband and others, who realized the water was too dangerous to enter, searched for anything in the area that might float, that they might throw to people who were fighting a washing-machine-like current and struggling to keep their heads above water. When firefighters arrived, they helped those would-be rescuers from the water with flotation devices. They were bruised and bloody from being thrown against the break wall by the waves. One of the young girls was still missing.

Two hundred community members gathered to mourn thirteen-year-old Darihanne Torres. One of her eighth-grade classmates had managed to grab hold of Darihanne's hand at one point during the crisis but could not hold on. Her friends had no flotation device to throw her.

To Quezada, the solution was clear: emergency flotation devices were needed on the beach. There had been no shortage of brave people eager to help each other, but they lacked the necessary tools, and some had nearly lost their lives attempting to help. If there had been a life ring available, Quezada felt sure things would have been different. Quezada and other activists started Chicago Alliance for Waterfront Safety (CAWS), a movement to educate Chicagoans on beach safety. CAWS pushed for better signage, indicating which areas were dangerous for swimmers, and the installation of safety devices.

CAWS began circulating petitions. Quezada researched the issue relentlessly and shared her findings with the city. CAWS reached out to Great Lakes advocacy groups and bereaved families, talked to the media, hosted meetings, and challenged their alderman who represented their neighborhood on the Chicago City Council to take action. The alderman launched a task force to address the issue, but a year went by, and as Quezada says, "The work of the task force never left paper." Then, in September 2021, nineteen-year-old Miguel "Maicky" Cisneros drowned on the same beach, only blocks away from where one of the teenage girls had been lost. Cisneros was within feet of the pier, and witnesses felt sure they could have saved him, if only they had access to a life ring.

The teen's death was the last straw for Quezada and her friends, who were tired of tangling with bureaucracy. They ordered a life ring online and installed it on the pier themselves. As expected, the park district removed the unauthorized rescue device—and local media captured the removal on film. Other community members joined the effort and replaced the life ring, which the parks department removed again. Four days in a row, the rings were replaced and removed and replaced again. Each time another life ring was taken down, public outrage grew. The park district was losing a narrative war. Lawyers for the city had previously argued that if the city installed life rings, the devices would only be stolen, creating a new liability in the event of wrongful-death lawsuits over drownings. But now it was the city stealing life rings, and community members were loudly naming that the park district would be responsible for the absence of those devices the next time someone drowned.

Public pressure grew, and finally the city yielded, installing its own life ring on the pier. Quezada and other local activists also worked to help pass legislation that made the change a matter of law. Quezada stresses that it was the power of direct action that made these victories possible.

"The fact of the matter is, we had worked for three years while people, including kids, died preventable deaths due to known hazards in public parks and nothing was being done," Quezada told us. She said people in power had the solutions and the funding to enact those solutions, but they also had what Quezada describes as "a competing need to be the authority." These officials "deeply resisted" being told by the community, or even their own experts, what needed to be done. "A single lawyer who wanted his job litigating wrongful-death suits to be easier was suddenly more important than preventing those wrongful deaths in the first place," Quezada said. The city government was unwilling to prioritize human lives, so Quezada and others had to place human life ahead of the rules.

"When our community took action, hanging our own rings without permission and hanging them again when they were taken down, we changed what the park district had authority over,"

Quezada said. "This direct action meant the choices in front of them were no longer life rings or no life rings; now they were left only with the choice of installing their own rings or dealing with ours." The direct action Quezada and her neighbors carried out reframed the crisis, and the life ring controversy became a narrative war the city could not win. For the government to reclaim its authority and to avoid being blamed for the next tragedy, says Quezada, "they had to first cede to what we wanted."

Thanks to the legislation Quezada and others pushed for and efforts supported by a new alderwoman in Quezada's neighborhood, there are now life rings stationed throughout Chicago's lakefront beaches and overlooks. Two people in Rogers Park have been rescued using the life rings since their installation. Those lives were saved by a community's willingness to commit defiant acts of care at the intersection of direct action and mutual aid.

Sometimes, systems of power can obscure our ability to act on our environment directly and make changes that can have transformative impacts. In Rogers Park, there are people who are alive today because some of their neighbors decided to break the rules together. This is a story worth remembering when we consider how we, as Gilmore says, make and remake the world.

CHAPTER 5

Rejecting Cynicism and
Building Broader Movements

None of us is exempt from the creep of cynicism in our movements, or in our own hearts and minds. But it must be actively fought. As we mentioned in chapter 1, Kelly did not initially believe that the Reparations NOW campaign could be won. This is a useful example of how even a hopeful person who believes in people power can mentally foreclose certain possibilities. In this case, friendship, solidarity, and comradery overwhelmed doubt, and Kelly enthusiastically joined the effort, co-organizing direct actions and creating online content for the campaign, even though she did not initially believe that victory was possible. Kelly's cynicism about the system made her doubt that the city would ever mention police torture in the Chicago public school curriculum, but her faith in her friend and co-strugglers who were uplifting the issue was stronger than that doubt. She also believed in the mass movement against police violence, which would take up the call for reparations locally, and in rallying and marching with those people, Kelly came to believe that victory was not only attainable but very much within reach.

When we believe in each other, we are more likely to take risks and to invest ourselves in possibility, even when our own hopes are not fully formed. In this way, our relationships and the work of relationship building can change our sense of what's possible.

As you develop your tactics and strategize, it's important to be aware of the pervasiveness of cynicism among many of those you may be trying to reach. Cynicism is a dominant force in today's political discourse, with some good reason, and a favorite approach of the world's political hobbyists. As writer Eitan Hersh explained in a 2020 *Atlantic* article, "Many college-educated people think they are deeply engaged in politics. They follow the news—reading articles like this one—and debate the latest developments on social media. They might sign an online petition or throw a $5 online donation at a presidential candidate. Mostly, they consume political information as a way of satisfying their own emotional and intellectual needs."[1] According to Hersh, a political hobbyist debating the latest headline protest is "no closer to engaging in politics than watching *SportsCenter* is to playing football."

It is important to understand the distinction between activists, organizers, and political hobbyists. Hobbyists often have very strict political standards around respectability or radicalism, to which few activists ever seem to rise. If you organize anything political, you are likely to attract the criticism of hobbyists, since for some people, critique is a pastime.

Of course, organizers make genuine mistakes that political hobbyists may react to, but the fact is, making mistakes is a consequence of trying. The more you take action, the more errors and missteps you will make along the way. A person who has attempted nothing can easily point to the fact that they have never failed, but what have they built? What have they healed? As Barbara Ransby says of some vocal political hobbyists, "You're not making any mistakes because you're not doing anything."

Political hobbyists have the luxury of pontificating about what organizers should do without any knowledge of the moving parts of a campaign or what actually moves people to act. In a moment of crisis or public outrage, hobbyists will frequently insist that "something" be done but often aren't terribly particular about what "something" consists of—or whom it might actually harm or serve.

As an organizer, you do not owe political hobbyists your time and energy. This does not mean you should brush off input, but it does mean that you should take uninformed critiques with a grain of salt (even as you take criticism seriously when it comes from people who share your objectives). Getting into heated debates with people who do not understand the work you are doing or the context in which you are doing it, or who do not share your values, is wasted energy and can create distractions that take you off message and disrupt your efforts.

Remember whose opinions matter most and direct your energies accordingly. Do not let the political hobbyists live in your brain rent free.

Rejecting Cynicism

One persistent form of cynicism on the "left" comes in the form of the dismissal, "This is nothing new." To explain that something is not new and to share important histories are good things, but such interventions should be the beginning, not the end, of a conversation. When the public is reacting to an injustice, our role as organizers is not to dismiss but to invite. For example, during the Trump administration, when the infamous child-separation policy was revealed, the ensuing chorus of moral outrage provoked many proclamations that the policy was "nothing new." After all, Black and Native children have been forcibly parted from their parents since the dawn of colonialism. From slavery to residential schools to the modern immigration system and the prison-industrial complex, child separation is very on-brand for the United States. Some Democrats and liberals treated Trump's violence toward immigrants as wholly novel, as though Trumpian policies interrupted the otherwise noble history of a country that welcomed all—which is nonsense. But rather than simply dismissing or admonishing people whose analysis was lacking, some activists took action to highlight the history and continuous nature of child separation in the United States. As Dorothy Roberts documented in her book *Torn Apart*, a group of activists in New York City put up a sign at the 125th Street subway that read, "They separate children at the border of Harlem too," calling attention to the crisis of family separation perpetrated by so-called child protective services in the United States. Those activists understood that "this is nothing new" should not be a dismissal but a call to understand and to act.[2]

Of course, Trump's child-separation policy is only one of countless examples. It's easy to dismiss any given injustice as "nothing new," because there is always a parallel to highlight in this country's bloody history. And since the education system imparts US history so poorly by design, it's easy to bombard people with facts that make a mockery of their shock and outrage that their government could enact a policy as grotesque as child separation. But is making people feel foolish for being shocked really our goal as organizers? Instead, the activists who connected family separations at the border to the removal of children from their families in New York City were inviting people to make broader connections and support a local struggle. As organizers, when we find ourselves correcting people's ignorance, we should ask ourselves what we are inviting those people to do. What are we directing them toward? What do we ultimately want from them? And are our words in line with those goals?

Making people aware that an atrocity is in keeping with the character of their country is not an end in itself. In some ways, comparisons that nullify—or reproach—shock can lead to normalization and resignation: the sense that we are experiencing an unchanging and inalterable cycle, so there's no point in getting riled up about it. For this reason, as organizers we must leverage history lessons as calls to action in the present.

It is true that the ruling class has never stopped finding ways to exploit, brutalize, and annihilate human beings. But it is also true that people have always defended their communities and one another against these tactics, at times upending death-making structures entirely. We do not suffer oppressions identical to those of our ancestors, but the struggle against our oppressors has never ceased. Our struggles have shifted in shape, form, and context *because* our ancestors resisted. The histories of those struggles and the specifics of what people endured are intentionally buried in US culture because they are dangerous: full of revelations and tactical knowledge that could help us more effectively challenge authority or even shift the course of human experience. Rather than shaming people for their lack of historical understanding, organizers should distribute the stories and histories we have amassed like shared weapons. Helping people understand the connections between historical events can spur new strategic action, alliances, and growth.

Instead of responding with cynicism to newcomers' shock at injustice, we should seize flashes of outrage as opportunities to draw people into our movements. An organizer should approach people's shock over an atrocity by urging them to consider the broader context of that atrocity. The stories and histories we carry position us to warn people that they cannot fight the evil that currently inflames them without understanding its relationship to the past and to other elements of the present.

It's also important to remember that we are all ignorant of many aspects of this system's history and violence, because the violence of imperialism is so vast that coming to thoroughly understand any one aspect of it can be a lifelong endeavor.

Finally, we must consider the fact that even if some of the oppressive violence that surfaces on a daily basis seems like "nothing new," we can develop creative new organizing strategies to respond to that violence—and build the transformed world we want to live in. Part of what's exciting about organizing is *making* something new amid a world replete with heartbreakingly repetitive cycles of violence. It's important to communicate this potential—and this excitement—to your audiences.

As you strategize in the face of cynicism, ask yourself these questions:

- What is the outcome you want?
- Do your words and actions lend themselves to the creation of that outcome?
- If not, how can you change them?
- What is the impact you would like to have?
- Do you believe you are capable of making that impact?

- If so, how will you go about making it?
- What power do you possess, and how are you leveraging that power in relation to the issue at hand?

We ask these questions not to prescribe answers but to provoke them.

Our aim is to be effective and invite people into a process of making change. Many, many people will decline the invitation, but even fewer will accept an invitation that is never offered. If we are determined and committed to improving our practice of organizing, some people will accept the invitation, and we will build power.

Reactions We Get Stuck In

Sometimes cynicism can be rooted in or linked to our experiences with trauma. As we build together, activists and organizers regularly confront painful issues that many people avoid so as not to experience the ache of awareness. At a visceral level, human beings have fundamental responses to threats: fight, flight, freeze, appease, or dissociate. But, according to somatic healer Staci K. Haines, in the wake of trauma, our responses often become overgeneralized. Reactions become embedded, and survival strategies take hold, even as we enter new environments where the same threats may not exist. We have all seen or experienced this phenomenon: someone is responding to a perceived harm or slight, which may be real, but the reaction we are witnessing is clearly connected to another, much more serious set of events where the stakes may have been much higher. For the person reacting, however, the stakes in the present moment may feel exactly the same, because when their safety or sense of dignity or belonging feels threatened in some way, their reaction is a reflexive one. The survival strategies summoned by this internal alert may have little connection to the situation at hand or how the person hopes to respond to conflict. As Haines writes, traumatized people are often frustrated by their inability to rein in their reactions.[3]

Traumas abound in our society, and the many disasters ahead are sure to leave an ever greater number of people feeling traumatized. Navigating a crisis—or even a misstep by an organizer or activist—is much more difficult with unchecked trauma responses ricocheting around a room. Many of the social patterns and behaviors that lead us to reject one another and revert to individualism are the products of trauma, so to do the work of being human together, we must make space to address these emotional and physiological realities. Grief work, healing work, and conflict resolution have always been important to our movements, but in this age of catastrophe they are more crucial than ever. A strong organizing community is more than a labor force for social justice. It is an ecosystem of care, learning, relationship building, and action.

Make Connections, Not Comparisons

In addition to providing a window into the dangers of cynicism, the moment in which people were activating to push back on Trump's child-separation policy also brings up the issue of comparison versus connection. In responding to the child-separation policy, some commentators compared child separation to the removal of Native children, who were sent to residential boarding schools in the US in the nineteenth and twentieth centuries. Unfortunately, this comparison inevitably led to debates about which was worse. Similarly, comparing Native genocide and the enslavement of Black people can lead to debates about which group has suffered more. Such debates are always self-defeating. With regard to chattel slavery and Native genocide, in both cases we are talking about unspeakable horrors that occurred on unthinkable scales, at the hands of the same system. The character of and connections between these atrocities frame every horror that the United States has perpetrated since, including the violence of border imperialism.

As strategists, we must ask what is the value of attempting to rank atrocities. If two people have been wounded by the same attacker, should the afflicted expend their strength arguing about whose injuries are more severe? Or should they carefully assess the harm done to each so that their injuries can be attended to and they can unite in their efforts to heal and create safety? In such a scenario, most of us would view the assessment of harm not as a competition but as an examination of what must be done to preserve people's lives and well-being and to heal the damage done. We would likely focus on our immediate safety and the prevention of further harm. In such a moment, it would be clear to many of us that our mutual survival could depend on our ability to cooperate, extend care, and strategize. The stakes in our larger struggle against this death-making system are no lower, but they can be less visible to us because systemic violence is more widely distributed and largely normalized.

Effective organizers emphasize the connections between struggles, instead of making totalizing comparisons. Every year, Kelly's collective works to make such connections during annual visits to the Village Leadership Academy, a social-justice-based grade school in Chicago, to facilitate Indigenous People's Day workshops for middle schoolers and junior high school students. Kelly and her Black and Indigenous comrades in Lifted Voices give presentations about various Indigenous struggles, like the fight to stop the Back Forty Mine on Kelly's reservation or the movement against the Dakota Access Pipeline at Standing Rock. During their presentations, members of Lifted Voices draw connections between the contamination of drinking water on reservations and the contamination caused by lead pipes, which affects the drinking water in Chicago. Black and Native communities both bear the brunt of environmental racism, and by drawing connections we can help build solidarity between our communities and find points of alignment. At the end of each Indigenous People's Day presentation, the young people make banners or protest signs around the issue that was explored, which the collective then delivers to Native organizers who are working on those fronts of struggle. The river-shaped banners the children made in support of the Standing Rock movement hung in one of the Oceti Sakowin camp's kitchens for months.

The task of understanding the connections between historical harms and the dynamics they have created over time is much more challenging than venting our emotions through debate or even successful "awareness raising." Sometimes becoming "aware" or "bearing witness" is simply an act of consumption. Given the sheer amount of media available to any person with an internet connection, we have no shortage of "witnesses" to atrocity. Forcing people to behold injustice is not enough. Nor is the goal to simply generate a reaction—any reaction—to injustice; such noise can easily become a passing clamor. The goal is to pull people into an active formation and build something. To do that, we have to draw people into conversations about the harms that have been done to our communities, how we can help one another, and how we can thwart the forces that are harming us. Through that work, the generation of new visions born in collectivity becomes possible.

Drawing connections between our struggles, rather than making comparisons, also lends itself to empathy, which is essential in our work. Organizers help people understand their own social and historical position in relation to other people, which means reframing their own history and the histories they know in relation to other histories and experiences. When we organize people, we are inviting them to relate to others. We are also reminding them, or perhaps even telling them for the first time, that their fate, their liberation, and their particular social concerns do not exist in any kind of singularity. Individualism has programmed people to view our fates and histories as divided. Movement education is, in part, a deprogramming process. It is a path toward unlearning mythologies and liberating ourselves from the isolation of individualism and enclosed narratives.

CHAPTER 6

"Violence" in Social Movements

In spring 2020, when the United States saw mass rebellion, protests that included acts of property destruction struck fear into officials around the country, as support for the uprisings ran high. Cities across the United States saw billions of dollars in property damage. Local governments offered scattered, sacrificial indictments of killer cops in an effort to appease the public. The words "Black Lives Matter" began to appear in large block letters on roadways in major cities. Painted by municipal workers or by community members at the invitation of government officials, rather than by protesters, the block letter murals were co-optive (symbolic) efforts to placate an outraged public and to depict nervous mayors and other rattled officials as "allies." As philosophy professor Olúfẹ́mi O. Táíwò has pointed out, the mayor of Washington, DC, had a Black Lives Matter mural painted on streets near the White House "atop which protestors continued to be brutalized."[1]

By mimicking protest art, officials sought to refashion Black Lives Matter into a mainstream phenomenon—something that belonged to everyday people and politicians alike. After all, how could city officials be part of the problem if they were not only making the philosophical concession that Black lives mattered but also offering a public visual to affirm it? While some appreciated the murals, others regarded them as pandering gestures, often from officials who played key roles in perpetuating—and sanctioning—police violence.

106

The murals were a predictable response to the upheaval of the protests. In a time of isolation and crisis, when so many people felt left behind, or even left to die by their government, the George Floyd protests saw not only unprecedented participation but also startling levels of public approval, even after a police precinct burned to the ground in Minneapolis. The fact that the public remained supportive of the protests, even in the wake of that fire, put officials around the country in an unstable position. When a radical concept or movement forces its way into the mainstream, the first reaction of authority is to eject it. But if that radical presence cannot be ejected, structural maintenance workers—such as public officials and others who benefit from the status quo—will attempt to defang and reconfigure it so that the concept or movement is no longer disruptive to the order of things. When such efforts are successful, disruption gives way to mere expression, and the powerful applaud themselves for welcoming or even participating in that expression. What was once an intervention becomes political wallpaper. Radicalism that is not successfully co-opted or defanged, that continues to linger within the mainstream, will be met with increasing hostility and, ultimately, condemned as associated with violence. As Táíwò writes in *Elite Capture*, "Where co-optation fails, regular old repression will do."[2]

Over time, support for the 2020 protests predictably dissipated. It was a presidential election year, and fears that the protests would help fuel a Trump victory led some liberals to insist that the protests should cease entirely. Others argued that the protests should continue but that they should remain orderly, "peaceful," and nondisruptive. In some places, like Portland, rebellions continued for months as protesters faced off with Donald Trump's fed squads in the streets. But, in cities around the country, we also saw the rise of the Defund the Police movement, which uplifted longstanding abolitionist efforts to redirect funds and resources away from police departments and toward potentially life-giving services for communities.

These efforts were targeted fiercely by liberal pundits, public officials, and their political fandoms. The idea of defunding the police was too radical, they insisted. Some suggested a return to the tired and failed rhetoric of "reform," arguing that such language would be better accepted by the public. Many mainstream Democrats, including Joe Biden, actually insisted that to *fund* the police was critical to reform.

It's true that the language of reform is more easily accepted by the public, because language that lacks substance is generally inoffensive. Yet "reform" poses no threat to the order of things and in practice often leads to policies that further entrench that order.

"Reform" is not a battle cry. It is a political pacifier.

The Defund the Police movement was challenging the order of things and would ultimately be blamed for the electoral losses of politicians who never embraced it, as well as for supposedly rising crime rates. To understand why, we have to understand how violence is framed in relation to social movements.

On Violence and Nonviolence

The terms "violence" and "nonviolence" don't have static and indisputable definitions. Different people deploy these terms in a wide variety of ways to serve their distinct political purposes. To some people nonviolence is a strategy, a practice, and an approach, and to others it is a moral ethos. Popular definitions of violence tend to include property destruction. But under these definitions, the destruction of property is usually viewed as violent only if it disrupts profit or the maintenance of wealth. If food is destroyed because it cannot be sold while people go hungry, that is not considered violent under the norms of capitalism. If a person's belongings are tossed on a sidewalk during an eviction and consequently destroyed, that is likewise not considered violent according to the norms of this society. Those destructive acts are part of the "order of things."

As organizers, we are practitioners of nonviolence, but we also recognize that fetishizing distinctions between violence and nonviolence can lead to the indulgence of rhetoric about "good" and "bad" protesters, where "peaceful" protesters are celebrated and "violent" protesters—for example, those who engage in property destruction that disrupts profit—are viewed as disposable and disreputable. This licenses people to care about the cause being protested without caring about what happens to the "bad" protesters. For example, even as significant numbers of people supported the uprisings following the racist murder of George Floyd, many fewer people vocally defended the rights of protesters who were arrested for acts of property destruction and funneled into the racist carceral system.

In moments of unrest, it's important to remember that, as Martin Luther King Jr. stated, there is no greater purveyor of violence in the world than the US government. From war to policing to incarceration to border violence to the slashing of the social safety net, the US government kills untold millions. The violence of rebellion is infinitesimal by comparison. Moreover, gender-based violence is pervasive in this society, and police officers themselves are fifteen times more likely commit acts of domestic violence than people who are not involved with law enforcement. While it is unusual for police officers to be arrested for acts of domestic violence, one study found that, of officers who are charged and convicted of domestic abuse, more than half keep their jobs. Researchers have also found that people who perpetrate incidents of mass violence, such as mass shootings, often have a history of domestic violence. One study argued that "prioritization of measures to decrease access to firearms to perpetrators of domestic violence may also reduce the incidence of mass shooting."[3] The frequency with which police kill people—both while on the job and in their own homes—also illustrates this connection between domestic violence and more widespread violence, but the United States is not about to disarm its police officers.

We are surrounded by violence in this society, even under conditions that government authorities would characterize as "peaceful," because violence has always been embedded in the norms and functions of this system.

Some people blame the uprisings of the late 1960s and early 1970s for the derailment of the civil rights movement, and we saw a resurgence of those arguments in 2020, from people who condemned some forms of protest and discouraged certain illegal acts. But that assignment of blame is ahistorical and erases the responsibility of racist white people, who organized en masse to destroy the civil rights movement by using tactics like the formation of White Citizens Councils, which sought to socially and financially suppress Black communities, in addition to enacting physical violence against Black people. It also erases the responsibility of the United States government, which ramped up imprisonment, brutality, and assassinations and launched programs of infiltration and disruption, like COINTELPRO, to destroy Black-led movements. Racist white people have always lashed out against Black-led movements, and white liberal support for Black-led movements is historically fickle and unreliable.

As moments of rebellion subside, even people who support the cause tend to have short attention spans, and criminalized people—often, those who've been accused of "violence"—are often left behind. Prison and court support work is usually maintained by small, committed groups of people who are overworked and under-resourced. If we are serious about supporting people who rebel, we must understand that support as a long-term project. We must never abandon our co-strugglers who've been cast as "violent" and thereby subjected to the violence of the state.

As scholar and organizer Barbara Ransby told us,

> [People can become] distracted by the next thing that's happening. So many things have been happening, and the bodies are piling up of people killed by racist cops, and so people are on to the next thing. But when people are tried and convicted of charges involved in movement work, we really have to rally to their defense, and I don't think we do a good enough job, and that's certainly a lesson from the '70s. Many people were set up by COINTELPRO, went to jail for many years, and we didn't do an adequate job to publicize those cases and defend those political prisoners.

Defending people who've been incarcerated for acts the state deems violent is an essential act of antiviolence—challenging the vast harm perpetrated by the state itself.

They Will Call You Violent

If your tactics disrupt the order of things under capitalism, you may well be accused of violence, because "violence" is an elastic term often deployed to vilify people who threaten the status quo. Conditions that the state characterizes as "peaceful" are, in reality, quite violent. Even as people experience the violence of poverty, the torture of imprisonment, the brutality of policing, the denial of health care, and many other violent functions of this system, we are told we are experiencing peace, so long as everyone is cooperating. When state actors refer to "peace," they are really talking about *order*. And when they refer to "peaceful protest," they are talking about *cooperative* protest that obediently stays within the lines drawn by the state. The more uncooperative you are, the more you will be accused of aggression and violence. It is therefore imperative that the state not be the arbiter of what violence means among people seeking justice.

In the past, activists frequently leveraged the violence of police, taking actions they believed police would likely respond to with violence, in order to expose the brutality of policing and force the public to witness and confront it. Many of those actions, including protests carried out by the Southern Christian Leadership Conference or the Student Nonviolent Coordinating Committee during the civil rights movement, took place in a context that was very different from today's world of pervasive mass media. Today, people are much more accustomed to witnessing violence, including violence against protesters, as such imagery is shared widely on a regular basis, particularly through social media. The public has largely become inured to such imagery.

The violence of the state in response to protest is rarely scrutinized to the degree that protesters are scrutinized. The idea that if you are defiant in the face of authority you should expect to incur its wrath is firmly entrenched in our culture. When people who defy police are abused, we often hear people ask, "What did they think was going to happen?" The ubiquity of the abuse puts the onus on the abused to avoid it, because they simply "should have known better." Protesters are expected to remain "nonviolent" at all times, regardless of the circumstances, while the state is assumed to be justified, at least sometimes, in inflicting violence to quell "unrest."

Protesters are expected to absorb violence but never inflict it—to function as shock absorbers to be acted upon, whose sympathetic value is nullified by any deviation from that standard. This expectation briefly wavered during the height of the George Floyd protests, striking fear into the hearts of public officials, but largely restabilized over time.

Whitelash

Leftist organizers are currently confronting a surge of white supremacist violence, reaching levels the United States has not experienced in decades. When activist Heather Heyer was struck and killed by a man who plowed his car into protesters during the 2017 "Unite the Right" rally in Charlottesville, Virginia, public outrage was tremendous and widespread. Even some Republican officials felt the need to denounce the vigilante attack and distance themselves from the white nationalists who had besieged Charlottesville (with the notable exception of Donald Trump, who maintained that there were "very fine people on both sides").[4]

But between May 27, 2020, and September 5, 2020, there were at least 104 incidents of people striking protesters with cars, 96 by civilians and 8 by police.[5] Some might argue that those incidents were simply lost in a larger blur of political chaos and unrest. Yet in June 2021, Deona Knajdek was struck and killed by a car that drove into a crowd of protesters in the Uptown neighborhood of Minneapolis. While the attack did garner media coverage, Knajdek's name did not echo across the country and her death did not spark calls for politicians to denounce the attack or its perpetrator. Deona Knajdek had two daughters and was just shy of her thirty-second birthday when she was killed. She was struck while protesting the killing of Winston Boogie Smith Jr., who was gunned down by federal marshals on June 3, 2021. Like Heather Heyer, Knajdek was an antiracist white woman killed by a white man who intentionally rammed his car into a protest, but Knajdek's death did not galvanize or polarize the country, because the violence she experienced had already become a standard feature of an ongoing (culture) war.

There are a number of factors that have propelled this uptick in vehicular violence, including the fact that hitting protesters with cars became a right-wing meme after Heyer's murder in Charlottesville. Racist white people on social media and forums like 8chan have avidly shared images of protesters being struck and egged each other on, encouraging further violence. The Trump administration also stoked racial hatred. More broadly, we are witnessing a rise in right-wing nationalism and violence across the country that has led to increased violence against marginalized people and activists demonstrating solidarity with marginalized groups.

Republicans in at least thirty-four states introduced eighty-one antiprotest bills in the 2021 legislative session. Much of this legislation seeks to conflate all unpermitted protest with riotous acts of rebellion. Many of the bills include provisions that would legalize hitting protesters with cars if protesters are unlawfully obstructing roadways, even though obstructing streets is a common protest tactic that is generally considered nonviolent. Other bills would increase penalties for tearing down monuments, blocking sidewalks, and writing or drawing on someone else's property. Many of those bills did not pass,[6] but even in states where such bills do not become law, their proposal sends a message of validation to would-be white vigilantes. By forwarding these bills, Republicans are telling white people who are angry at Black protesters that even if it isn't legal to hit them with cars, it should be, and that people who commit these acts have the backing of some government officials.

There has always been a reciprocal relationship between racist elected officials and white vigilante violence, and we are witnessing a moment of intensification on both sides. This kind of order-making, through the state sanctioning of outright racist violence, is deeply embedded in the United States as a political project. Ruth Wilson Gilmore refers to this phenomenon as "the delegation of violence."[7]

As organizers, we must understand that these latest antiprotest laws are part of a long and unceasing tradition that becomes louder and more recognizable in the face of resistance but never abates.

Recent antiprotest bills have notably been accompanied by a fresh barrage of voter suppression bills, propelled by conspiracy theories about the 2020 election being "stolen" from Donald Trump. These mythologies have fueled a phase of Republican politics that some are calling Jim Crow 2.0, as Republicans double down on voting restrictions and work to criminalize protest at the state level, while also lending legitimacy to white vigilante violence. According to Toni Watkins, a voting rights organizer with the New Georgia Project, some activists are now taking precautions usually reserved for protests—such as writing their lawyers' phone numbers on their bodies and wearing glasses instead of contacts, in case of pepper spray—"when we go to poll monitor or even to vote," due to escalating police harassment and right-wing interference.[8]

An example of the current onslaught is the antiprotest law HB 1 in Florida, which Republicans promoted as an "antiriot" bill. One federal judge has stated that the law "arguably criminalizes mere presence at a protest where violence occurs—even if that violence is caused by counter protesters."[9] Among its many draconian provisions, HB 1 aims to prevent local officials from reducing funding for police departments while severely escalating penalties for protest-related offenses. It also prohibits protesters from posting bail prior to their first court appearance, ensuring they'll remain incarcerated during that time. As Ransby has written, the antibail provision of the law "is reminiscent of the detention without charge policies that characterize dictatorships around the world and regimes like the former apartheid system in South Africa."[10] The law also provides an affirmative defense for motorists who strike protesters with cars.

As of this writing, HB 1 is being challenged in the courts by groups like the Dream Defenders, the NAACP Legal Defense and Educational Fund, the ACLU of Florida, and the Community Justice Project and was denounced by the United Nations Committee on the Elimination of Racial Discrimination. Still, the bill enjoys broad-based right-wing support and is consistently referenced as a tool against the "violence" of protest.

The elasticity of violence as a concept allows vigilante violence to be legitimized by the state or even attributed to its victims, if they are protesting the white supremacist order. The conceptual elasticity of violence also allows police to commit casual acts of brutality and gender violence and to kill three people per day in the US, while robbing countless others of life and dignity, without being viewed as inordinately violent. The everyday violence of policing is protested by a select few, while the broader public views the need for intervention narrowly, only supporting protests in cases where police violence is popularly deemed extraordinary, and even then only if the victim is viewed as helpless and relatively innocent. In such cases, much of the public may join calls for the offending police officer to be indicted. Such indictments are rarely granted, and most do not lead to convictions. Occasionally a conviction or a hollow reform is offered up. In such cases, many perceive the system to be redeemed—an officer has been convicted, so it must be working! This perception erases the pervasive violence of the system itself. The status quo is then restored, until the next time.

Meanwhile, organizers campaigning to defund the police and redirect funds toward life-giving services are blamed for alleged spikes in violent crime, even though no correlation exists between defund efforts and crime rates. Elites have merely conjured an association between violence and efforts to disrupt the status quo, and that narrative has been allowed to gain traction in the mainstream. It is a thematic association, propagated through rhetoric, in the hopes that fearful people will reject Defund the Police and eject its radical ideas from the mainstream. Because, under capitalism, "peace" is the maintenance of violence on the state's terms. Organized efforts to disrupt those harms will always be characterized, by any necessary stretch of the imagination, as violent.

As Ransby writes, "The challenge to social movements, then, is to be ever courageous and creative in speaking truth to power, no matter what censoring measures those in power attempt to impose in Florida and beyond."

Land and Water Defense as Violence

In recent years, amid a rise in Indigenous-led efforts to defend land and water, we've witnessed a push to designate these types of protest as "violence" and to simultaneously permit brutally violent state-sanctioned tactics to quell them. Indigenous land defenders and other environmental activists have been targeted with dystopian antiprotest provisions, including enhanced penalties for those who hinder "critical infrastructure" projects, like pipelines, through acts of protests. According to the Brennan Center for Justice,

> Since 2016, 13 states have quietly enacted laws that increase criminal penalties for trespassing, damage, and interference with infrastructure sites such as oil refineries and pipelines. At least five more states have already introduced similar legislation this year. These laws draw from national security legislation enacted after 9/11 to protect physical infrastructure considered so "vital" that the "incapacity or destruction of such systems and assets would have a debilitating impact on security, national economic security, national public health or safety."[11]

The fact that these laws draw on national security legislation created in the wake of 9/11 is illustrative of two important facts: laws that supposedly target "terrorists" will always be used to target activists, and those who would interrupt systemic violence will in turn, be associated with violence by those who maintain the system. While Indigenous land and water defenders face surging rates of targeted violence around the world, it is the potential disruption of "critical infrastructure" projects that is associated with the catastrophe of 9/11, and it is environment activists who are depicted as terrorists.

Much like the antiprotest laws forwarded in the wake of the George Floyd protests, these "critical infrastructure" laws invoke vague terminology that conflates passive acts of resistance with more destructive acts and ramps up the penalties for both. As Kaylana Mueller-Hsia writes, "Vague language like 'damage,' 'tamper,' and 'impede' in critical infrastructure laws makes it unclear if, for example, knocking down safety cones and starting a fire next to a natural gas facility are the same under the law." Some state laws seek to criminalize those who "train" or "conspire" with protesters.

In June 2021, antipipeline activist Jessica Reznicek was sentenced to eight years in prison and ordered to pay nearly $3.2 million in restitution after she pled guilty to damaging an energy facility. This hefty penalty was due to a terrorism sentencing enhancement enabled by the Patriot Act. No one was harmed by Reznicek's acts of property destruction, which were intended to halt construction of the Dakota Access Pipeline, but the judge in Reznicek's case determined that she could be considered a terrorist because "not only the flow of oil, but the government's continued response were targets of this action."[12] Regardless of whether one agrees with the validity of property destruction as a political intervention, it is important that we consider the imbalance of power when it comes to the state's targeting of pipeline protesters and how the label of "violent" is assigned. For decades, oil executives have knowingly contributed to catastrophic climate change while suppressing knowledge about the severity and trajectory of the problem, endangering all of humanity and many other species. These executives' actions have already contributed to the death and displacement of millions of people. Meanwhile, activists who challenge those executives' acts are designated "violent" terrorists deserving of lengthy prison sentences.

Contributing to mass death while destroying the Earth for a profit are not considered violent actions, while damaging equipment in an effort to interrupt those harms is considered terrorism.

In examining how—and to whom—labels of "violence" are assigned, we must also consider the ways that the fossil fuel industry has directly merged its extractive power with that of the carceral state. The Standing Rock movement's efforts to stop construction of the Dakota Access Pipeline reportedly cost Morton County, North Dakota, $40 million. Rather than serving as a deterrent to further pipeline construction, these astronomical costs led the Minnesota Public Utilities Commission to create a mechanism by which oil companies like Enbridge could fund policing to protect pipeline construction themselves. When the commission issued Enbridge a permit for work on its controversial Line 3 pipeline in December 2020, they included a provision that required the company to establish an escrow trust that would reimburse local law enforcement for mileage, wages, protective gear, and training related to pipeline construction.

Meanwhile, Line 3 protesters also faced escalated charges; two were charged with "attempted assisted suicide" for entering a pipeline to halt construction. Line 3 opponents also encountered intensified police-perpetrated brutality. In September 2021, not long before Line 3 became fully operational, water protector Tara Houska told Kelly in *Truthout*, "The level of brutality that is experienced by Indigenous people and allies in struggle with us is extreme." Houska is the founder of the Giniw Collective, whose Namewag Camp became a hub of resistance and care for water protectors taking action against Line 3. "I was a part of a group that experienced rubber bullets and mace being fired at us at very, very close range," Houska told Kelly. "I was hit several times, but I also witnessed young people with their heads split open, bleeding down their faces . . . and sheriffs have been using pain compliance [inducing pain to force people to comply with orders] . . . which is essentially torture. They dislocated someone's jaw a couple weeks ago."[13]

Police arrested over a thousand people struggling to stop Line 3,[14] and, as of this writing, hundreds of water protectors were still facing charges, including bogus felony charges. Thanks to the escrow fund Enbridge established, police agencies received a $2.9 million infusion for their efforts. From militarized "field force" trainings and helicopter and drone excursions to overtime and mileage costs, the escrow fund served as a piggybank for policing.

Water protectors who resisted Line 3 have been subjected to carceral violence. They have been jailed, and some are being threatened with years of incarceration. In retaliation for their protests against profit-driven resource extraction, they are being threatened with what Ruth Wilson Gilmore characterizes as the extraction of time. In her essay "Abolition Geography and the Problem of Innocence," Gilmore writes,

> Today's prisons are extractive. What does that mean? It means prisons enable money to move because of the enforced inactivity of people locked in them. It means people extracted from communities, and people returned to communities but not entitled to be of them, enable the circulation of money on rapid cycles. What's extracted from the extracted is the resource of life—time. If we think about this dynamic through the politics of scale, understanding bodies as places, then criminalization transforms individuals into tiny territories primed for the extractive activity to unfold—extracting and extracting again time from the territories of selves.[15]

A Giniw Collective member named Siihasin also tied the struggle against pipelines (resource extraction) to the struggle against prisons (time and life extraction) when she spoke to Kelly in November 2021 for an episode of *Movement Memos*. Siihasin, a Diné and Mescalero Apache water protector, was still facing protest-related charges. She said that in addition to showing direct support for water protectors facing charges, people could act in solidarity by "showing support for people who are advocating for the abolition of prisons and for the ending of incarceration" and "tying the struggle that we have had as water protectors in this fight against Line 3 to the struggles that are happening across the world around extraction, [and] to our borders where children are being held in concentration camps." Siihasin emphasized that "[these] systems and structures of violence" are "all one in the same."[16] Siihasin was providing a corrective, emphasizing that the main perpetrators of violence are these extractive systems, which—in varied but connected ways—extract the resources that sustain life.

An effort in Atlanta known as Stop Cop City further illustrates the connection between environmental destruction and the extractive violence of policing and prisons. Stop Cop City is an organized effort to prevent the destruction of 381 acres of Weelaunee Forest for the construction of "a police military facility funded by corporations."[17] Waging struggle at an intersection of state violence and environmental destruction, Stop Cop City protesters have been the targets of extreme charges and extraordinary violence—including the first known killing of a forest defender at a protest site by law enforcement in the United States.[18] As Atlanta organizer Micah Herskind told us,

> On January 18, 2023, a joint police task force marched into the Weelaunee Forest and murdered a queer, Indigenous Venezuelan forest defender named Tortugita. And as of February 2023, nineteen forest defenders have been charged with domestic terrorism in an attempt to suppress and intimidate others in the movement against environmental devastation and police expansion. These charges are not about individual protesters' conduct—they're about using the state violence of cuffs and cages to undermine a movement that threatens Atlanta's ruling class.

As climate change intensifies, legal efforts to suppress environmental activism are not limited to the United States. In the United Kingdom, the Police, Crime, Sentencing and Courts Act has ramped up police power to curtail protests. Among other powers, the law gives police the authority to choose start and stop times for protests and to impose noise limits on protests when their sounds affect "activities of an organisation" or have a "relevant impact on persons in the vicinity." The bill also gives the home secretary (a member of the UK cabinet) the power to create laws, without legislative approval, that dictate what constitutes a "serious disruption," giving police further license to restrict the actions of protesters. These rules apply to all protests, even those that involve just one person, and any refusal to comply with police directives, or directions police claim protesters "ought" to have known about, can result in heavy fines.[19] The provisions are largely a response to the massive Extinction Rebellion protests of 2019, in which activists shut down roads and bridges, occupied public spaces, and intentionally incurred arrests in order to draw attention to the climate emergency. Critics say the UK antiprotest law's provisions violate international human rights laws and seek to extinguish all forms of disruptive protest, including the occupation of public space.

From the United States to the UK and beyond, the suppression of dissent is being ramped up, not to "keep the peace" but to preserve a status quo so violent that it is incompatible with most life on Earth.

Rescue as Violence

In an era when nation-states are experiencing and anticipating the instability of climate collapse, laws are being passed to ensure our continued cooperation with the system responsible for those catastrophes—by casting rescue efforts as acts of violence. With millions of people being displaced by climate disasters, rescuers who have retrieved drowning migrants from the Mediterranean Sea are being charged under laws that supposedly target "human smuggling" operations.[20] Similarly, Scott Warren, an activist with the humanitarian organization No More Deaths, was charged with a felony by the United States government after giving food and water to migrants crossing the Arizona desert in 2018. In such cases, activists are being penalized for disrupting what Harsha Walia calls a "violent warscape of premeditated fatalities." Acts of care and rescue disrupt the deterrence strategy of governments whose border security measures herd desperate refugees into deserts and oceans. "The doctrine of deterrence *requires* mass border deaths to instill fear and prevent migration," Walia explains in her book *Border and Rule*.[21]

In order to ward off surplus people and discourage migration, governments narrow migration routes to scenarios that will necessarily result in mass death. At least seven thousand migrants are believed to have died along the US–Mexico border from 1998 to 2017. More than thirty-three thousand migrants died at sea trying to enter Europe between 2000 and 2017. People who disrupt this cycle of violence are accused of human trafficking and smuggling because they chose to preserve life. This should not surprise us. When laws encode violence and law enforcers maintain it, those who attempt to prevent this violence are indeed breaking the law and challenging its enforcers. Such is the perversion of "violence" under imperial and colonial rule: the maintenance of state-sanctioned violence is considered peaceful, while the disruption of those death-making processes is deemed violent.

In March 2021, Italian prosecutors charged more than twenty rescuers from NGOs including Save the Children and Doctors Without Borders with crimes carrying sentences of up to twenty years. The charges, which include collaborating with smugglers, have been vehemently denied by rescuers and contradicted by a forensic study by academics at Goldsmiths, University of London. Italian officials have complained that NGO-led rescues hamper their investigations of human smuggling at rescue sites—investigations that often amount to questioning migrants about who steered a rubber boat, held a compass, or even bailed out water as the boat sank, so that migrants themselves, who have been thrust into survival roles, can be charged as smugglers.

Among the rescuers facing charges is Pia Klemp, a German biologist who commanded two rescue ships for the nonprofit organizations Jugend Rettet and Sea-Watch between 2016 and 2018. Her ships rescued about fourteen thousand migrants during that time. In 2019, with Klemp's future in jeopardy due to criminal charges, the council of the city of Paris announced that Klemp and another rescue captain, Carola Rackete, would receive the Grand Vermeil Medal, the top award of the city of Paris, for rescuing migrants at sea. Klemp's rejection of the award, posted on Facebook, subsequently went viral. Addressed to Anne Hidalgo, the mayor of Paris, the post read,

> Madame Hidalgo, you want to award me a medal for my solidarian action in the Mediterranean Sea, because our crews "work to rescue migrants from difficult conditions on a daily basis." At the same time your police are stealing blankets from people that you force to live on the streets, while you raid protests and criminalize people that are standing up for rights of migrants and asylum seekers. You want to give me a medal for actions that you fight in your own ramparts. I am sure you won't be surprised that I decline the medaille Grand Vermeil.

Paris, I'm not a humanitarian. I am not there to "aid."
I stand with you in solidarity. We do not need medals. We
do not need authorities deciding about who is a "hero" and
who is "illegal." In fact they are in no position to make this
call, because we are all equal.
What we need are freedom and rights. It is time we call
out hypocrite honorings and fill the void with social justice.
It is time we cast all medals into spearheads of revolution!
Documents and housing for all![22]

Klemp's statement calls out the hypocrisy of governments that
would obscure their own violence with symbolic gestures. From
block-letter street murals to state-sanctioned awards that exception-
alize individual activists as "heroes" while death-making policies remain unchanged, we must reject the empty PR maneuvers of those
who sustain the oppressions we struggle against.

Poetry as Violence

On July 31, 2018, Palestinian poet, activist, and filmmaker Dareen
Tatour was convicted in an Israeli court of "inciting violence" and
"supporting a terrorist organization." Tatour's crime, as defined by
the state of Israel, took the form of a poem. The poem, titled "Resist,
My People, Resist Them," was written in response to the extrajudicial
execution of Palestinian student Hadil Hashlamoun and the burning of two Palestinian children, Mohammed Abu Khdeir and Ali
Dawabsha. While the idea of a poem being criminalized may sound
unthinkable to some, Israeli investigators argued, "The content, its
exposure and the circumstances of its publication created a real possibility that acts of violence or terrorism will be committed."[23]
Arguing that her work had been mischaracterized, Tatour received support and expressions of solidarity from around the world.
She had already been under house arrest for nearly three years at the
time of her conviction. She would ultimately serve two months in
prison before being released in September 2018.

In 2019, Tatour's conviction for inciting terrorism via poetry was overturned, while other convictions regarding her social media posts remained intact. It's important to note that Israel's belated acknowledgment that Tatour's poem was not a crime does nothing to address the violence the state of Israel inflicted on Tatour. Her arrest, house arrest, and imprisonment were not undone by the court's eventual acknowledgment that Tatour had a right to artistic expression. State violence around the world is routinely dealt out in such a manner: the state reserves the right to overstep its own laws, and even when it subsequently acknowledges its mistakes, it has already subjected people to the indignity of arrest, deprived them of their liberty, or subjected them to other violence. Such abuse is intentionally crafted to discourage others from expressing themselves or taking action, because it sends a message: even if the government is in the wrong and is ultimately forced to acknowledge as much, it can make you suffer and ruin your life in the meantime.

In her poem, as translated by Tariq al Haydar, Tatour wrote,

> Resist, my people, resist them.
> In Jerusalem, I dressed my wounds and breathed my
> sorrows
> And carried the soul in my palm
> For an Arab Palestine.
> I will not succumb to the "peaceful solution,"
> Never lower my flags
> Until I evict them from my land.

There is a long history of the Israeli government seeking to suppress Palestinian art and cultural expression. The US passed similar laws as it sought to stamp out Native cultures in the United States. In Israel, Palestinian activist Lea Kayali told us that, at one time, it was illegal for Palestinians to use the colors of the Palestinian flag—red, white, green, and black—in combination in any single piece of art. "I grew up on stories about [how if] you were stopped with red, white, green, and black paint that you would just claim you were painting watermelons instead. So then watermelons became a symbol of resistance."

In 1981, Israel Shahak wrote about art being confiscated from Palestinian shops because it was illegal to use the colors white, black, green, and red "too closely" in any publicly displayed work. Other works of Palestinian art were also targeted. As Shahak wrote, "A horse wildly rearing on his hind legs was confiscated because, so the governor said, the name of the picture, which was 'The Horse Refuses,' is of course a 'nationalistic incitement.'"[24]

As Kayali told us, the Israeli government's definition of violence "contorts itself to repress any and all forms of our resistance." Kayali explained that even during periods when it was not officially illegal to raise the Palestinian flag, nonstate actors enforce its prohibition by removing or destroying flags that are displayed in public and targeting those who carry them. She noted that this kind of delegated violence, as Ruth Wilson Gilmore would call it, is also occurring in the United States, where nonstate actors have been rallied to enact violence against the same communities targeted by state violence. In Israel, nonstate actors participate in acts of ethnic cleansing, such as the mass theft of Palestinian homes, in which mobs of Israelis invade and move into the homes of Palestinian residents, forcing them from their communities en masse, in addition to other acts of violence.

Given the regular theft and demolition of Palestinian housing, the frequent murder of Palestinians at the hands of the Israel Defense Forces, and the overall violence of Israeli apartheid, one can easily understand why Tatour would write,

Resist, my people, resist them.
Resist the settler's robbery
And follow the caravan of martyrs.
Shred the disgraceful constitution
Which imposed degradation and humiliation
And deterred us from restoring justice.

Kayali points out that under international law, Palestinians have the right to violently resist Israel's unlawful occupation of Gaza, but she also cautions against placing an overemphasis on "structures of law and legality." As Kayali told Kelly on *Movement Memos* in May

2021, as Israeli bombs were raining down on Gaza, "What this comes down to, in my mind, is kind of the omnipresence of neoliberalism and its tight grip on our framing of justice."[25] Kayali explained, "After the Oslo Accords, which were the peace deals that happened in the 1990s, we saw a really detrimental shift in international discourse about Palestine that really framed everything in terms of the rights of the individual, everything centering the individual and the ascendance of the state as the ultimate goal of the Palestinian people." Kayali says this shift ushered in an era of discourse about a "two-state solution" and protecting the "human rights" of Palestinian people. Discussions of human rights are inherently limited, she noted, because rights are afforded to individuals by larger structures of power and can be revoked by those structures. "I want my existence and liberation to be valid, whether or not the UN agrees with me," Kayali told us. "So I think what this framing can deprive us of is an understanding of collectivism and an understanding of liberation."

Even though Israel blatantly and regularly violates international law, the United States and others routinely defend Israel as an important ally, insisting "Israel has the right to exist." This language not only positions all Palestinian struggles for self-determination and survival as an existential threat, but it also confers upon a state a fundamental right that Israel does not extend to Palestinians, who are not treated as though they have an inherent right to exist.

In the United States, Israel's many crimes are often glossed over or defended by those who insist the situation is "complicated." With rare exception, the word "violence" is seldom invoked by US officials to describe the executions, imprisonment, and torture Palestinians experience at the hands of the Israeli government or the apartheid conditions in which Palestinians are forced to live. As is the case in the US, institutionalized violence is normalized. When people in the United States do rally against Israeli violence, it is usually in response to an active bombing campaign being perpetrated by Israel against Gaza. During such times, marches and other protests may take place in the US, but once the bombs temporarily stop falling—when supposed "peace" is "achieved"—most Americans typically turn their attention elsewhere.

Yet, even within the US itself, state violence against Palestinians continues. The Boycott, Divestment, and Sanctions movement (BDS), which "works to end international support for Israel's oppression of Palestinians and pressure Israel to comply with international law" has been criminalized in multiple countries, including many parts of the US.[26] In June 2022, the US Court of Appeals for the Eighth Circuit upheld an Arkansas law forbidding public contractors from participating in the BDS movement, arguing that boycotts are not a protected form of speech. Arkansas is just one of more than thirty states that have passed anti-BDS laws in the last several years. In the United States, Canada, France, Germany, and the United Kingdom, Palestinian activists—as well as Jewish activists working in solidarity with them—have been targeted and accused of antisemitism for condemning Israeli apartheid.

Kayali noted that, from Israel to the US and beyond, Palestinians' armed struggle and nonviolent struggle are both treated as "terrorism," or as an attack on Israel, or even all Jewish people: "Student activism [in Palestine] is criminalized, nonviolent struggle in the diaspora is criminalized, international mutual aid or charitable supports, including purely humanitarian support, is illegal. Nonengagement through boycotts and diaspora is criminalized."

The repression of Palestinian resistance offers a profound example of the elasticity of violence as a concept and shows how, while the powerful can wage war on particular communities with impunity and claim innocence, the oppressed can be deemed a violent threat simply for attempting to assert their rights or defend their humanity. As Tatour wrote,

> They burned blameless children;
> As for Hadil, they sniped her in public,
> Killed her in broad daylight.
> Resist, my people, resist them.
> Resist the colonialist's onslaught.

The maintenance of global capitalism necessitates mass death, just as the maintenance of capitalism in the United States requires the violence of the carceral system. If these systems function without interruption, you will be told you are experiencing "peace." After all, police are often cast as "peace officers," and soldiers are called "peacekeepers."

If you choose to disrupt these systems, passively, destructively, or by way of extending mutual aid, the concept of violence may be stretched and manipulated by the powerful to encompass your work. That is why we must not allow the frameworks of the powerful to define the bounds of morality in our politics and our action. The elastic concepts of criminality and violence, as controlled by the powerful, will always be bent against us.

Instead, we must expose and dismantle the supposed moral frameworks of the death-makers. We must craft our own narratives and uplift our own frameworks, which implicate the system itself. We must, as Tatour says, "resist the colonialist's onslaught."

CHAPTER 7

Don't Pedestal Organizers

The powerful encourage us to put individual activists on pedestals. Charismatic leaders who are viewed as essential can be co-opted, discredited, or destroyed, thereby harming or even undoing movements. Thus, a movement structure that relies too heavily on hyped-up individuals is highly vulnerable.

Of course, this is not to say that we should not admire and learn from experienced and inspiring people. Organizers who do admirable work and say motivating things can move us to think and to act. They can play a crucial role in our intellectual development. They can even help raise us up as activists and organizers by nurturing our political growth. But, in a culture of individualism and celebrity, admiration can sometimes lead us to overidealization that not only leaves us vulnerable to co-optation and discrediting by the powerful but also can harm the person being pedestaled and the work itself.

For example, when people we've pedestaled say things that we find disappointing, our reactions are sometimes outsized because we are experiencing those failings in comparison to an idealization rather than a person. The snapshots of a person's life and work that become popularized can become enlarged, eclipsing the rest of their humanity. And, as with any infatuation, the gaps in what we know are often filled in with fantasies about who we would like such people to be and how we would like to relate to them. This kind of

129

thinking and parasocial attachment makes it easy to completely miss points of disagreement or misalignment. It can also create the illusion of someone whose actions, ideas, and politics will never let you down when, in reality, no such person exists.

If we were to view the people we admire as flawed but capable human beings with whom we sometimes agree and sometimes disagree, any disagreements we might have with them would be viewed as normal and healthy occurrences—after all, no two people agree on absolutely everything—rather than signs that our organizing world must be thrown into chaos. But we do not witness the totality of the people we put on pedestals. In the age of social media, we often take a meme- or tweet-sized sampling of someone's humanity and project it, large-scale, over the whole of their being.

It is dehumanizing to pedestal people in this way, for a number of reasons. It erases the wholeness of their being, papering over the truth of their life, work, and beliefs with fantasy and adulation. It also sets people up to be dismissed or widely condemned when they are inevitably wrong about something, because those moments will always come, for all of us. No one's politics are infallible, and we all have terrible days where we say or do the wrong thing, even if we believe the right things. We all cause harm and experience harm, and doing righteous work in one arena does not purify our politics in all others. We have all waded through the muck of a racist, homophobic, transphobic, ableist, misogynist, classist, and otherwise harmful society. The normalization of harm that we have experienced is genuinely horrific. The process of disentangling those oppressive forces from our politics, and undoing that normalization, is a lifelong journey. We sometimes like to imagine that the people we admire have completed that journey, but no one ever really has.

If you look back at your own political stances over the past ten years, or even less, you can likely spot numerous instances when your own assumptions, beliefs, predictions, or strategic positions were off base or outright wrong. As organizers, we are always learning, and we don't know what we don't know. This never ceases to be true, however accomplished and admired someone might become.

When people spend a lot of time in the public spotlight or attain a certain celebrity status on social media, they will eventually be wrong in public. The extent to which they are wrong, and how you will reconcile it, may vary. If, for example, someone is indulging in bigotry, a forceful rejection of their commentary may be necessary in defense of at-risk and marginalized communities. In matters of strategic disagreement, it may be enough to simply state disagreement or say nothing at all. After all, having a large platform does not make anyone the arbiter of what we do. But when we feel personally disappointed in—or even betrayed by—figures we do not know, it is important to interrogate our reactions and how we are relating to those people.

Feelings of personal "betrayal" can be misplaced, because we sometimes imagine ideological compatibility that does not exist. If we looked into someone's previous work, writing, or practices, we might discover that they have long held some positions that we disagree with or that their organizing style may not align with our own. This does not mean that we cannot praise someone's work without running a background check or familiarizing ourselves with their entire body of work. It does mean that we should be specific about what we admire: the campaigns they have co-organized, their leadership style, their written work, or even specific words they have shared, rather than reducing them as people to emblems of good politics whose unknown words, actions, and beliefs have been overwritten with idealization. Such idealizations are a trap, both for the admirer and the admired.

The idealization of individual leaders can also encourage us to embrace ideas that are harmful or excuse behavior that should be challenged. If we become too invested in someone's leadership, or even fetishize that leadership, we can abandon our own strategic analysis or fail to develop that analysis. Good organizers do not want "fans." They want committed and thoughtful co-strugglers. An organizer who wants your allegiance rather than your solidarity and co-investment in struggle is not someone whose leadership you should trust.

Putting organizers on pedestals also creates psychological distance between everyday people and movement work. Exceptionalizing organizers does not help everyday people imagine themselves within the struggle. It makes organizing seem like something orchestrated by heroic individuals rather than interdependent communities composed of people like themselves. To succeed, our movements need everyday people to not only imagine themselves doing the work of organizing but also be drawn to that work with great enthusiasm. As Dr. Charles Payne has written, "Ordinary, flawed, everyday sorts of human beings frequently manage to make extraordinary contributions to social change."[1]

Navigating Visibility

What about those pedestaled organizers themselves? How can one navigate visibility while staying true to one's movement roots? These are important questions for people of all ages, but our movements have fallen especially short when it comes to helping young people navigate the perils of sudden popularity.

When a movement gains new momentum and an organizer's leadership, public speaking, or social media presence draws significant attention, individual platforms can grow quickly. Organizers may be deemed "celebrities" over the course of a few weeks or months. At times, that visibility is accompanied by financial opportunities, and a few people may become rich, but the vast majority of activists and organizers who experience high levels of visibility will never have access to the material resources that people associate with "fame." Still, they sometimes experience common pitfalls of celebrity, absent those material benefits. Some organizers may not become anything like "famous" but may find that they are being evaluated with additional scrutiny, overidealized, or frequently treated as the arbiter of a particular topic because they are part of a group or community whose movement is presently in the spotlight.

This form of heightened visibility can also have negative consequences for the person being afforded extra attention. In a culture that is preoccupied with fame and idealized individuals, organizers who experience heightened visibility are often subject to the kind of scrutiny and harassment that traditional celebrities may experience but without any defensive infrastructure in place to protect them against things like harassment and doxing. Highly visible organizers may also experience depression, anxiety, or other mental health impacts as a result of close public scrutiny and overexposure.

We ourselves have struggled with the contradictions of visibility. When it comes to deciding whether to engage with criticism, or whether to follow through on an opportunity, there are no handy rulebooks for organizers. Being idealized, of course, is a trap, as you will invariably disappoint people with your imperfections, human failings, and contradictions. All people cause harm at some point in their lives. This is inevitable. Therefore, it's important to figure out how to utilize your platform in a way that uplifts your beliefs and your cause without losing your way. That's no simple matter in a world that would rather treat you as a brand to be sculpted, co-opted, projected upon, or destroyed.

In the hopes of further illuminating the journeys of those who are entering those waters—as well as our own journeys—we discussed the matter with organizers who offer a jumping-off point for people grappling with these issues.

Individual "Success" Is Not Movement Success

Longtime scholar and organizer Barbara Ransby reminds us to avoid the illusion that mainstream recognition of any individual activist— even if that activist is you—qualifies as movement success.

"We're all trained to be kind of individualistic and wanting a certain kind of traditional success," Ransby told us. "So, how do we resist celebrity and the seduction of people bestowing all kinds of praise on you, and understand what is also happening in that process that is corrosive?"

Part of the problem, says Ransby, is that the powerful create the illusion that movements have succeeded by singling out people to embrace. Usually, after attempting to co-opt the image of a particular individual activist, the system moves to either defeat or co-opt the demands of the social movement itself and sometimes tries to defang larger efforts toward justice in the process. For instance, the mainstream whitewashing of the legacy of Martin Luther King Jr. has led to many politicians and right-wing forces attempting to weaponize King's words and memory when criticizing contemporary protesters. Pundits will often chastise protesters in King's name, claiming that he would not approve of their tactics, despite King's own deployment of the same tactics.

Inclusion is a compromise the powerful sometimes offer in order to avoid more significant systemic alterations. Ransby points to academia as an example of inclusion being offered on very strict terms. "Most of the sort of Black intellectual tradition has been on the margins or outside of predominantly white institutions because of how racist and exclusionary they were. But then certain demands were made, and the demand was for justice. The demand was not just for representation, but the demand gets kind of contorted into something that the system can absorb without convulsing." Ransby says the "diversity, equity, and inclusion" approach of academic institutions creates "a kind of cosmetic diversity," but she stresses that those who are included are expected to conform to the norms of the institutions that have deigned to include them, rather than rocking the boat or expressing their own values. In this way, "victories" of inclusion often lead to disappointment.

Both Critique and Affirmation Are Necessary

Ransby acknowledges that organizers who are highly visible are sometimes bombarded by critique, but she also believes that good-faith critique is essential to movement building. "I do think we should, in a principled way, critique behavior within the movement that is counterproductive, and I think we have to promote a movement culture that has a certain expectation of all of us, of how we behave, how we present ourselves as organizers and activists and how we treat each other." Ransby believes in critique that "acknowledges the effort and the rightness in what [organizers are] intending to do and then how you see the weaknesses or mistakes in that. Finding a way to do it such that we are still encouraging and humble ourselves, I think, is a challenge."

Critique comes with its own complex set of challenges. "I've had experiences critiquing people privately and lovingly, and them, let's just say, not taking it well," Ransby says. On the flip side, "somebody might tell you you're wrong when you're not. . . . I find sometimes the people who are the most dogmatic about 'this is wrong, this is wrong' sometimes are wrong themselves, and they can't see it." Criticism often comes from people who have no connection to the work and may have no idea what they are talking about. When this happens, we can check in with ourselves and, if necessary, our co-strugglers or personal touchstones about whether the criticism merits consideration. Meanwhile, Ransby encourages organizers to commit to a process of self-reflection that includes questioning and challenging their own positions. This advice may be particularly relevant to high-profile organizers whose positions are continually praised.

Ransby also notes that it is natural for people to want to be affirmed and that we should affirm and reward one another in our work. If recognition and affirmation are fostered in healthy ways within a community or a group, organizers are more likely to engage in a reciprocal culture of affirmation, recognizing and uplifting one another rather than treating one another as competitors. Ransby also notes that it is easier to invest trust in organizers who are eager to share the mic with others. "I'm always impressed when people don't want the spotlight," Ransby told us, noting that when an organizer is determined to redistribute opportunities to speak or be uplifted, "then you say, 'Hey, maybe that's the person we want to represent us in this situation.' Because you understand that they've not internalized any kind of lust for that."

Solidifying Your Community and Sharing the Spotlight

Page May is a middle school teacher, cohost of the *Lit Review* podcast, and a cofounder of Assata's Daughters, a queer, Black, woman-led, and youth-focused organization rooted in the Black radical tradition. As an organizer whose work began to receive significant media attention during the Black Lives Matter protests of 2014, May knows the pressures of sudden visibility. For her, a heavy sense of obligation arose as opportunities to speak or draw attention to an issue presented themselves. "I would feel like I was being lazy or something, if I would say no to stuff," May told us.

However, May found that after she cofounded Assata's Daughters, the sense of pressure and obligation became less overwhelming because she was accountable to a community of people who could weigh in on decisions together. "[Having an organization] can give you more permission to say no," May said. "It can also help you think through talking points."

When decisions about who will speak and what the group's talking points will be are decided jointly, it can also make subsequent critiques feel less personal. "Knowing that there was a crew of people that I trusted a lot . . . it was really, really helpful." May described a process at Assata's Daughters in which, when speaking requests would come to the group or to May, they'd be shared out and anyone could volunteer to step up. Sometimes, May would end up speaking anyway, but even in those cases, "having it go through that process takes [off] a lot of the pressure."

May also stressed the importance of using the spotlight to elevate new leadership. "As a leader, you tend to have a lot of publicity, but there are ways that you can start to transition and to train up other people that are coming up behind you to take that on, and just sharing that spotlight as much as possible."

In highly energetic moments, young organizers or others whose work is in the spotlight are sometimes fetishized. For example, we will sometimes hear that it is time to "follow the leadership" of women, youth, Black youth, Indigenous people, or some other group, usually because a particular effort has caught the spotlight. People who are understandably impatient for large-scale change often want to believe that there's a shortcut: that one group, movement, or demographic is the truth and the way and that merely cheering on that contingent will spur a revolution. This places undue pressure on whatever group or demographic is being fetishized as a savior troupe. While there are

moments when it makes sense for us to take leadership from particular groups, particularly when the struggle at hand centers on their
lives, land, or water, there is no one group—and certainly no one
person—who can defeat capitalism, end imperialism, or bring down
white supremacy alone. Attaching oneself to such fantasies may feel
like solidarity to some, but in reality it is dehumanizing, nonstrategic,
and an abdication of one's responsibility to forge struggle.

Rather than becoming co-strugglers, some people who fetishize
movements, groups, or individual activists can become part of fandoms. Having "fans" can go to an organizer's head, because it can
mean that whenever we are wrong, there is a flock of people waiting
to tell us that we are right and, potentially, reinforce our worst or
least strategic impulses.

"This is why it is so important to have people that aren't just
your fans," May told us. And, she says, it's another place where having an organization—or some other small-scale community—to
turn to can be crucial, to "keep you in check." May said that at first,
she "naively" failed to realize how "dangerous and messed up" the
spotlight could be. It was her co-strugglers who alerted her to the
dangers and downsides of celebrity-organizer status. "I knew I didn't
want to be *that* person, because I had friends that would complain
about those kinds of people," she said.

"I want to get free," May told us. "First and foremost, the goal
is about liberation, right? And that's going to take longer than our
lifetimes. So for me, I think a lot about how I am trying to be in this
world. And I don't want to be some celebrity activist that makes a
shit ton of money because I talk at things, right? I have a vision of a
community that I am a part of, where everyone knows that if there's
a cat that needs help, come to that lady."

In other words, organizers need to develop a vision of who they
want to be in relation to their community, their movement, and
other people, instead of focusing on self-elevation. What role will
they play in the context of the larger group? What are their skills and
knowledge base? What will they *not* do? These are questions that
must be answered together with others in the struggle.

Having people whom you are accountable to, whom you can honestly engage with about visibility, is a must, May said. "Having more honest and consistent space to talk with your people, and that being a part of check-ins—maybe not at every single meeting, but just like once a quarter, or at least a couple of times a year, just being able to have an honest space [and asking], 'Who's visible right now? How is that going? What needs to change? Who is on a track to become more visible?'"

May also suggested that rotating the role of "spokesperson" among members of a group is a way to avoid placing one organizer on a permanent pedestal. "The media is going to turn [some people] into spokespeople regardless," she said. "Having that be understood as a role that can be switched out would go a long way."

"Ground Yourself"

Aly Wane has been "an activist in some capacity" since around 2001. He has worked with the American Friends Service Committee, the Black Immigration Network, BLM Syracuse, and the UndocuBlack Network. He is also on the steering committee of the Syracuse Peace Council and lives in Syracuse, New York.

"I've preferred to keep my work at the grassroots level," Wane told us. He explained that his organizing around state violence and immigration "organically" led him to embrace abolitionist politics. "I felt pretty early on that the immigration system cannot simply be reformed into anything resembling justice," he said.

Over the decades, Wane has seen organizers rise and fall in mainstream popularity, including some who became wealthy. "I really genuinely feel for people who become sort of 'movement celebrities,'" Wane told us. "I think that's a very dangerous space to enter. I mean, listen, I'm offering this from a place of love. I'm forty-four years old. If I was given the money and the opportunities and the platform that some of my friends who I know have become movement celebrities, would I maintain my politics or would I maintain my direction?" he said. "I feel like I'm old enough to know that I would, but certainly the younger I was, the more tempting it would have been to maybe go a different way."

Wane echoed May's sentiments that a highly visible activist needs to be accountable to a community. "I think that once you start to get that level of attention, you need to absolutely ground yourself in a community of people who have been there with you before you became a celebrity, or before you became sort of a bigger brand name. The folks who you have in your corner, who you know love you, but who will call you in lovingly when they feel like, 'Hey, you're starting to zig where you should have zagged.'"

Wane emphasized that organizers who've been thrust into the spotlight need to persistently return to their grounded communities for critique and guidance, because movement celebrities tend to become surrounded by people who are *not* their communities—people who view them as a "commodity" or a "resource." Having the support of disingenuous people, as well as people who overidealize us, can also compromise our ability to address conflict. Wane stressed that it is very hard for most people to "see past their egos" when navigating conflict. When an activist's popularity surges, some people may begin to view them as a brand or a product. This can be perilous, Wane warned, because people who are invested in you as an idea or an image "are invested in protecting your brand rather than allowing you to address harms you may have perpetuated."

Wane said it is deeply important to ground yourself in a community of people who were there for you before you became highly visible. He emphasized the importance of friends who offer loving correction when we cause harm. "It's so important to have those people who are going to ground you because once you become a sort of a big name, it's so easy to be unbalanced on both sides," he said. Wane acknowledged that criticism will also be plentiful for any highly visible activist and that much of that criticism will be nonsense or the product of envy. Still, he added, "You're going to have tons of people who are there to gas you up," and he warned that, without trusted co-strugglers to keep you grounded, "You're going to lose your sense of self."

Wane reminded us that it doesn't have to be this way—organizers who get swept up in the spotlight sometimes return to more grounded work, especially if they have a trusted community to return to:

> There's a friend of mine who definitely moved into the big-wig sort of movement celebrity space who started to appear on MSNBC and all of these sorts of channels and was approached by all of these foundations and the Democratic Party. And at a certain point, he was just like, "Nope, this is changing me. This is starting to change who I am as a person." So he intentionally stopped accepting all of those offers. He decided to go back to the organizing group that he worked with and to do a retreat with them, to recommit himself to a model of horizontal leadership. Now he's doing a lot of good work.

"Be Suspicious"

For Ruth Wilson Gilmore, the increased popularity of prison abolition in 2020 brought a new wave of attention to her work but also some amount of unhelpful and unwelcome pedestaling. Gilmore, who always warns against the flattening and oversimplification of histories and systems, shared with us that she found she was being credited as a cocreator of prison abolition by some organizers. "There was an awkward period over the last year where some newer, younger people absolutely believed that abolition was something that was invented by two Black women, me and Angela Davis. And it's like, 'No. It's really lovely that you want to look up to your Black women elders in this way, but boy, that's so far wide off the mark.'"

Gilmore's anecdote is worth remembering anytime you may be credited or complimented for something that was the product of a group effort. This will frequently occur, as people in this society are accustomed to looking for an individual to credit in the wake of a great achievement—because individualism has taught them to search for a person to praise, rather than a community that they might relate to or even join. But, as an organizer, if you are given credit for a group effort, you are in the happy position of telling a larger story—and issuing an invitation to become part of that story. It is important to name the wholeness of what we do, because becoming individualized—and divorced from the histories and webwork of community that fuel our work—is a death knell for organizing.

While it's important to dispel oversimplifications that may exalt individuals, Gilmore does not believe that having a large platform is an inherently bad thing. "I do want to share with people who want to hear what I think about this world, because this is what I've been thinking about. Not because I've got all the answers, but I've been thinking about it so hard. And I cherish the opportunity to be able to point some things out to people and point people in directions." But Gilmore warns organizers who are frequently being afforded a platform that they should "be suspicious." Gilmore said, "While I don't encourage paranoia, there's an outward-looking suspicion that can also help keep us true to the fight—which is to wonder, Why the attention? How come people are clamoring for me/us? What's the opportunity and what are the pitfalls of heightened visibility?"

When They Come for You

In the summer of 2021, Harsha Walia, an organizer for migrants rights and Indigenous justice and author of the book *Border and Rule*, became the subject of a targeted harassment campaign orchestrated by conservatives and right-wing trolls after using the phrase "burn it all down" on Twitter. Unknown individuals had recently set fires at two Catholic churches in British Columbia, following the discovery of previously unknown mass graves at residential "school" sites in Canada where generations of Indigenous children had been held. Walia's statement was obviously metaphorical—a call for decolonization and social transformation made by a scholar who has expressed similar sentiments on many occasions. Variations of the phrases "let it burn" and "burn it all down" have a rich history of metaphorical usage on both the left and the right, but in Walia's

case, the language was seized upon, and she was beset with harassment, including death threats, as well accusations of terrorism and
inciting arson. Some of her critics called for her to be imprisoned,
and Walia was informed that some people had filed police reports.
Today's activists face the threat of targeted harassment, doxing, and
even "swatting" (the practice of calling in a fake emergency so that a
SWAT team will descend on someone's home).

Walia resigned from her role as executive director of the British
Columbia Civil Liberties Association over the controversy in July
2021. As Walia explained on Twitter shortly after her resignation,
"I wasn't dismissed; I did resign on my own terms. But through
the days, my leadership was undermined, my hiring was questioned,
and there was no consideration for my safety. The board leadership
acknowledged this all 'served to push her out in any event.'"[2] Others
were vocal in their support of Walia, including the Union of British Columbia Indian Chiefs, which made a statement on Twitter
declaring, "UBCIC stands in strong solidarity with [Harsha Walia]
in condemning the brutally gruesome genocide of the residential
'school' system."[3] Activists and scholars across Canada, the US,
and beyond pushed back against the racism and misogyny that was
being leveled at Walia and celebrated her work. As Walia tweeted
after her resignation, "Everyone's support means so very much—a
reminder that struggle, kinship and grounded relationships is home.
That when oppressive power structures come for you, there are so
many who show up with generosity and ferocity and reciprocity to
co-create resistance and care."[4]

It's important to note that in cases such as Walia's, where respectability is at issue, right-wing and centrist forces aren't the only source
of attacks. Liberals who are committed to maintaining some form of
the status quo often distance themselves from bold forms of dissent.
The extremity of this reflex can result in displays of absurdity, such
as when the Orange County Republican Party headquarters was fire-
bombed in October 2016. The words "Nazi Republicans leave town
or else" were painted on the side of the building. Eager to distance
Democrats from the event, a Harvard researcher started a campaign

on GoFundMe titled "Dems Raise Money to Reopen NC GOP office." The campaign raised approximately $13,000. At a time when Republicans were campaigning against the humanity of trans people, immigrants, Muslims, and other oppressed groups, the people who donated to that GoFundMe could have been supporting targeted communities or antifascist organizing. Instead, they were willing to pay $13,000 to establish that they did not approve of someone else destroying the property of fascists.

While Walia's experience was an extreme case, the targeted harassment of leftist activists and scholars, including efforts to criminalize people or terminate their employment, have become increasingly common. "When organizers find themselves targeted by political opponents online—by which I mean specifically conservatives, liberal, centrist forces—I think it's useful to remember a few things," Walia told us. "The first is to create a support network. What are the movements and communities you are part of and accountable to that share your views? What support can they offer publicly or privately to defuse the individual targeting? We are only as strong as the constellation of communities that hold us up. By building our collective capacity to respond, we also challenge the 'single person/leader' phenomenon."

Walia noted that "our political opponents have a hard time accepting that our movements are nonhierarchical and decentralized and really believe that targeting one person can challenge the legitimacy of an entire movement." The right's investment in individualism means that they may assume they can topple entire social movements by harming single individuals, and those kinds of illusions put organizers at risk.

Walia also cautioned that activists should be "strategic and thoughtful about what deserves our attention." She advises activists to "block freely" on social media and think twice before engaging with a "pile-on." Walia's guidance is important: on social media, we should not hesitate to block, mute, or otherwise avoid people we do not wish to engage with. If you are public about your politics, many people will want to argue with you, and most of those arguments will be unworthy conflicts. "Consider if any of it is worth your energy," Walia told us.

Walia also stressed the importance of cybersecurity protocols, such as using two-factor authentication and frequently changing passwords. "There are important resources for organizers, especially racialized women and gender-diverse people, on keeping safe as a public leftist on the internet," she told us. If you need help developing a personal digital security plan, resources like the Surveillance Self-Defense project can help you examine potential threats and take appropriate cautions.[5]

Ultimately, Walia told us, "it is impossible not to internalize the hatred of those who target you. It might be hard to admit because we like to think we can just brush off trolls, but it will most likely impact your mental, physical, and spiritual well-being. Take the time to process that harm and know that you deserve care and safety."

We're All in the Spotlight of Surveillance

Walia's advice to organizers in the spotlight can be applied more broadly, in today's online world. It's worth remembering that each of us is being watched, even if we are not elevated to the status of "celebrity."

Many of us live much of our lives online, where our behavior is under constant surveillance, packaged as data, and manipulated by content engineered to promote more engagement. Digital algorithms, researcher Robert E. Smith has written, "are now the most powerful curators of information, whose actions enable such manipulation by creating our fractured informational multiverse."[6]

Algorithms are finite sequences of instructions and rules that allow a computer or a program to function. In the case of social media, algorithms work to promote user engagement, which means content that provokes a response or reaction becomes more visible, often rewarding users for extremity. Algorithms exacerbate divisions around identity, culture, and even casual disagreements to calamitous effect, Smith says: "Given the simplifying features that algorithms use (gender, race, political persuasion, religion, age, etc.) and the statistical generalizations they draw, the real-life consequence is informational segregation, not unlike previous racial and social segregation."[7] Social media algorithms that produce and amplify this stratification have already proven catastrophic to the health of our societies: Facebook algorithms can create political rabbit holes that can lead conservatives to embrace QAnon conspiracy theories in as little as two days' time.[8]

When we navigate the digital world, we are experiencing forms of commercial surveillance that aim to map human behavior in order to craft interventions that generate profit and to reduce uncertainty by influencing people's behavior (curating content to anticipate and accommodate our habits, preferences, and whims, as tracked in real time). Apps built on algorithms of stratification curate content aimed at prompting users to react in observable ways. Any response, from the "likes" we click on Twitter or Facebook to our willingness to engage with a question posed on a social media platform, is potentially valuable data. That data can be used to not only predict what we might do or buy but is also mined for larger purposes.

In this landscape of surveillance, corporations attempt to exploit what Shoshana Zuboff has termed "behavioral surplus." Zuboff writes that Google's path to profitability took shape when the company discovered that all of the extraneous data it gathered in the process of improving its products had additional value "for uses *beyond* service improvements," and it was "on the strength of this *behavioral surplus* that the young company would find its way to the 'sustained and exponential' profits that would be necessary for survival."[9] Many online surveillance mechanisms are commercial—but under capitalism, there is no clear divide between corporate data harvesting and governmental surveillance, just as there is no clear divide between government propaganda and the corporate media.

Take, for example, the Hemisphere Project, a partnership between AT&T and two federal entities, the Drug Enforcement Administration and the Office of National Drug Control Policy. "The Hemisphere Project is a massive database," sociologist Brendan Mc-Quade told us. "Four billion records are added every day. It provides twenty-six years of data that can be requested by federal, state, and local narcotics officers. The Hemisphere Project's signature intelligence product uses an algorithm to match a 'pattern of life analysis' from a 'dropped phone' to locate the user's new number." The analysis is based on the metadata of a person's entire call and text history. "With this type of surveillance," Brendan explained, "disposable phones—the 'burners' used and abandoned by people selling illegal drugs in the informal economy—no longer provide a degree of protection from police."

This is not to say that social media cannot be leveraged for organizing purposes—and, if we deal in the realities of where people are and what they are doing, it must. But we should engage with it carefully, with full understanding of how these structures function, who they actually serve, and why. Marginalized people have utilized social media brilliantly, creating visibility for work, stories, and movements that might not otherwise find an audience. We have accomplished projects on Twitter that would not have been replicable in the physical world. We have also seen social-media-based tactics help catapult campaigns to victory, free imprisoned people, expose corruption, unmask white nationalists, and more. But we should recognize that social media were not designed to provide opportunities to oppressed people; instead, oppressed groups have often figured out how to leverage these platforms in useful ways, in spite of those platforms' corporate-driven limitations.

Mass connectivity does not have to be harmful, but it is currently managed under capitalism, which means the motives that govern corporate platforms will never be grounded in our interests, no matter how brilliantly we use them. Our presence in those worlds will be monitored by law enforcement and surveilled and mined by corporations for behavioral surplus. All of us must move through digital corridors with this knowledge, regardless of whether we perceive ourselves to be in the "spotlight." We must also remember that corporate algorithms elevate content geared toward increasingly insular groups—reinforcing echo chambers—and they reward conflict. Facebook researchers told the company's executives in 2018, "Our algorithms exploit the human brain's attraction to divisiveness."[10]

The most divisive, oversimplified content rises to the top, and the algorithm presents people with increasingly divisive content over time, in an effort to hold their interest. We must take advantage of social media platforms as best we can, connecting with people we would never otherwise meet or be exposed to, while also understanding that the algorithmic fragmentation of common ground is an ongoing disaster we will have to navigate in our work.

Perhaps most urgently, we must also remember that there is a distinction between connection and communion. "Connectivity"—connection with other people that is mediated by technological platforms—is often presented as an inherent good, but as many of us witness daily on social media, it alone does not necessarily generate understanding or inspire reflection on our shared humanity. In fact, what we attempt to cultivate in our work is at odds with the extractive economy of "connectivity." Political communion necessitates both connection and purpose, as well as a profound recognition of the shared humanity of those participating, whether in digital or in-person spaces. We must engage with the tools of the digital world with this in mind, no matter how deeply or publicly we use these platforms.

Navigating the complexities of visibility in these times will be an ongoing struggle for activists and organizers. Our enemies would like us to fashion ourselves into dueling brands that can be bought off or smeared into irrelevance. Even those who support us will at times seek to reduce us to a tweet, a brand, a projection, or an idea. We must learn how to push past those reductions and to engage meaningfully with people who are looking not for an object to admire but a co-struggler with whom to build.

CHAPTER 8

Hope and Grief Can Coexist

Why write love poetry in a burning world?
To train myself, in the midst of a burning world,
to offer poems of love to a burning world.

—Katie Farris, *Why Write Love Poetry*
in a Burning World[1]

In October 2020, as the United States reached the milestone of having officially lost one hundred thousand people to COVID-19, the lack of commemoration was striking. While gathering often was not possible due to COVID restrictions, Kelly and other Chicago organizers felt that there needed to be some outlet for the grief people were experiencing—or, worse, not allowing themselves to experience. With society on the brink of full-blown fascism, many of us worried that a lack of memorialization played into a larger erosion of empathy that would ultimately empower fascists. In an effort to help people process and hold the moment together, in spite of the physical distance between them, Kelly's collective, Lifted Voices, and others set out to plan a week of action and memorialization.

Taking into account that people could not safely gather, the group worked with friends and allies across Chicago on a weeklong event called "Signs, Shrines, Collages, and a Mixtape: A Remote COVID

Vigil." Participants were encouraged to make signs, shrines, and collages and to share photos of their work on social media using the hashtag #WeGrieveTogether. Scans of memorial artwork created by participants and volunteers were available online and could be printed for use in the creation of shrines and collages. Organizers dropped off signs outside the homes of people who wanted to photograph themselves with the artwork but didn't have printer access. Activists also hung dozens of banners bearing the words "We Grieve Together" in neighborhoods across the city. The banners, many of which depicted the names of people lost to COVID-19, appeared on park fences, outside of schools, across a set of church doors, at the First Nations Garden, in storefronts, and in front of people's homes. Young people from the Chicago Freedom School also carried out a banner drop—a protest tactic in which large banners are displayed in a public location—downtown. As organizers, we typically associate banner drops with disruption, and the same was true in this case, as organizers were disrupting the erasure and suppression of grief.

A lineup of activists also recorded speeches they would have given at an in-person memorial, and Chicago performing artist Ric Wilson cut those speeches into a mixtape called *Let This Radicalize You* as a loving nod to Mariame's oft-quoted words, "Let this radicalize you rather than lead you to despair," which are also the inspiration for this book's title. The week culminated in a noise action: a small group of activists gathered outside the Metropolitan Correctional Center in downtown Chicago and played the mixtape on a loudspeaker so those incarcerated inside the federal jail could hear it. The tape was also released online so that people could listen at home. Some of the speakers featured on the mixtape addressed the imprisoned people directly, condemning the system's abandonment of them as COVID raged behind bars expressing solidarity with the people being held inside the prison. The speeches from the mixtape were also compiled in a zine that activists and loved ones mailed to many imprisoned people.

Loved ones of some of the people imprisoned inside joined activists as they waved from the sidewalk and held up a banner that read "We Love You." People caged inside the prison acknowledged the action by flickering the lights in their cells.

The week's actions offered people who were coping with grief and isolation the opportunity to reach out and to extend the truth of their shared grief—and the reality of our interconnectedness—across time and space. As people grappled with illness, mass death, and the rising threat of fascism, they were able to create a sense of political communion and push back against the further normalization of mass death. As Kelly wrote in the introduction for the memorial zine,

> There is a reason our collective grief has been suppressed with lies and political circus acts during this pandemic. It's because there is power in solidarity and collective memorialization, and the powerful are afraid of that empathy and solidarity. This pandemic, like the horrors of the prison system, has demonstrated how harmful it is to human beings to be deprived of connection. We were already being starved of it by the cult of individualism.
>
> The answer is more empathy and connection. The answer is to become an immovable force when we are together and a constellation of power and empathy when we are apart.[2]

An Unthinkable Question

In the twenty-first century, an unthinkable question haunts many organizers and activists: Is our world dying? Amid rising temperatures, record hurricane seasons, and sprawling wildfires, we have heard stern warnings from scientists about the need to curb carbon emissions—calls to action that wealthy nations like the United States have largely ignored. As the damage continues, fears that the end of life on Earth is near leave some organizers to wonder if the work of social movements still holds meaning. We believe it does.

We do not seek to minimize the severity of the moment we are living in. We know that human activity has warmed the Earth's climate at an unprecedented rate over the last two thousand years.

According to the Intergovernmental Panel on Climate Change's 2021 report, "Global surface temperature will continue to increase until at least the mid-century" in all foreseeable scenarios, which means that climate catastrophes will continue to worsen.[3] While we as human beings still have some ability to affect how high temperatures rise in the coming years, we recognize that, despite our best efforts, the effects of climate change will claim many lives and that many precious creatures and ecosystems will be destroyed. We feel deeply for those who are suffering and for the young people who have inherited this era of catastrophe. We share in their heartbreak and their fury.

We also know this: hope and grief can coexist, and if we wish to transform the world, we must learn to hold and to process both simultaneously. That process will, as ever, involve reaching for community.

In a society where fellowship and connection are so lacking, where isolation and loneliness abound, we are often ill equipped to process grief. Our fumbling efforts to do so often end in suppression, desensitization, or despair. Such ineptitude can prove dangerous, as in the wake of 9/11, when a manipulative government fashioned the grief of the masses into a nationalist fervor and complicity in endless warfare. Grief can also lead us to retreat and recoil and, too often, to abandon people to suffer in ways that we cannot bear to process and behold. We saw such behaviors manifest among some people during the COVID pandemic.

We say this not because we are interested in blaming individuals but to convey that we, as people, do have power. Depending on our choices, we can turn away from injustice and let it continue, or we can confront our grief and move forward to shift the course of societal action in the face of a massive failure of leadership and institutional abandonment. Grief, after all, is a manifestation of love, and our capacity to grieve is in some ways proportional to our capacity to care. Grief is painful, but when we process our grief in community, we are less likely to slip into despair.

To maintain the current social and economic order in the unstable years ahead, capitalist governments will have to rely on the further normalization of mass death. As climate-driven migration continues to intensify and droughts and other disasters cause food shortages, the consolidation of wealth will continue, and the disposal of human beings who have no place in the economy will escalate, unless we fight for another way of living in relation to these crises. If the public at large accepts preventable mass deaths as inevitable, the system will maintain itself. The pandemic gave us a preview of how the government will address future experiences of catastrophe and collapse: by prioritizing the economy over human lives. They will rely on us to doggedly pursue normalcy instead of rising up and upending the culture of greed and human disposability that has already caused so much death. Our oppressors rely on our hesitation to feel for one another. They rely on our suppression of empathy and grief and on the desensitization that often takes hold as a defense mechanism in the face of so much suffering. They are hoping that the battery of catastrophes we witness in real time will shorten our attention spans until the fallen are forgotten in the blink of an eye.

Fortunately, the system's reliance on us to deaden and dull our capacity for grief presents us with a lever for change. Our oppressors are wholly unprepared to confront a multiracial, intergenerational movement of people who share a loving practice of grief and who are prepared to care for one another and act in one another's defense. As Cindy Milstein writes in *Rebellious Mourning*, "Our grief—our feelings, as words or actions, images or practices—can open up cracks in the wall of the system. It can also pry open spaces of contestation and reconstruction, intervulnerability and strength, empathy and solidarity. It can discomfort the stories told from above that would have us believe we aren't human or deserving of life-affirming lives—or for that matter, life-affirming deaths."[4]

As in the "We Grieve Together" project, wholly confronting our grief in connection with each other can be a rebellious political act in the face of top-down attempts at normalization. Even just acknowledging that we are not alone in our grief can, as Milstein notes, brings a sense of solidarity and collective strength. That strength kindles our energy to face the future, sparking the fire of hope.

We know that hope is essential to social change because in order to make change, someone must first imagine that it can be so. Some find it difficult to practice hope amid the stark climate projections we face, but it is important to remember that people have always found ways to cultivate hope, even in the face of daunting or insurmountable odds. Many of our ancestors experienced the end of the worlds they had known. During times of siege and enslavement, amid open warfare and famine, behind bars and while living as fugitives, and with the threat of nuclear annihilation looming overhead, previous generations have found ways to organize for change and for collective survival. We must learn from their histories and traditions as we face an uncertain future. We can also learn from organizers among us today who face seemingly insurmountable odds and find ways to move forward in hope. Following their example, we must allow our grief and hope to coexist and courageously hold on to both.

"Dancing Things Back into Place"

For Native organizers defending the natural world, the violence of capitalism has inflicted a great deal of grief and trauma. Morning Star Gali, a member of the Ajumawi band of the Pit River Tribe, is the project director for the group Restoring Justice for Indigenous Peoples. She is also the tribal water organizer for the organization Save California Salmon. Gali told us, "Ninety-eight percent of our juvenile salmon populations were killed off last year." This mass death of salmon is, according to Gali, part of the California economy's historical and ongoing "gold, greed, and genocide framework." Gali explained that mercury was used to enhance the recovery of gold during the California gold rush of 1848–1855. About three million pounds of mercury were lost in runoff at hard-rock mines, contaminating local waterways. "We call it the toxic legacy of gold mining and how these environmental health effects still continue to affect us today, in terms of the water being polluted with mercury and other toxins. . . . Our communities have been so greatly impacted by not having clean water, by not having the salmon running freely within our rivers, that only 2 percent of them are surviving." Gali notes a parallel between the mass death of the salmon and the genocide of Indigenous peoples: "Only 1 to 2 percent of us in California survived."

Gali emphasized that the struggle against colonialism has always been a struggle to prevent the destruction of the natural world. Everywhere land and water have been stolen from their Indigenous stewards, contamination and extraction have followed. The gold rush also brought disease, massacres, enslavement, child separation, and other horrors to Native communities, which were targeted for extermination. White settler communities often placed bounties on the heads, scalps, and ears of Native people, creating a human-hunting industry that was eventually subsidized with millions of state and federal dollars. Thousands of Native people were massacred, and hundreds of thousands died of starvation, disease, and overwork.

Today, Native people are once again faced with mass death. One study found that COVID-19 mortality among Native people was 2.8 times as high as that of white people and considerably higher than other groups as well, due to a perilous assemblage of risk factors. Native people have also proven vulnerable to epidemics that are fueled by poverty, trauma, and despair. Between 1999 and 2015, Native people experienced a larger increase in opioid overdose deaths than any other racial or ethnic group in the United States, according to the CDC. Another CDC study found that suicide rates among Native people went up 139 percent between 1999 and 2017—the highest increase among any group. Native people also suffer disproportionately from the health impacts of environmental racism.

To Gali, the work of saving Native lives imperiled by trauma and despair and the struggle to preserve all life on Earth are part of the same ongoing struggle Native people have waged since the onset of colonialism. "That was a battle against colonialism, when our lands and waters were being decimated by toxins in the gold mining process," Gali told us, connecting the world-crushing impacts of the gold rush to the disasters of the present—water shortages, mass death, the loss of the salmon. "We go out and gather acorns. There's so many oak trees that are sick now and are not producing the [acorns] as they should be," she told us. "We have these rampant wildfires here in California, and with the high rising temperatures, we're having to worry about a fire season that's not just going to be three or four months here, but it's going to be possibly anywhere between nine to eleven months out of the year."

Yet amid all these crises, Gali told us, "There has to be hope." How does she cultivate it? As ever, hope comes through community. In solidarity with family members of missing and murdered Indigenous women (MMIW) and missing and murdered Indigenous relatives (MMIR), Gali co-organizes support for berry-picking efforts in the spring and summer that are led by the families. The berries are redistributed in Native communities as a form of mutual aid. "That's a way that we can support them in their healing journeys," Gali told us, noting that the elderberries and chokecherries are used to make traditional foods.

But now, when groups go up into the mountains to pick berries, "they have to carry bear spray," Gali said. "They have to be very careful about the areas that they go," Gali told us,

> because we understand that this is the bear's food source. Because of the wildfires, because of the scarcity of water, because of all of these various factors, they're not getting the food supply that they're used to, and they're starving as well. There's just all of these different factors that you have to take into consideration now that you didn't have to before. And that means less for us, which is fine, but how are all of those animal relatives being sustained when their habitats are being burned out? There's very, very low to no water within the springs and there's not enough food for them to eat.

Still, Gali does not see despair as an option. "It hasn't been a choice to wake up and decide that we are going to fight for the protection of Mother Earth," she told us. "It's a responsibility that we just understand in that sense. We understand that for us to be healthy, that Mother Earth needs to be healthy, that there is that symbiotic relationship, whether it's with the water, with the salmon, with the oak trees, with the bears in the area, all of it. We all are dependent on one another to survive."

Even though the salmon are perishing, Gali still teaches her children how to make traditional fish traps. "That's what we did," she told us. "We lived along the creeks and the rivers and had our salmon camps in the summer. Even if the salmon are no longer there, we still have to pass that knowledge down of how to create those lava rock traps within the streams just as our ancestors have done for so many years." Gali believes there is an understanding of our symbiosis with the Earth embedded in those practices that must not be lost, even as the Earth changes. "By continuing those practices, and our ceremonies and dances, we understand that there's a relationship, and we are dancing things back into place as they should be, even with all of the turmoil that's being experienced in the outside world. We still have a responsibility to continue in that way," she told us.

Gali notes how scientists and society at large disregarded Indigenous knowledge until it became horribly apparent that "the Earth is being destroyed." Climate scientists in recent years have stressed the need for a return to Indigenous practices. "Now, they're just catching up to say, like, 'Oh yeah, those Indigenous burning methods and those practices were helpful,'" Gali said. The colonizers, she points out, did not simply ignore or demean Indigenous knowledge that could have averted countless catastrophes, but also criminalized and sought to extinguish those beliefs and practices.

But, despite grim projections and resentful feelings, Gali told us, "At the end of the day, I have four children between the ages of eight and eighteen. I know just for myself personally, I can't be in this doom-and-gloom mindset space because I have to have hope for what their life is going to be. We have to think ahead of the impact. They say seven generations ahead." The Haudenosaunee principle of planning for the well-being of the next "seven generations," as opposed to simply providing for one's own family and immediate survival, is widely invoked by Indigenous people. It means that leaders must be accountable not only to themselves and those around them but also to the next seven generations to come. It may be difficult for some people to imagine seven generations into the future under current conditions, but this task is no less overwhelming to Native people who have survived the apocalyptic onslaughts of colonialism: plagues, siege, forced relocation, and efforts to exterminate their culture and communities.

Gali acknowledged that the idea of ensuring the well-being of the next seven generations is daunting in our current context. "It is frightening that there are projections, especially in the Bay Area, in the next twenty-five to thirty years that they're going to be out of water. They're going to be out of clean drinking water. I don't want that for my children. I don't want that for potential grandchildren in the future." But Gali reminded us of how far-fetched the existence of Native people living today must have seemed during past moments of mass murder, siege, and survival—and yet Native ancestors did not abandon their hopes for future generations: "Our ancestors prayed for us. They prayed for us. They prayed for our health. They prayed for us being here and living today."

Gali observed that there are many catastrophes ahead but again reminded us of Native ancestors who survived mass death and the destruction of the world they knew. "There are ways that we have been able to navigate our own survival. I have hope that in the future that we can care for the Earth and she can care for us in a way that is mutually sustainable, that we can participate in Mother Earth's healing as we tend to our own healing."

On the day we talked with Gali about grief, she was preparing to speak at the memorial service for "one of our sister warriors" who had died of COVID-19. Gali's friend, a formerly incarcerated Pueblo woman, was only thirty-eight when she contracted COVID, which was complicated by diabetes, and she had a massive heart attack.

Gali is no stranger to heartbreaking loss. "I lost my father when I was fifteen years old," she told us.

And at that time, he had been incarcerated in San Quentin. He had spent seven years in there. I was just so grief stricken. I remember being fifteen years old, just turning sixteen and just being, like, "What am I going to do?" I just had really no idea. We were very much grounded in our ceremonies, but I didn't understand how to move that grief. At the time, this was the mid-'90s in the midst of the AIDS epidemic. My mom was working at the time as the homeless and HIV case manager. And she's working for the Native American AIDS Project. She was losing not only her clients who were community members, but she was losing her co-workers, her staff. I mean over a hundred people within the community in just a few years, and very similar to what's happening now.

Gali's mother also lost her best friend to multiple sclerosis. "She was just not in a space where she could care for herself, let alone care for us. She had actually ended up leaving," Gali told us. Gali and her sisters worked as teenagers to provide for themselves and a nephew.

She explained that, for her, these ongoing losses have not led her to withdraw or despair—they've moved her to organize. "I was just thinking of how it was from holding and carrying that grief to the organizing that we do today," she told us. "We have so much loss and so much grief that we're dealing with all the time—if it's not within our immediate family, it's within our community, within our extended family. It's just so many losses that we stopped even counting how many within the last few years of the pandemic. So many relatives that have been lost."

In the face of so much grief, Gali said, hope is not optional; it's a necessity: "There has to be hope. There has to be hope. There has to be some light ahead that we can follow."

Gali described what hope looks like in the context of her work with MMIW families and MMIR families, in which she regularly deals with "unthinkable situations" such as "having to write a press release for a prayer vigil for my sister that was just murdered by her partner, and there's no charges being brought against him because he called it in as a suicide. Trying to hold that space and ask her family members for a quote while they're trying to make funeral preparations." Hope may not be the immediate emotion in these moments of acute grief, but Gali believes that "in the larger context we are moving towards healing. Through our organizing that is healing work, through us supporting the families, that it is an opportunity for them to heal and for us to hold those spaces."

Organizing makes it possible to grieve in ways that make a different future visible: "This is bringing our communities together in a way when we are addressing injustices, when we are addressing the invisibility and how misogyny and patriarchy play an essential role in the disappearance of Indigenous women," Gali said.

On the day we spoke with Gali, a prayer run was taking place in Sacramento. Gali expected the event would draw fifty people or so. She and her co-organizers had invited around a dozen MMIW and MMIR families and had prepared breakfast burritos for their 8:00 a.m. start time. When Gali arrived, there were more than six hundred people waiting for the event to begin. "It was beautiful, and it was just incredible," she told Kelly on *Movement Memos*.[5] "We had local Miwok youth, local Native youth [who] were leading this march of six hundred relatives holding signs and banners calling for justice for their loved ones and chanting 'No More Stolen Sisters' [and] 'Whose land? Miwok land.'"

Gali emphasized the importance of events like the prayer run in helping community members process their grief. "It's just being done with this very spiritual foundation, in this very prayerful way of understanding that we have to move the grief through our bodies and move the trauma through our bodies. They say every step is a prayer. Every step is a prayer, and with every movement our ancestors are with us. They're supporting us from the other side in this way." To Gali, the collective experience of community, healing, and comradery people experience during the prayer run is itself an answered prayer.

Gali told us that amid the heartbreak of MMIW and MMIR organizing, hope comes in many forms, including in witnessing profound transformation. "Over six months ago," said, "we had a sister that was the youngest sibling of one of our relatives that was killed. She was very, very deep in her addiction, and we always came from a place of nonshaming and supported her."

Gali and her co-organizers helped the young woman attend ceremonies and vigils when she was able and "just did what we could to keep those lines of communication open, recognizing that when they were ready that they would absolutely be welcomed and embraced within our communal spaces." Eventually, something shifted for the young woman. "Six months ago, she made a decision for herself that she was ready to go into treatment. It meant us physically driving up and helping pack her apartment and putting her belongings into storage." Gali and her co-strugglers helped the young woman navigate the extra testing and paperwork she faced due to the pandemic and drove her to a Native-run treatment facility.

"As of today, she is six months clean and sober," Gali told us. "She is working full-time. She is in transitional housing. She's participating in the MMIW prayer run this weekend, and we were able to cover her lost wages for work, so that doesn't become a financial barrier. We were able to not only cover her transportation to participate but cover her lost wages."

Gali's story reminds us that accompanying each other through grief can help pave new paths forward. "It's situations like that that give me hope," Gali told us, "and I'm just so proud of her."

Walking into Possibility

> What is there possibly left for us to be afraid of, after we have dealt face to face with death and not embraced it? Once I accept the existence of dying, as a life process, who can ever have power over me again?
> —Audre Lorde, *The Cancer Journals*[6]

Anoa J. Changa is a Black Atlanta-based organizer and journalist whose work focuses on electoral justice and voting rights. In the run-up to the 2020 election, Changa's work highlighted voter suppression tactics in Georgia and documented the struggles and unlikely victories of the multiracial, grassroots coalition that overcame a highly sophisticated antidemocratic apparatus. But while she was working to educate the public about voting rights, Changa was also fighting a more personal battle.

"I started getting sick in the middle of 2019 and landed in the ER," Changa told us. She was uninsured at that time and noted that she still probably has collection notices "floating around somewhere." Changa was shaking and experiencing extreme fits of nausea. The doctors told her she was experiencing acid reflux, but due to the severity of her symptoms, Changa had doubts. The episodes continued, followed by long bouts of fatigue lasting a week or more.

In January 2020, Changa had a new job and new insurance. During her second full month of work, she experienced another episode and ended up in the hospital. This time, Changa brought a friend with her to the emergency room. Changa's friend advocated for her, arguing with doctors who, Changa says, "were acting like I was exaggerating about the pain." Changa's friend rejected the doctors' dismissiveness and insisted they run more tests.

Finally, the doctors relented and ordered a CT scan for Changa. When the on-call doctor entered the room, Changa could tell immediately that the news was bad. "He tells me, 'So, we got your scans back'—and those doctors, they have that voice whenever they tell you something is not good—and he says, 'We saw some things on your liver.'"

Changa was admitted to the hospital. Within the week, she was diagnosed with inoperable stage IV neuroendocrine cancer. Doctors cautioned Changa against "doomscrolling" about her condition on the internet and assured her that recent medical advances could potentially help her "live into older age," but the situation was critical. Changa found a specialist and began advanced treatment, including radiation therapy.

As an otherwise healthy forty-year-old woman, Changa had been accustomed to moving at a certain speed. Cancer, she said, has slowed her down—and that deceleration has been intensified by the fact that, shortly after her diagnosis, the pandemic hit. Changa struggled to balance her treatments and symptoms with the need to earn a living in COVID times while also coping with anger and grief.

"The fact that they could have done scans much earlier, but they didn't, probably because I was uninsured at the time—that just made me so mad," she told us. Changa also knows too well that medical racism may have played a role in her delayed diagnosis, as the concerns of Black women are often written off or dismissed by doctors. She wrestles with that outrage as well.

Some people in her life have tried to comfort Changa by reminding her that our fates are never certain. But, she says, these platitudes are not a comfort. "The fact that uncertain things could happen to us does not really help when we have this idea or vision for our future laid out," she said. Instead, she began to grieve her diagnosis—not because her fate was decided but because her feeling of certainty that she'd reach old age was gone.

In the early months after her diagnosis, Changa struggled to articulate her grief "for what I had thought of my life." Previously, Changa had felt optimistic about her longevity. "I thought, I'm going to be an old woman like my grandma, and like my great-aunts, and all of them. I've seen myself as a white-haired old woman with grands and great-grands and still talking up and talking stuff as an older person. That's what I have seen for myself." While Changa is pursuing treatments that could allow her the opportunity to grow old as she had envisioned, she is also grappling with "the possibility of not making it to fifty."

Changa has also struggled with acknowledging and accepting her physical limitations. She understands that coming to terms with those limitations is part of "grieving the person who I thought I was on track to be." For Changa, practicing hope while also holding space for her grief means recognizing that "I can still very much shape my experience. But I have new limitations, in some ways, that I have to also factor in."

Yet her limitations have not prevented Changa from acting in pursuit of justice and transformation. Her passion for universal health care and voting rights has only intensified since her diagnosis, as she continues to write stories that she hopes will help fuel movements. While she does struggle with anxiety, Changa's practice of hope is a grounded one. "I've been defying odds my entire life," she told us. "I'm a single mother who went through three different academic degree programs, with children, and done a bunch of other things, too, that people say I shouldn't be able to do."

Others facing difficult diagnoses have pointed to this practice of working toward justice in hopeful ways, without dismissing fear and grief. Writer and organizer Audre Lorde battled cancer for fourteen years. She wrote in her book *The Cancer Journals*, "I realize that if I wait until I am no longer afraid to act, write, speak, be, I'll be sending messages on a ouija board, cryptic complaints from the other side. When I dare to be powerful, to use my strength in the service of my vision, then it becomes less important whether or not I am unafraid."[7]

Reflecting on the state of the climate while facing her own mortality, Changa refused to embrace notions of all-out terror and doom. "The doom, it's possible, but it's also possible that we can stave it off. So, I choose to walk into possibility. It's not a lack of realism; it's just choosing to work from a different framework."

Changa said she's learned to focus less on the potential scarcity of time. "The clock is definitely ticking," she told us, "but instead of worrying about how little time we have left, I'm thinking about what we can do with the time we have—or who we need to move to extend the time we have." As we work to use and extend our time on this planet, we should also avoid becoming mired in assessing our chances of success, Changa advised.

"In organizing, the odds are always stacked against you," Changa told us with a knowing smile. "That's always been the way. So you find a window. And if the window is small, you still aim for it. And you go."

Waging Acts of Care

On April 11, 2020, with Illinois schools shut down and a statewide shelter-in-place order in effect due to COVID-19, the residents of Chicago's Little Village neighborhood were faced with another disaster as the world outside their windows disappeared in a haze of toxic smoke. The plume of dust that consumed the neighborhood looked like something out of a war zone. Some residents were caught in it on their way to work, or to pick up groceries, or outside with their children as the toxic cloud overtook the community.

"This toxic dust infiltrated people's homes with no warning," organizer Juliana Pino told us. "Just imagine being in your home, and all of a sudden, every surface that you're coming into contact with is coated with a layer of powder that you don't recognize, and knowing that this dust cloud is coming from a coal plant that had been responsible for forty-one premature deaths a year, thousands of emergency room visits, hundreds of days of missed school and missed work. People who were caught outside were blasted by the dust."

The dust cloud was the result of a hastily approved implosion of a decommissioned coal stack, carried out by the company Hilco Redevelopment Partners. Local organizers had objected to the disastrous demolition plan, but with only a few hours' notice, they had little time to mount an intervention. Most residents had even less warning and were wholly caught off guard when the dust enveloped the neighborhood.

Fernando Cantú, a seventy-eight-year-old resident of Little Village, died shortly after the demolition. Like many residents of the largely Latinx neighborhood, Cantú had asthma, and residents believe the dust from the implosion may have aggravated his respiratory system. As for the long-term effects on residents' health, Pino told us, "that's a story that continues to unfold."

Pino is the policy director for the Little Village Environmental Justice Organization (LVEJO), a community-based frontline group based in Little Village that organizes for environmental justice and the self-determination of immigrant, low-income, and working-class families. During the 2000s, LVEJO and its co-strugglers waged a decade-long and ultimately victorious battle to close the environmentally hazardous Crawford Generating Station coal plant. In 2020, they were faced with reckless demolition efforts waged by Hilco— the new owners of the property on which the Crawford plant stood.

"Hilco thinks of itself as a cleaner-upper of businesses and facilities," Pino told us. "They came into the community, snatched up the coal plant, and said, 'We're going to put a warehousing distribution facility here.'" Community members had a different vision for the site: a cleaned-up and repurposed space that could be used for workforce training programs and an indoor market. But their vision had been rejected in favor of a plan that would generate even more pollution in the area.

Pino believes Hilco leveraged the chaos of the pandemic to gain speedy approval of their demolition plans. The city authorized Hilco's plan despite obvious indicators that the implosion could prove disastrous. "Little Village is a super-dense community," Pino told us. "The nonindustrial part of the neighborhood is more dense than Manhattan. So we have many families and a very small amount of space, where you have industrial facilities positioned right next to people's homes."

The impacts of environmental racism have long been part of daily life for Little Village residents. "Residents deal with toxic pollution every day, with people suffering from respiratory illnesses, not knowing if they are going to wind up in the emergency room or if their kids will develop asthma or if their water is safe coming out of the tap."

Pino explained, "Little Village is also one of the youngest neighborhoods in Chicago, so a huge proportion of folks in Little Village are under eighteen, and an even larger number are under twenty-five. So you have social and economic factors that add up to the neighborhood being really heavily policed. The Chicago Police Department, ICE in some cases, and the FBI are hanging around all the time, surveilling young people, harassing residents."

But in spite of the pollution and the heavy-handed policing residents experience, Pino told us, "the neighborhood really, I think, is a beautiful place. Folks have a lot of love for where they come from, and they stay there, and fight back, in spite of the oppressive conditions that are foisted upon them."

LVEJO was already in crisis mode prior to the implosion due to the neighborhood's vulnerability to the pandemic. By May of 2020, Little Village had more confirmed COVID cases than any other single zip code in the state.[8] Throughout the pandemic, the neighborhood has had some of the highest case rates and death rates in the city.[9] Little Village residents pleaded with the city government for a rapid expansion of COVID testing, but their requests were denied. They asked for additional resources to prepare for the pandemic's disproportionate impacts on the neighborhood but were dismissed.

"We knew that Black and brown communities that are heavily impacted by air pollution were going to be hit hard because they already experience high rates of respiratory illness," Pino said. "We knew that this was going to be really difficult for families who don't have access to safe water. There was already this kind of acute grief about what was happening outside of Little Village, and then things got worse in Little Village really quickly."

LVEJO kicked into high gear, making tough choices at every turn. "We made a decision as an organization to take our work out of the office," Pino told us. "So we weren't going into the office, but our organizing work still maintained in-person components, because it was really important to be in touch with the community. And I think for us, there was this additional layer of, how is this manifesting in our bodies? We needed to attend to ourselves, and our group, as a sort of small community, as well as the neighbors in the neighborhood."

Pino and other organizers were also concerned about community members being held in Cook County Jail, which is located in Little Village. On March 23, 2020, two people imprisoned in the facility, which is one of the nation's largest jails, tested positive for COVID-19. In a little over two weeks, the virus had spread through the jail, infecting more than 350 people. On April 23, 2020, the *New York Times* reported that Cook County Jail had become the "nation's largest-known source of coronavirus infections."[10]

"So many people [in Little Village] had family members who were incarcerated at the time," Pino told us. "People were fighting desperately to make sure that their family members survived, and some of them didn't due to the county's negligence and complete lack of care for people in the jail as community members."

Pino stressed that, in addition to the fact that nonincarcerated Little Village residents have family members in the jail, everyone inside Cook County Jail is part of the Little Village community. "It's an arbitrary wall that separates them physically from everyone else, but there's no difference in our mind," she said. "When people are being held in Cook County Jail, it doesn't matter if their residence is somewhere else—they're part of the Little Village community, and they're impacted by things that happen in the community. And the lack of regard for their lives impacts the rest of the community."

The pandemic threw the Chicago government's disregard for incarcerated people—and their place in the Little Village community—into sharp relief. The negligence exhibited toward those in the jail reverberated throughout the neighborhood.

"They didn't want to distribute masks or allow anyone else to distribute them," Pino said. So, for Little Village organizers, "it was a question of, how do we support people, person by person and family by family, to at least get people the information that they need, if we couldn't get people supplies that they needed."

In spring 2020, *Health Affairs* published a study that found that "jail-community cycling was a significant predictor of cases of [COVID-19], accounting for 55 percent of the variance in case rates across ZIP codes in Chicago and 37 percent of the variance in all of Illinois."[11] The study also found that jail-community cycling "far exceeds race, poverty, public transit use, and population density as a predictor of variance." The authors of the study suggested that the cycling of people through Cook County Jail was associated with 15.7 percent of all documented COVID-19 cases in Illinois and 15.9 percent of all documented cases in Chicago as of April 19, 2020. As of this writing, one in seven people in the 60623 zip code, which encompasses most of Little Village, has had a confirmed case of COVID-19, making it the hardest-hit zip code in Chicago.

Like the rest of the community, people confined in Cook County Jail were exposed to the damaging respiratory effects of the Hilco implosion along with COVID-19. "It's all connected," Pino told us, "because structural violence is cumulative and compounding."

Eleven days after the Hilco implosion, Chicagoans participated in a car caravan protest to demand accountability from the city and

Hilco for the demolition and to honor the memory of Fernando Cantú and other victims of environmental violence. The caravan was a sprawling demonstration with a line of cars that stretched out for three miles. "There's a legacy in environmental justice work of doing toxic tours, where you show people an overview of some of the facilities in a neighborhood," Pino explained:

> This was kind of a modified version of that because it wasn't just the toxic part of it. The caravan started in the industrial corridor, deep in the heart of Little Village where a lot of folks from outside the community had no idea that it was just facility after facility after facility. And they drove past those facilities and then immediately into a main commercial and residential area. And I think the contrast really hit people in the heart. I think that for a lot of people, they imagined that these things were nearby but didn't really understand—we're talking about schoolchildren and major sites of pollution being separated by a fence line.

The caravan moved through the Little Village and Pilsen neighborhoods and ultimately encircled city hall. The protest included livestreamed audio that offered a guided tour to drivers, explaining the history and continuum of environmental racism residents were struggling against, including those trapped in Cook County Jail. Impacted residents shared their stories, and participants were able to ask questions as they learned.

"We needed to help people understand it's not just that communities are facing one facility; it's hundreds," Pino said. "And it's not just that it's one community. Most Black and brown communities in Chicago are facing some kind of environmental racism problem that's unacknowledged, and people's lives are often decades shorter because of it, and because of all the violence that they face otherwise. Making this seen through the windows of the cars, and showing the city that people were angry, was important," she told us. "The decision makers had to know we were determined to make the unseen seen."

The car caravan protest was a coalition effort that brought together labor groups and frontline community organizations, like LVEJO and El Foro del Pueblo.

"It was extremely important for there to be a bearing of witness," Pino told us, "and the telling of the stories was an important intervention, for the sake of grief, for the sake of care, and to sustain a spirit of resistance." Pino said residents felt the need to memorialize the moment and their losses in order to push back against the oppression they were experiencing. Pino told us, "I think it was both hard and important that there was a specific person who was lost, whose life had meaning, and that there were so many other people who are struggling to get by, who were struggling to breathe and who were worried about their families and who were losing family members at the time, that in a way it was about Señor Cantú but it was also about the mass death occurring in the community."

Pino said the caravan allowed people in the community to combat the potential erasure of their suffering by the city and the press. "People needed to say, 'This is happening. We are feeling it. These are people who meant something to us. And even if the state wants to disappear our experiences, these lives had value, and we will fight in their honor, and for our own lives, and for change.'" Storytelling, paired with community care, were defining elements of LVEJO's response to the pandemic and the implosion.

The caravan was a powerful action that drew mass participation, but on the ground in Little Village, organizers were also feeling the grief and pressure of the moment. The exacerbation of existing structural violence, such as industrial pollution, police harassment, and the deprivation of resources, was taking its toll on the community. For some, the implosion felt like a catastrophic blow. "People felt the grief and felt it hard," Pino told us. She said that acknowledging feelings of despair, rather than simply trying to push past them, was important. "In so much of our work, the odds are super long," Pino explained, "and folks really were having moments of feeling, like, 'Wow, what are we going to do? Is there anything we can do?'"

For some community members, the implosion felt like the realization of a complete dystopia, and some organizers acknowledged that they could feel despair creeping in. But even as the culmination of COVID-19, carceral violence, and environmental racism bore down on them, Pino and her co-strugglers did not lose hope. "I think it's important that we recognize that our work happens in opposition to statistics," she said. "Our work happens in opposition to what is likely, or what others in power think will happen. I think remembering that allowed us to push back the hopelessness, and to find each other, as people committed to the work and community, in that sort of relational space, and that's where we found the energy to fight back." Pino told us that strained organizers "really went back down to basics": checking in on individuals, going door to door to make sure residents had access to water, providing transportation, and making sure people knew about COVID tests and where they could access them. Organizers acted as problem solvers in the community, asking people, "'Do you have everything you need to get to the end of the day? If not, let's figure out how to make that happen.'

"We sometimes think about our organizing work in terms of these big campaigns that we wage, but there are also these sort of micro-campaigns, where literal acts of care are what we are waging," said Pino. "We wage acts of care, and that's how we navigate loss and create hope. We say, 'We will wage this act of care in defiance of the state, which tells us that our bodies are worthless and expendable.'" Pino said that by waging acts of care, organizers in Little Village raged against the normalization of mass death and against the erasure of the inequities they experienced in the face of disaster. "That was the navigation," she told us. "It was in the waging. It was in the care we extended. It was in the rejection of disposability. It was in the constant check-ins. It was seeing each other's faces over video and looking into each other's eyes and saying, 'Are you OK? Do you have what you need?' It was like we were all just holding little candles in the night, trying to collectively see together, and see each other, and make sure we kept warm."

Pino told us,

I think the only way for us to navigate grief and loss in a meaningful way, at the time, was to be able to sort of weave those things together. Well-being was at the center, instead of the things that we are trying to achieve on a broad scale driving everything. Those things matter, of course, but how we're doing matters just as much. And I think that really hit home in a different way during the pandemic than it ever had before. How are we waging acts of care? What is our own practice of care? How are we making sure that the community is cared for?

In Little Village and elsewhere, the people most impacted by environmental racism are the very same families that are staring down police violence. They are the same people that are losing mental health clinics and schools. And all of these things cumulatively are killing us. And so weaving that narrative, at that moment, felt really important to folks. And it also felt like an opportunity to really attend to the community's broader set of needs in a new way. In a way that only the timing of the pandemic and this sort of intersection of issues, as they were presenting themselves, made possible. Collective survival was just underwritten into everything. And I think that the nature of those kinds of actions was different, necessarily, because of that.

There was also so much work done to make sure folks had access to medicine and food, basic survival. Folks really ramped up their efforts to feed each other in the days after the implosion and to make sure people were able to get to the store to get what they needed, to get their asthma inhalers. The volume on that kind of care turned up, not just because the need was greater, but because folks felt deeply recommitted to sustaining each other. And that was part of the resistance. It was the community's way of saying, "They're trying to kill us. We want us living. That's the battle. And so we're going to wage care and resistance on those terms, against these forces that would destroy us."

In the fall of 2020, Pino participated in the creation of *Let This Radicalize You: A COVID Memorial Mixtape* and was one of the organizers who prepared a speech that was included in the tape.

Pino's speech concluded with the words,

Together, we transform water dripping with poisonous particles.

Together, we clear the air, thick with pollution, COVID, and lies.

Together, we honor the soil ground down with waste of industry and the bones of ancestors.

Together, we remember the souls snatched away from our family, always too soon.

Together, we turn chains to dust, returning the minerals in steel and concrete to the plants.

Together, we rest in community without being disposed of in our own beds.

Together, we rise to deprive the monster of its simple story, and replace it with our own.

Ask a Palestinian

In his essay "The Walls of the Tank: On Palestinian Resistance," author Andreas Malm writes, "How do you keep on fighting when everything is lost? Ask a Palestinian." According to Malm, "A Palestinian is someone who is wading knee-deep in rubble. Palestinian politics is always already post-apocalyptic: it is about surviving after the end of the world and, in the best case, salvaging something out of all that has been lost."[12]

Palestinian organizer Lea Kayali is well acquainted with the work of salvaging something out of all that has been lost. Her great-grandparents, grandmother, and other relatives fled during the Nakba, a period of massacres and violent displacement in Palestine that occurred during 1947 and 1948 as British troops destroyed hundreds of Palestinian villages in order to make way for the creation of the Israeli state. "My family fled by boats and by foot and bus from Jaffa, Palestine, under fire to Gaza, and it was horrific," Kayali told Kelly on *Movement Memos* in May 2021.[13]

Thousands of Palestinians were killed during the Nakba, and hundreds of thousands were displaced. In the decades since the Nakba, Palestinians in Gaza have lived in what some describe as an open-air prison, with Israel exercising violent and often arbitrary control over people's movements, confiscating land, destroying homes, criminalizing cultural expression, and murdering and disappearing Palestinians with impunity. Israel has also engaged in periodic military assaults on Gaza, in bombing campaigns Israeli leaders cynically characterize as "mowing the grass." During these bombing campaigns, it is not unusual for Palestinian families to send one of their own children to another home while welcoming someone else's child into their own, in the hopes that a single bomb will not destroy an entire family.

In June 2021, Palestinian organizer Linda Ereikat wrote,

> Being Palestinian arguably does not allow for the body to return to homeostasis due to the consistent trauma of loss. It's as if we are in constant and continuous mourning.[14]

Ereikat described the climate of grief in her parents' home in California in May 2021, as Israeli bombs once again rained down on Gaza: "My mother doesn't allow music to be played in our house and declines invitations to gatherings during these times. My father suddenly stops speaking and the news is on, full volume, for more than eighteen hours a day."[15]

Yet, that same month, as Israeli bombardments of Gaza continued, Palestinians engaged in a historic general strike. Amid the bombings and protests, a message written by anonymous Palestinian organizers was circulating in Palestine, spreading fast on social media and beyond. "The Dignity and Hope Manifesto," addressed to the people of Palestine, states, "Here we are, writing a new chapter of courage and pride, in which we tell a story of justice and of the truth that no level of Israeli colonial repression can erase, however cruel and brutal that repression may be."[16]

"The Dignity and Hope Manifesto" describes how Palestinians have been separated by forced migration, bureaucracy, acts of violence, militarized isolation, and forced dispersal across the globe. The document states, "In these days, we write a new chapter, a chapter of a united Intifada that seeks our one and only goal: reuniting Palestinian society in all of its different parts; reuniting our political will, and our means of struggle to confront Zionism throughout Palestine."[17] The statement calls this struggle "an Intifada of consciousness" and "an Intifada to overthrow off the filth of quietude and defeatism." The manifesto calls on all Palestinians to unite around their right to return home.[18] Notably, the vision the manifesto invokes is global, stating that "this Intifada will be a long one in the streets of Palestine and in streets around the world; an intifada that fights the hand of injustice wherever it tries to reach, that fights the batons of cruel regimes wherever they try to strike."[19]

Like the protests against police violence that sprung up in the US in 2020, the 2021 Palestinian protests did not yield an immediate transformation, but "The Dignity and Hope Manifesto" conjured a powerful vision of global Palestinian solidarity that organizers have not abandoned. As Kayali told us in a conversation in August of 2022, "An all-out rejection of fragmentation gives strength and credence to our ability to hold the line and not cede to violence that's happened over the last seventy-five years."

While Kayali believes that resistance should "materially challenge the conditions of our oppression," she also believes that Palestinian traditions "that have been stolen from us over the last seventy-five years" can be sources of politicization, renewal, and hope. "I recently joined a *dabke* troupe," she told us, referring to a type of folk dance with origins in Palestine, Jordan, Syria, and Lebanon. "That maybe saved my life, being able to dance with my people and learn those dances and practice that weekly has just been amazing." Kayali convinced the troupe that they should also form a reading group. She sees great potential in pairing "our inherent desire to reconnect with our culture and our traditions" with political education and strategic efforts to advance a larger political project. She also finds solace in her family's traditional recipes and in reconnecting with her language, but she acknowledges, "I wish we could live our messy lives without needing to cling to these pillars of joy as resilience, instead of just as joy."

Kayali also finds mutual aid efforts in Gaza inspiring, as people in the diaspora collaborate with their co-strugglers in Palestine to address unmet needs on the ground. In June of 2022, Kayali co-organized a local fundraiser in Boston that raised $7,000 to send to mutual aid organizers in Gaza. The event included a *dabke* performance.

At the close of her reflection on Palestinian grief, Ereikat reminded readers of a video of two Palestinian children who searched through the rubble of their home in Gaza, which was destroyed in a bombing in May of 2021. The children smiled triumphantly as they held up a jar containing their pet fish. "We saved it from the house," the boy declared. "We saved it," the girl repeated, before adding, "And we want to go back for the birds."[20]

Ereikat wrote, "I hope they save the birds too. For we are all birds who aspire to one day fly back to Palestine, our wings able to fly with more freedom and in less grief."[21]

The Practice of Hope

When someone we love faces a difficult diagnosis or our community is hit by disaster, we come to more deeply understand the value of time and care. If we discover that we may have less time with someone than we had hoped, time does not become pointless or less meaningful; it becomes more precious. When our communities experience disaster, we understand that care and rescue efforts are essential, even if some loss is inevitable. In those moments, we know that care matters and that trying matters, come what may. It may be difficult for some people to imagine extending such sentiments to the larger world we live in, and to all of our relations, but it is possible.

Sometimes we expect the energy and feelings that we need in order to build movements amid crisis to flow naturally, as though they are embedded in our personalities. That is the influence of individualism. Just as patience is a practice, rather than a feeling, hope and grief are not simply things we feel but things we enact in the world.

When we enact grief with intention, and in concert with other people, we can find and create moments of relief, comfort, and even joy—and those moments can sustain us. As Malkia Devich-Cyril writes, "Becoming aware of grief gives us more choices about how to respond to grief and opens up possibilities to approach grief not only with compassion for self and others, but also with joy. Joy is not the opposite of grief. Grief is the opposite of indifference."[22]

Hope, too, requires us to reject indifference. And like any indifference-rejecting phenomenon, it demands effort in order to thrive. When we talk about hope in these times, we are not prescribing optimism. Rather, we are talking about a practice and a discipline—what Joanna Macy and Chris Johnstone have termed "Active Hope." As Macy and Johnstone write,

> Active Hope is a practice. Like tai chi or gardening, it is something we do rather than have. It is a process we can apply to any situation, and it involves three key steps. First, we take a clear view of reality; second, we identify what we hope for in terms of the direction we'd like things to move in or the values we'd like to see expressed; and third, we take steps to move ourselves or our situation in that direction. Since Active Hope doesn't require our optimism, we can apply it even in areas where we feel hopeless. The guiding impetus is intention; we choose what we aim to bring about, act for, or express. Rather than weighing our chances, and proceeding only when we feel hopeful, we focus on our intention and let it be our guide.[23]

This practice of hope allows us to remain creative and strategic. It does not require us to deny the severity of our situation or detract from our practice of grief. To practice active hope, we do not need to believe that everything will work out in the end. We need only decide who we are choosing to be and how we are choosing to function in relation to the outcome we desire and abide by what those decisions demand of us.

This practice of hope does not guarantee any victories against long odds, but it does make those victories more possible. Hope, therefore, is not only a source of comfort to the afflicted but also a strategic imperative.

Practice Spaces

It follows that if we believe having a practice of hope and a practice of grief are important for organizers and movement work, we should be creating spaces and opportunities for this work to occur. As we move forward, we must ask ourselves, Are we making space for grief in our organizing work? Are we talking about the practice of hope, and how we can orient ourselves in these daunting times?

What would making room for grief in your spaces look like? Some groups with a physical space might have "altar hours," when members can visit the group's altar to grieve for COVID victims or victims of any struggle. These could also be art-making hours, with craft supplies available for people to add decorative commemorations. Making art and preserving stories are essential, particularly in this era of overnight erasure, when atrocities are washed away in a single news cycle. Grief spaces can provide opportunities for people to create and to hold space together and talk, or they can simply allow people to experience grief in a place where their love, their loss, and their continued existence are held sacred.

In Octavia Butler's novel *The Parable of the Sower*, characters who had previously been deprived of the opportunity to memorialize lost loved ones buried acorns together, to lay their memories to rest and create new life in their honor. Similarly, in our times, memorial gardens for victims of COVID-19, or whatever loss a community is enduring, can create a therapeutic space while also providing a resource for the community. In Chicago, the radical Black youth-directed organization Assata's Daughters dedicated its group's garden to Takiya Holmes, an eleven-year-old member who was killed by a stray bullet in February 2017. In July 2022, the Chicago-based groups Love & Protect and Prison + Neighborhood Arts Project invited community members to contribute to the creation of a "seed quilt"—a biodegradable quilt that will disintegrate into the ground as the seeds embedded within it take root. Even as participants stitched together squares to create this symbol of hope, they memorialized formerly incarcerated loved ones who were recently lost. The quilt will be installed outside Logan Correctional Center, in Logan County, Illinois, as a symbol of the work of prison abolition, which requires us to counter death-making institutions with life-giving efforts.

Memorials can also be biting or disruptive, and that, too, can be a source of healing for participants. As politicians and corporations push us to accept a society that does not grieve mass death, our grief and stories of the dead can function as resistance. Dirges should drown out their speeches. Pop-up memorials should force them to reconfigure their events. From guerilla art to direct actions, such as die-ins, where people use their own bodies to memorialize the dead, our practices of grief should overwhelm normalcy's narratives and imagery. A multilayered community memorial, for example, could draw connections between the forces causing so much death while disrupting a violent cycle of forgetting. Hundreds of memorial messages could be wheat-pasted throughout a city overnight. People could spontaneously disrupt events that erase or perpetuate deaths with poems, prayers, or songs. Acts of rebellious grief can take many shapes, but all are a rejection of mass death and an insistence on the humanity of those who have passed.

We must also create practice space for hope. As we've discussed, our movements cannot be echo chambers of doom. When the news cycle is depleting us or members are worn down by loss or defeat, we should acknowledge this and engage in conversations, activities, and exercises that can help us reorient ourselves. Cynicism is a creeping enemy. We must actively evade it. From group dialogues to artistic exercises and direct actions, we must create space for renewal and recommitment.

Sometimes the practice of hope takes the form of mutual aid. In her essay "Dust of the Desert," Lee Sandusky writes of grief, struggle, and mutual aid in the Sonoran Desert, where thousands of migrants have died while attempting to cross the US-Mexico border. Sandusky notes that the dead go uncounted, unidentified, and at least half the time, ungathered. Sandusky organizes with No More Deaths, a group that provides mutual aid to border crossers, many of whom are in distress. She and her co-strugglers also go on search missions for people lost in the desert and leave jugs of water for thirsty migrants to find. "The desert landscape is littered with thousands of black jugs carried from the south and clear gallons graffitied with well wishes brought from the north," writes Sandusky.[24]

Some of the jugs are slashed open by US Border Patrol agents. Some are found by people in need. By leaving jugs of water, mutual aid workers in the borderlands hold hope and grief simultaneously. Some of the jugs they scatter will alleviate suffering or even save lives, while others will become "plastic memorial stones for those who don't make it." But as Sandusky writes, "Border work is predicated on ending the deaths of those crossing—currently an insurmountable task—and much of the action we take is in response to grief, but also anger and hope; the three are inseparable motivations that sustain organizing and action within our community."[25]

How does your community practice hope and grief in collectivity? Are such efforts planned intentionally? Has your group created any space, physical or otherwise, for people to process their hope or grief about the pandemic?

One exercise that might allow for the practice of hope and grief simultaneously might be the creation of a memorial time capsule. Members of your group could write messages, detailing what they think activists one hundred years from now should understand about the moment we are living in, and what losses were being erased. This activity might not sound subversive or hopeful, but as it assumes the existence of activists a hundred years from now, there is hope embedded in the activity's basic premise. Even as we fear environmental catastrophe, we can prepare messages for the activists of the future—asserting their existence in order to help make it so.

This is also a time to cherish poetry, which has always played an important role in fueling hope and making space for grief in movements. Poetry, like prayer, can provide a sense of communion—a joint hope, plea, or promise projected onto the world. Our movements are rich in poems, and we should embrace their anchoring power, incorporating poetry into actions, meetings, and events, dedicated with the specificity that groups see fit. The system we are raging against erodes our compassion and confines our imaginations. In the face of such violence, poetry is a fitting weapon. We should wield it often.

Some will consider these actions insufficiently political. It's true that memorializations alone can sometimes be politically timid. But actions that help us remain whole, that prevent us from going numb, and that bring us into political communion with other people will be necessary to build a counterculture of care in this precarious era. You choose what you bring to a vigil that you plan. Created thoughtfully, vigils can introduce radical ideas, initiate relationships, foster solidarity, and build power while also fulfilling a fundamental, unmet need.

Regardless of how we choose to grieve or cultivate hope, we know that we are living in disastrous times and that we will need one another. We are wading through hell and high water, tasked with dreaming new worlds into being while the worlds we have known fall down around us. Here, on the edge of everything, the work of cultivating hope and purpose, of anchoring people to one another, is as important now as it has ever been, at any time in human history, because without those efforts, we would be lost in the dark. As James Baldwin emphasized at the close of his book *Nothing Personal*, "The moment we cease to hold each other, the moment we break faith with one another, the sea engulfs us and the light goes out."[26]

CHAPTER 9

Organizing Isn't Matchmaking

Organizing is not a process of ideological matchmaking. Most people's politics will not mirror our own, and even people who identify with us strongly on some points will often differ sharply on others. When organizers do not fully understand each other's beliefs or identities, people will often stumble and offend one another, even if they earnestly wish to build from a place of solidarity. Efforts to build diverse, intergenerational movements will always generate conflict and discomfort. But the desire to shrink groups down to spaces of easy agreement is not conducive to movement building.

The forces that oppress us may compete and make war with one another, but when it comes to maintaining the order of capitalism, and the hierarchy of white supremacy, they collaborate and work together based on their death-making and eliminationist shared interests. Oppressed people, on the other hand, often demand ideological alignment or even affinity when seeking to interrupt or upend structural violence. This tendency lends an advantage to the powerful that is not easily overcome.

Put simply, we need more people. What do we mean by this? We are not talking about launching search parties to find an undiscovered army of people with already-perfected politics with whom we will easily and naturally align. Instead, organizing on the scale that our struggles demand means finding common ground with a broad spectrum of people, many of whom we would never otherwise interact with, and building a shared practice of politics in the pursuit of more just outcomes. It's a process that can bring us into the company of people who share our beliefs quite explicitly, but to create movements, rather than clubhouses, we need to engage with people with whom we do not fully identify and may even dislike. We can build upon our expectations of such people and negotiate protocols around matters of respect, but the truth is, we will sometimes be uncomfortable or even offended. We will, at times, have to constructively critique people's behavior or simply allow them room to grow. There will be other times, of course, when we have to draw hard lines, but if we cannot organize beyond the bounds of our comfort zones, we will never build movements large enough to combat the forces that would destroy us.

Some groups have learned to navigate difference and animus out of necessity. Incarcerated people organizing within prisons, for example, often learn to put feuds, rivalries, and personal differences aside because they recognize the necessity of building with who is there.

As Kelly and organizer Ejeris Dixon wrote in *Truthout* in June 2020, when discussing solidarity in the face of right-wing violence and the rise of fascism,

> Not everyone we work with on a particular issue has to have deep ideological alignment with us. A skilled organizer should be able to work with people who aren't of their own choosing, including people they don't like. It's really as simple as being attacked by fascist police in the streets. Once the attack begins, there are two sides: armed police inflicting violence and everyone else. We need to be able to see each other in those terms, reeling in the face of unthinkable violence, scrambling to stay alive and uncaged, and doing the work to protect one another. . . .
>
> This [alignment] will not come easily, because white supremacy and classism have forced many wedges between our communities. Great harms have been committed and very difficult conversations are needed, but refusing to do that work,

in this historical moment, is an abdication of responsibility. It is no exaggeration to say that the whole world is at stake, and we cannot afford to minimize what that demands of us.[1]

This is not to say that we should seek no respite from the messiness and occasional discomfort of large-scale movement work. We all need spaces where we can operate within our comfort zone. Whether these take the shape of a collective, an affinity group, a processing space, a caucus, or a group of friends, we need people with whom we can feel fully seen and heard and with whose values we feel deeply aligned. In such a violent and oppressive world, we are all entitled to some amount of sanctuary. Many organizers have tight-knit political homes, sometimes grounded in shared identity, in addition to participating in broader organizing efforts.

But broader movements are struggles, not sanctuaries. They are full of contradiction and challenges we may feel unprepared for.

Effective organizers operate beyond the bounds of their comfort zones, moving into what we might call their "stretch zone," when necessary. No one has to be able to work with everyone, but how far beyond the bounds of easy agreement can you reach? How much empathy can you extend to people who do not fully understand your identity or experience or who have not had the same access to liberatory ideas? How much discomfort can you navigate for what you believe is truly at stake?

These are not questions anyone can answer for you, as we must all make autonomous choices about who we connect and build with, but if we do not challenge ourselves to navigate some amount of discomfort, our political reach will have terminal limits.

Navigating Trauma and Discomfort

"Like a lot of activists, I started out organizing out of trauma," Aly Wane told us in spring 2021. Wane is an undocumented human rights activist, originally from Senegal. "When I went into the work, I went into the work as a traumatized activist, and to a certain degree

I feel like I'm still traumatized by the system. I just feel like I know where to express that trauma better, I think now." Navigating his own traumas and trauma responses in organizing spaces became a challenge for Wane.

Many activists enter the work having already experienced significant trauma, sometimes due to the very forces against which they are organizing. Those who are not directly traumatized by systemic violence often enter from a place of outrage. The trauma and outrage that drive people into organizing spaces are real, but sometimes our valid feelings can manifest themselves in ways that ultimately hinder our work, as Wane experienced. "I went into organizing from a very self-focused, arrogant place to a certain degree," he told us. "If someone came into an organizing space and didn't know as much as I did, or would say offensive things about 'illegals' or 'criminals,' I would immediately go into fight or flight, saying, 'Well, you said this,' or 'You called me that,' and 'How dare you,' and blah, blah, blah."

Wane's anger about the use of dehumanizing language was valid. Throughout his life, he had heard words like "illegals" and "criminals" deployed to justify violence against undocumented people. But venting his outrage in meeting spaces came at a cost. "It felt good, but then next meeting, it would just be me and my four acolytes." Wane says his organizing approach in those days was "more of a crusade." After years of being silenced and degraded, Wane told us, "it was about proving that I was right."

Most oppressed people spend their entire lives being told that their experience of oppression is natural, correct, or their own fault. Entering spaces where our struggles are recognized can be incredibly empowering. It can also bring to the surface many emotions that society has never given us the space to process or express. "Every organizer knows that person who is an activist who just talks and talks and talks and talks in a meeting, and you can tell that they're emotionally downloading, and it's really not organizing," Wane said.

In his case, entering therapy helped him make more intentional choices about how and when to "emotionally download." While continuing to navigate his own trauma, Wane came to accept that in organizing, he was going to encounter ideas and language that might offend him. "I can't be reactive," he told us. "I can't immediately go into, 'Well, here's why I'm right.' I really need to think about where that person is coming from."

It is understandable that people who have experienced oppression and dehumanization their entire lives want to live and work in environments where they do not experience the dynamics that have made their lives more difficult. In moments when we feel especially empowered and realize that people can and in some cases do treat us with the understanding, empathy, and respect that we deserve, it is understandable that we would want to insist that all interactions be held to such a standard. After all, if some people *can* treat us in ways that make us feel good and whole, why shouldn't all people in movement spaces automatically do so?

But political transformation is not as simple as handing newcomers a new set of politics and telling them, "Yours are bad, use these instead." Instead, we will sometimes have to accompany people along messy transformational journeys. And we must also remember that no matter how far we have come, we are still on our own messy journeys, and our own transformations will continue as we grow.

To expand the practice of our politics in the world, we have to be able to organize outside of our comfort zones. People whose words and ideas don't yet align with our own often need room to grow, and some people grow by building relationships and doing work—often in fumbling and imperfect ways.

How do we as organizers cope with the frustration and discomfort that inevitably accompany organizing alongside people with whom we don't perfectly align? For Wane, resisting reactive responses was key. "I found that by not reacting, and [by] drawing out that person's story, I became a much more effective organizer, because people who I thought I would never have been able to be in conversation with were at least receptive to what I was saying in ways that they weren't before."

Wane recalled one occasion when he and his team set up an outreach table at an upstate New York farmers' market, predominantly filled with conservative white people. Wane and his co-organizers set up a table of fruits and vegetables and distributed literature about the issues undocumented farmworkers face. He and his co-organizers knew that many of the white people at the farmers' market would not be sympathetic to their cause, but they viewed their efforts at dialogue as a challenge: an opportunity to sharpen their organizing skills by engaging a difficult audience.

"We had so many good conversations with folks you would assume would be sort of anti-immigrant," Wane told us. Upon reading the literature, white people visiting the table would sometimes get defensive or make offensive comments about "illegals," but instead of arguing, Wane's team would ask questions. "We started asking, 'How do you make your money?' And asking how hard or easy it was for them to make their money in this economy." Encouraging people to talk about their own families' hardships opened up a space for exchange, and Wane found that people became more open to hearing about the struggles of undocumented families.

"We started having these conversations about this basic family struggle and how hard it is to make ends meet, and we were able to get so many folks who I would have probably considered conservative to sign petitions and to start to see the issue from a different perspective," Wane said. "And that's all because we set up this space to have this conversation."

Wane's handling of the situation was the product of growth and the concerted development of organizing skills. He knew from experience that even among people with shared values and objectives, it is easy to be derailed by difference or defensiveness. This practice effort, of engaging with people who Wane thought were likely to be hostile, allowed him to flex and test his communication skills. While the exercise was more focused on honing the craft of organizers than actually attaining signatures for petitions, some of the people Wane engaged with did sign the group's petition, which he considered a huge organizing victory.

When he was young in his organizing, Wane would not have had the patience to listen to some of what he heard that day. "I would not have had the capacity," he told us, to tolerate the deployment of stereotypes about undocumented people or the use of words like "illegals." But that day, Wane was not quick to react. "I just kept listening," he said.

Wane noted that having space in therapy and intentional space with friends to talk about such moments made his practice of patience possible. He knew he would not have to hold in his feelings indefinitely, but rather, he was waiting to share them with people who cared about him, with whom he could meaningfully discuss those events. Wane creates space in his life for navigating hurt and trauma, but he says that in organizing spaces, "What I'm trying to achieve is to get as many folks as possible at the table having conversations about the immigration system and how to change it."

Wane has also come to realize that the system deals out bias very effectively and that he himself probably wouldn't understand the realities of his oppression if not for his firsthand experience. "I know 100 percent that if I weren't an immigrant or if I didn't know someone who was an immigrant, I would have absolutely no idea how this system works or how complicated it is," Wane told us. "And I might have the same stereotypes that many of the folks who I would consider on the other side would have, because it's an opaque system just like the criminal justice system. These systems are intentionally opaque in order to sort of preserve the mythos around them."

Learning to Listen

To do the kind of work that Wane has described, a person has to hone multiple skills, including the ability to listen. When people delve into activism, they often grapple with questions like, "Am I willing to get arrested," when often the more pressing question for a new activist is, "Am I willing to listen, even when it's hard?"

For organizer and scholar Ruth Wilson Gilmore, it was her time in Alcoholics Anonymous that helped her transform her practice of listening. "The main thing that I learned," Gilmore told us, "especially in the first couple years that I was going to meetings, was the beauty of the rule against cross talk. It was the best thing that ever happened to me, that I couldn't say shit to anybody. I had to listen, and I had to learn to listen." The urge to interject or object ran deep for Gilmore. "I've always been a nerd, yet I've always been a know-it-all," she told us, "so there's this tension between my nerdiness that wants to know everything and my know-it-all-ness that wants everybody to know that I know it all already."

At first, listening did not come easily—or feel particularly productive—to Gilmore. "I would sit in these meetings, and I listened to people talk, and listen to them, and listen to them, and at first I was like, 'I don't get this, I don't get this.' And so for me in the early days, it was just a performance of words. I mean, my main thing was, 'I won't drink when I leave this meeting. I won't drink, and I won't use.'"

But over time, Gilmore began to appreciate the role of listening in the group's collective struggle to avoid drugs and alcohol—even when she did not appreciate what was being said. "I would be getting more and more wound up, because there'd be the sexist guy going on about women and his wife, and then there'd be somebody else talking nonsense about whatever, [but I was] learning to just sit there, and listen, and keep my eye on the prize, which was not just that I wasn't going to drink but that the only way I could not drink was if all of us didn't drink."

Being committed to the sobriety of every person in the room, which meant listening to their story and being invested in their well-being, helped Gilmore develop a deeper practice of patience. "That was kind of this transformation for me that carried into the organizing that I already used to do before I got sober," she told us.

It is our ability to constructively engage with other people that will ultimately power our efforts. We have to nurture that ability and respect its importance in all of the ways that our society does not. And that skill of constructive engagement starts with listening.

Radical educator and philosopher Paulo Freire wrote, "The more radical the person is, the more fully he or she enters into reality so that, knowing it better, he or she can better transform it. This individual is not afraid to confront, to listen, to see the world unveiled."[2]

This may sound like an attitude, and in part it is, but it's also a skill set. The impulse to interrupt, correct, or pull the conversation in another direction can be strong. The temptation to exert power over, rather than power with, by attempting to deposit our solution or perspective in a person's mind is ingrained by this system. In teacher-student relations, Freire called such efforts to deposit ideas the "banking concept of education."[3] He argued that instead of trying to deposit ideas into people, as though human beings were receptacles, knowledge must flow from a relational, nonhierarchical, and mutually creative process.

Freire argued for a form of political education he characterized as "problem-posing" education. While banking education "anesthetizes and inhibits creative power," Freire argued that problem-posing education "involves a constant unveiling of reality." The ability to examine and contemplate challenges in concert with people, rather than acting as an instructor, makes collective growth possible.[4]

Many people describe themselves as good listeners. In reality, most people are not. This disparity between perception and practice can be explained by the fact that most people think of being a good listener as a personality trait—like being friendly or upbeat. But while being a good listener may come more easily to some people than others, it is not, in fact, a mere personality trait. Like so many other aspects of organizing, listening is a practice, and at times, it's a strategic one.

This society has not conditioned us to be attentive listeners. When people say things that make us uneasy or impatient, instead of listening we often home in on what we want to say next or drift into contemplation of how the matter relates to our own plans or experiences. To stay in the moment with another person, to truly hear and consider what they are saying without slipping into reaction or retreating inward, can require intention. If we are bored, uncomfortable, or irritated, we may be inclined to either interrupt or escape. This tendency hinders us in a number of ways.

First and foremost, we might need to hear something true that makes us uncomfortable. Listening deeply makes space for that to happen. But even if the person who's talking is off base, we can often still learn by listening to them. Why do they feel the way they do? What sources informed or convinced them? What influences them? What strengthens their resolve? What makes them hesitant to get more involved or to engage more boldly? If you are in an organizing space together, how has that issue brought them into a shared space with you despite your differences? What points of agreement might you build upon? What is surprising about them? A good organizer wants to understand these things about the people around them, and you cannot truly understand these things about a person without listening.

Organizers will often repeat the maxim, "We have to meet people where they are at." It is difficult to meet someone where they're at when you do not know where they are. Until you have heard someone out, you do not know where they are, so how could you hope to meet them there? Relationships are not built through presumption or through the deployment of tropes or stereotypes. We must understand people as having their own unique experiences, traumas, struggles, ideas, and motivations that will inform how they show up to organizing spaces.

Some task-focused activists brush off activities that involve "talking about our feelings." This is a common sentiment among bad listeners. The fundamental skill of patiently absorbing another person's words in a respectful and thoughtful manner is desperately lacking in our society. For this reason, it is folly to expect this skill to manifest itself fully formed when it is most needed, such as in a heated meeting, if we are not building a greater culture of listening in our work.

A group culture that helps participants build their listening skills is an important component of successful organizing. Political education can create opportunities for people to practice listening to one another, without interruption, and interacting meaningfully with what others have contributed. For example, during the Great Depression, communist union organizers in Bessemer, Alabama, developed a practice of devoting thirty minutes of each meeting to political education. For thirty minutes, material would be read aloud—creating space to collectively listen while also allowing members who could not read the opportunity to hear the information. Members would then spend fifteen minutes discussing the material, listening to each other's thoughts in response to the work.

Poetry circles are another activity that can deepen a group's ability to listen, reflect, and grapple with ideas together. In 2010, Project NIA released a curriculum Mariame developed called *"Giving Name to the Nameless": Using Poetry as an Anti-Violence Intervention with Girls.* As the curriculum's introduction explains, "The use of literature and guided reading has been recognized as a viable option for helping young people address their concerns. Poetry is a particularly wonderful way to address sensitive issues (like sexuality, violence, and self-esteem). When young people (or adults for that matter) see something of themselves in a piece of literature (books, poetry), identify with the work, reflect on it, and undergo some emotional growth as a result of that reading experience, this can be considered a successful anti-violence intervention."[5] Importantly, this curriculum was the result of years of sitting in circles held by the Rogers Park Young Women's Action Team, a youth-led, adult-supported social-change project that empowers young women to take action on issues affecting their lives. Young people of color sat and read together and listened to how the texts related to personal and communal experiences. As part of the action team's circles, everyone had their turn to read, to speak, and to listen. The act of listening to one another, as participants read aloud and then share their thoughts and perspectives on the poems, is good practice in a society where people are often distracted or focused on what they might say next. Listening to someone talk about a poem and how it impacted them is an empathetic exercise—and it can also help us to practice patience by taking the time to consider someone else's point of view rather than rushing off to the next distraction.

In organizing, we sometimes expect people, including ourselves, to shed the habits this society has embedded in us through sheer force of will, when in reality we all need practice. Activities that help us hone our practice of listening can make us better organizers, improve our personal relationships, and help us build stronger and longer-lasting movements.

Rejecting Zero-Tolerance Attitudes toward Language

As we work to build more sustainable movements, we must think hard about our strategies for responding when organizers make mistakes. Social media can often foster a "zero-tolerance" attitude about political ignorance or missteps. Platforms like Twitter have helped facilitate tremendous accomplishments in movement work, but they have also created an arena for political performance and critique that is often divorced from relationship building or strategic aims. For many people, social media is not an organizing tool but a realm of political performance and spectatorship. A trend has emerged in which some organizers will demand performances of solidarity and awareness on social media but then critique or even tear apart those performances when they fall short or are deemed insincere. As with reality television, favorites emerge, and people are sometimes voted off the island.

When the performance of solidarity via the replication of the right words or slogans becomes our central focus, it's not surprising that responses might read as empty or even insincere. Sloganizing is not organizing, and paying righteous lip service to a cause, in the preferred language of the moment, does not empty any cages or transform anyone's material conditions. Rather than fixating on the grammar of people's politics, we organizers must ask ourselves what we want people to do.

When debates arise around language, we must also understand the extent to which the language of dissent and liberation has shifted over time. The terms and jargon we use today do not represent an "arrival" at the "correct" words that were always out there, waiting to be found, while our predecessors flailed about in search of them. The language we uplift in movements today represents an unending process of grappling—a search for words that embody the experiences of oppressed people in relation to their history, their current conditions, and the culture they are presently experiencing. Policing language, as though our phrasing is written in law, misunderstands that pursuit and the purpose it serves. If these words merely exist to divide us into categories—those who can properly discuss ideas and those who cannot—what is their value in the pursuit of liberation?

While it is important to trouble terminology and to engage with its evolution, the mastery of language does not spur systemic change or alter anyone's material conditions. The concept of "allyship," for example, is often grounded in presentation rather than substantive action. Similarly, people who believe they are "good people" often view goodness as a fixed identity, evidenced by their expressed feelings about injustice rather than a set of practices or actions. Goodness, to them, is a designation to be defended rather than something that they seek to generate in the world in concert with other people. Mainstream liberals often fall prey to this line of thinking because liberal politics play very heavily into political identity as being determinant of whether a person is good or bad (Democrats are good, Republicans bad). But the left can fall into its own version of this trap by treating politics as a test of how well we can perform language or recite ideas.

Our movements are not driven by getting the words just right. They are driven by the goal of enacting change through collective struggle as we endeavor to both understand ideas and turn them into action. Fumbling is inevitable, but, as Gilmore tells us, "practice makes different."

Longtime organizer and Vision Change Win founder Ejeris Dixon emphasizes that people will show up imperfectly and that organizers have to anticipate that mistakes and harm will happen. "I worry we're creating a culture now where people are so afraid to make mistakes," she told us. "They're afraid to not have the analysis before they open their mouth. The bonds that I'm really trying to build within organizing are the bonds where we can divulge the things that we are nervous about, or ashamed of, or the things we need to learn, all of those areas, because that's when I know we're building the kind of intimacy that takes care of each other around heightened threats."

Dixon points out that when trust is lost, organizing not only becomes more difficult, but it also becomes more vulnerable to surveillance and infiltration: "A huge piece of COINTELPRO was around seeding distrust." Therefore, she says, a key part of organizing is building bonds of trust, and that can only happen within a context where people are allowed to be vulnerable and make mistakes.

Learning and growing in front of other people can be embarrassing and even intimidating, particularly for people who have been put down or made to feel diminished in the past. Even seasoned organizers like Dixon often worry about derailing their work with a verbal misstep. "I have a small crew of other organizers where I think our text thread is mostly questions we are afraid to ask publicly," she acknowledged. "It's our own little political education circle, where we ask, 'What does this mean?' Or, 'Is this fucked up?' Or, 'What is the right way to say this? Because I don't think this is right.'" Dixon says that she believes "everyone needs that text thread," but she also hopes that more of our movement spaces can operate in the same spirit and offer opportunities for people to "feel safe in their process of transforming." Creating trust-based movement spaces also puts us in a better place to confront harm and conflict, Dixon says.

"The biggest part of the work is how we maintain relationships while navigating harm," she told us. "Because that's the thing, that will break your group. That'll break any project." Dixon stresses the importance of conflict resolution and accountability mechanisms within groups—that is, group- or community-based methods of confronting harm, such as peace circles and transformative justice. But she also reminds us that in order for accountability mechanisms to serve their purpose, people need room and opportunities to grow. "People need to build skills and mechanisms to navigate conflict. Sometimes we're not apologizing. Sometimes we're not accountable. Sometimes we have done harmful things. Sometimes we're doing things we were never told go against the norms [of the group] and then are being held accountable." Dixon offered the example of a young person in one group who made a comment about how a supply closet looked like it had been attacked but used an inappropriate, triggering term to describe what had apparently happened to the closet. "Next thing you know, she is in an accountability session. She is bewildered. She is in a straight-up shame spiral. And I was like, 'Shit, it was just a lack of political education.'"

In an organizing space, accountability should not be about policing or punishment, but our punitive impulses can sometimes twist accountability mechanisms into those shapes. It's easy to forget how imperfectly we have shown up in movement spaces and throughout our lives. Sometimes our aggravation with others is rooted in pain or trauma we have experienced; sometimes it is rooted in our uneasiness about things we may have said or done that were equally upsetting because we did not always know what we know now. And regardless of how much we believe we have learned, as the saying goes, we don't know what we don't know. Many of us would not be in this work today if someone along the way had not been patient with us.

Practicing Patience

Sometimes we strive to practice patience in contexts that are uncomfortable or even offensive. At a training about eight years ago in a church basement in Chicago, a community group was planning a blockade action as part of a campaign demanding more affordable housing in a rapidly gentrifying neighborhood. The group had asked for the help of Lifted Voices, the collective Kelly cofounded, in building barricade equipment and preparing to use it for their protest. Kelly and her team knew it would be a challenging action and wanted to offer a demonstration of how it could play out so participants would understand what kind of equipment they would be using and what kinds of power tools police would likely use to cut them out of their blockade devices. After giving a talk about direct action and blockades and presenting the equipment demo, Kelly asked the crowd if there were any questions. An older Latinx gentleman in the back of the room called out, "Where are the men?"

As members of a Black and Indigenous collective of women and nonbinary organizers, Kelly and her team were certainly put off by the comment. After all, they had just demonstrated their competence, and it was this group who had invited Lifted Voices to help on the basis of the group's expertise. The organizers who had invited Kelly's group cringed, and there was a felt anxiety in the room among people who realized the comment was inappropriate. In an effort to pivot, Kelly joked loudly in a firm voice, "At home, making me dinner." Most of the room erupted in laughter. Others proceeded to ask real questions before making plans for action rehearsals.

Later, Kelly would check in with her team about whether her joke had been an acceptable way to shift the energy in the room. After all, "We can be macho, too!" was not an ideal response to misogyny. But group members agreed that, under the circumstances, the joke was a good way to push back without derailing the project or the work of relationship building that they were trying to do. They, too, felt that some kind of response was needed in order to move on, but no one wanted the situation to escalate. The pushback was gentle, and it made people laugh, but it also demonstrated that Kelly's group rejected the idea that their team was lacking in some way.

This is not to say that we can joke our way out of problematic moments. When someone has said something sexist or otherwise harmful, a joke is rarely the way forward. But in that moment, Kelly assessed the room she was in and devised a way to stick up for herself and her collective without getting into a messier conversation that might have derailed the urgent antigentrification effort. That kind of assessment and improvisation will be familiar to many organizers— and to many people who have had to deescalate messy situations in their own lives. Kelly knew there were varying degrees of misogyny in the room and that her collective was not going to correct those issues that day. A successful coalitional blockade to defend affordable housing, however, seemed wholly attainable.

Kelly's solution, however imperfect, smoothed over an awkward moment, and the two groups proceeded to collaborate effectively. While grumbling persisted among some of the men who did not feel they needed so much practice and training, everyone was steadfast in their commitments to the action. On the day of the protest, police were more aggressive than expected, using sledgehammers to destroy cement "lockbox" devices that were linking people's arms. This escalation by the police was not only dangerous, it was horrifying for onlookers, including Kelly and the other trainers. But the participants were not deterred, and they proceeded to hold the roadway until the last blockader was forcibly removed.

Kelly and other supporters awaited the arrestees outside the police station, deeply concerned about their co-strugglers inside. Kelly kept picturing the police swinging hammers through the air and thinking about how rattled the arrestees must have been. But when the blockaders were released, each of them emerged from the police station smiling. The group was not traumatized by their experience but instead felt powerful and excited about what they had accomplished. They credited the many hours they had spent practicing together and also thanked Kelly's collective for insisting that so much rehearsal was needed. As they executed the action, the group had felt prepared to face the police, and they had confidence in each other, too. Later, at a celebratory dinner, members of both groups shared words of appreciation for one another.

As she enjoyed that moment, and a piece of homemade cake, Kelly was aware that all of this—the trainings, the blockade, the dinner, and the solidarity—could have been derailed by a dramatic exchange weeks earlier if she or her team had responded differently to the question, "Where are the men?" A different reaction would have been justified, because the comment was not acceptable, but in that moment, Kelly and her team were not looking to be justified. They were looking to build a blockade with people who were fighting gentrification.

If the exchange had occurred a couple of years earlier, Kelly might have responded in a less constructive manner. But, like Aly Wane, she had been trying to develop a new practice of patience and to rein in reactions that might obstruct her work. In that sense, her joking pivot was a big win.

There is no formula for moving from a problematic comment to a celebratory dinner where people announce their mutual respect and appreciation, and such happy endings will not always occur. But such outcomes are possible, and do sometimes happen, when people grapple with their differences long enough to develop mutual respect and understanding.

Even if we never get to that celebratory dinner—or develop a sense of mutual respect and understanding, or even come to like the people we're working with—we can still build power with them. In many cases, we must. After all, the whole world is at stake. We must ask ourselves, *How much discomfort is the whole world worth?*

CHAPTER 10

Avoiding Burnout
and Going the Distance

For organizers, burnout is a stubborn enemy. In our struggles for justice, people's lives and liberty are forever at stake, and the urgency of our movements can become all-consuming. Countless organizers have worked themselves to the point of collapse, sometimes destroying their health and compromising their material well-being. But what activists call "burnout" is rarely characterized by exhaustion alone. If people experiencing burnout were simply exhausted and nothing more, they could likely rest away the problem. But for activists, burnout often describes a deeper issue: a profound exhaustion paired with an injury to our dignity or sense of belonging or a violation of our boundaries. As Dean Spade told Kelly on *Movement Memos*, "Burnout usually means I went way past my boundaries, or I deeply believed I wasn't good enough unless I did more than I could do."[1] People experiencing burnout may feel unappreciated, betrayed, exploited, blamed, or as though they no longer belong, in addition to feeling physically and emotionally depleted. Too often, burnout marks the end of an organizer's work, as many depart our movements resentful, weary, or even in despair. This cycle of self-destruction weakens our movements. But it also flies in the face of what we are fighting for: a world where people are not treated as disposable or ground down in the name of their productivity.

These destructive dynamics are perpetuated in part by a culture of martyrdom embedded in movement work. The idea that we should be willing to die for what we believe in resonates with many organizers and lends itself to the notion that we should be willing to work ourselves to death. This can lead us to make commitments that exceed our capacity. We know that movement work can endanger our lives, but if we also believe that human lives have value outside of capitalism and structures of productivity, we must value our own. We must preserve our health and well-being. So, how can we reconcile the urgency of our work—as we operate with too few people and square off with intractable enemies—with preserving our health and well-being?

People who commit themselves to justice work should not see their lives ruined or shortened because they chose to fight for a better world. Such losses are themselves a form of injustice. We must also understand that when we lose activists and organizers to burnout, our movements suffer. We do not simply lose their labor. We also lose knowledge and experience, hard-fought bonds of solidarity, and people who model what the world should be. As we struggle to balance our lives with what the work demands of us, we must ask ourselves whether the manner in which we organize reflects the world we want to build.

The two of us have learned that care must be a community practice and, further, that our personal care practices may require discipline. Sometimes we must apply the same level of effort and focus that we bring to our projects and campaigns to the maintenance of our health and well-being. Like many of you, we sometimes push our limits and exhaust ourselves, but we also endeavor to make space for rest, learning, and joy, because we know that without those things we will not endure as people or in this work. As organizers, we do not want to inspire a culture of martyrdom or self-destruction. We believe in a culture of care, where people who engage in struggle are more supported than they otherwise would be, not less. If we exempt ourselves from that vision, we cannot model or rehearse it in the world.

We also believe that developing group practices around conflict resolution and cultivating belonging can help to mitigate some of the issues that can lead to burnout.

Still, the balance is a struggle. In this section, we talk with several organizers whose thoughts and experiences have helped us better understand what it means to sustain movements while also sustaining our own well-being.

Be Part of the Future You Are Fighting For

Sharon Lungo is an Indigenous organizer, mother, facilitator, trainer, and founding member of the Indigenous People's Power Project (IP3). Lungo is also the former executive director of the Ruckus Society and has been an international nonviolent direct-action trainer and practitioner since 2001. When we talked with Lungo in summer 2020, we asked what advice she wished she had been given as a young organizer. She told us, "I wish that people would have been more staunch in reminding me that I get to prioritize myself at times, that I get to center myself in my own well-being, in addition to everything that I can give to the movement."

Lungo told us, "I feel like I wore this work as an identity for a long time, and it was the thing that I was, and stepping outside of that meant that I wasn't supporting my people or supporting the Earth, that I wasn't doing my job for humanity when I was capable and had gifts that would support this movement and support our people." The feelings of guilt and obligation that Lungo described are common among heavily engaged organizers and activists.

Movement work defined Lungo's life for over two decades. She coordinated countless protests and facilitated nonviolent direct-action trainings for thousands of activists, including many who became trainers themselves. But while her work was rich, Lungo deprived herself of many comforts. "I wish that more people had reminded me that it was OK to gift myself things, and take pleasure in things, and allow myself certain luxuries—and that it wasn't just about sacrificing my youth and all the energy that I had," Lungo said.

After devoting over a quarter of a century to movement work, Lungo wishes she had prioritized other ambitions and her mental health alongside her organizing and not allowed justice work to serve as an eclipsing force in her life. "I should have taken more opportunities to learn, to find a mentor, and indulge in learning things that weren't necessarily in service of the movement—skills or crafts that I found interesting, but didn't take time for, because I told myself I needed to give 100 percent to my work." Looking back, Lungo believes she should not "have settled for living on couches, and ridiculous wages, while the white folks around me took big vacations. I should have given myself permission to love myself by saying no to things."

Some of our movement cultures exacerbate this problem. While organizing work often involves sacrifice, such sacrifices are not evenly distributed. Most communities have stalwart organizers who will work through the night to make sure an important event happens or that a deadline gets met. The personal sacrifices of those organizers are rarely acknowledged, just as their labor is generally assumed rather than supported or reinforced. In this way, committed organizers often carry the weight of knowing they are both a strength and a potential vulnerability to their cause, since their sudden absence or removal could bring important work to a halt. Too often, organizations that have the resources to lighten the workload of such organizers, or to offer volunteers compensation for particularly grueling projects, instead treat such people as assets to be exploited. Many Black, Indigenous, and women and trans people of color also experience what Leah Lakshmi Piepzna-Samarasinha has termed "hyper-accountability,"[2] where, in addition to performing a disproportionate amount of labor for a cause, a person (usually a marginalized person) is expected to respond immediately and flawlessly to any and all claims that their work or behavior is somehow lacking or problematic. These dynamics can become draining and destructive to a person's physical, financial, and emotional well-being.

For a long time, Lungo felt she must simply endure these blows until the bitter end. "I kind of saw myself as disposable and thought, 'This is it, I'm going to do the work, and then one day I'm just going to implode because it's been too much, or I'm going to, like, fall off a cliff and it'll be done,'" Lungo said.

In her forties, Lungo experienced a profound level of burnout and faced a reckoning: Was she truly disposable, or was she deserving of care, healing, and recovery? After years of self-neglect, Lungo chose to heal. "I gave myself permission to go to therapy, to get massages and other treatments that support my body, to sleep in hotel beds instead of [on] couches, and to not feel bad about not going to every march or rally," she said.

As she began to care for herself, Lungo realized that in treating herself as disposable, she had failed to envision herself in the future she had been striving to create. "The consequences are personal, but they are also strategic," she told us. By failing to imagine her place in the world she was fighting for, Lungo impeded her ability to fully envision that world. "I think it limited my ability to think strategically and also to have hope. Hopelessness is not a good place to be, and it's not a good place to come from when you're trying to do this work."

Preparation Is Preservation

Lungo also emphasized the importance of understanding that movement work is "a life journey" and that "things happen slowly over time." Such pacing can be difficult to reconcile for people who are mobilized during highly energetic moments or who organize around local or global emergencies. However, we often carry the energy of high-intensity moments into our everyday organizing work, convinced that we must always operate in crisis mode.

"I was so politicized by spaces like the World Trade Organization meetings in 1999, and to see this amazing, huge burst of energy in people and to be part of these monumental moments," Lungo said, "but I feel like we chase those things around then for the rest of our activist lives. We're trying to re-create these giant surges in energy."

We must understand that "surges" cannot structure our whole organizing lives. For the most part, transformation is slow work, and as such, we must find ways to sustain it for the long haul. "Real change, real development, real growth, real organizing happens slowly," Lungo said. "It happens over time. It happens on the day-to-day, and in encouraging each other to find the balance between these big bursts and moments."

Lungo finds this lesson especially relevant in her greatest area of expertise: direct action. From sit-ins to shutdowns and beyond, direct actions serve as interventions and moments of social confrontation in pursuit of political reckonings or social transformations. "We're looking to create these bursts of energy, these big moments that will catalyze something larger, that will initiate movement or change in our opponents and get them to the table, or whatever it is that we want to do," she said. But, in reality, no direct action will magically transport a movement to its end goal. Instead, Lungo said, "It's kind of a staircase, as we say in IP3. It's like you make a jump to the next stair, but there's all this work that you have to do in order to get to the next level."

Lungo warned that a "thirst for something big or monumental" that would "move and shake people in big ways" can inhibit an activist's ability to pace their work, which can lead to both burnout and strategic failure. "We actually don't need to move everyone, all at once," she explained. "We need to move a smaller portion of people than we actually think" to initiate major shifts in political thought and action. "The shift and change, it takes time." Lungo noted that smaller actions and "the everyday work that you do with each other and other humans" is as important as "creating big giant marches or beautiful actions or big takeovers."

Many activists are frustrated that they cannot manufacture the kind of energy that Lungo characterizes as "organic"—such as spontaneous uprisings stemming from specific atrocities or disasters. Rather than relentlessly attempting to force a mass activation in the absence of momentum, Lungo hopes more organizers will use less energetic moments to cultivate skills that will help them move strategically and cope with pressure and trauma in higher-intensity moments. She told us,

Taking the time to learn and to study and to grow your skills is as important as getting off your ass when shit is happening, and heading to the streets. Building with each other in the "off season" . . . building in the spaciousness of that time to have conversations about history and strategy. Asking, "What if we tried this?" And exploring all of the different scenarios and being able to do that in a moment where you can breathe, and you can think, and you can take care of yourself spiritually and emotionally—and factor in all the trauma that comes with your body and your life. In those moments, we can stop and expand [our practice] and have a larger view of things.

Creating space for exploration outside of high-pressure moments allows organizers to develop a deeper understanding of the strategies, tactics, and histories that inform their work and to build stronger relationships.

Burnout doesn't just cause people to leave movements; it can also have lasting emotional and physical impacts. "How many of our people have we lost due to mental health struggles, or just the trauma of being out on the streets in shitty moments?" Lungo asked. She urges us to ask ourselves how we are recognizing that reality and shaping our movements to respond to it.

"That is as important as driving ahead with your campaign or continuing to get the signatures or doing the work for the next thing," Lungo told us. "Stopping and giving yourself that space to converse, to learn, to explore, to try the things on that you've been wanting to do. To test your body's reaction to somebody being up in your face. To test your own personal sense of fear in horrible moments or when weapons come out. To really get to know and understand yourself in situations that could potentially be hard, so that when you're in those moments, we can support each other in navigating to a better place."

Solidarity and Getting in the Game

What does it mean to support each other and take care of ourselves during urgent times? Ejeris Dixon, the New York–based organizer and founder of Vision Change Win, notes that merely prescribing rest or "self-care" does not reduce the stress level of an organizer who knows a particular set of tasks must be completed in order to seize a political opportunity or support a community in need. As Dixon said, "We can't go hard all the time, but sometimes, we have to go hard, and that's just the reality of the task or the fight."

When the stakes are high, it can be difficult for an organizer to rest when pausing means the work simply will not happen. Dixon said, "The best way for me to feel cared for when I feel like we're in these David and Goliath fights—and my friends know this about me—is that they've got to fucking get in the game with me."

We do not all have the same skill sets or capacity for risk, but "getting in the game" to take pressure off of organizers can take many shapes. "To get in the game with me can mean asking, 'Hey, Ejeris, are you eating? Can I send you food? Hey, how do I take something off your plate?' Not, 'You should slow down,' but, 'I see what you're doing and what we're up against. How do we do that together?'"

Dixon believes in care strategies that involve assessing conditions and making sure organizers are not going it alone. "I think the best way to burn out an organizer is to leave them alone," she says.

Dixon described a period of her antiviolence work when every time she tried to take a break, a murder would occur, and she would feel pulled toward rapid-response organizing to support victims' loved ones. She felt that if she went on vacation, she'd be abandoning a family that needed her. However, one of her co-strugglers suggested a path forward. "I had a coworker say, 'Well, why don't we all get trained up on rapid response around murder, so then we have a whole crew of us?'" Dixon said. She continued:

> I think the best way to do collaborative and collective care is to ask, How are we backing each other up? How are we encouraging each other to take the breaks we need, but not making ourselves make impossible choices? How do we make sure the goals of our work are covered so that nobody has to

burn themselves out because they're politically committed? Are we making sure that every role has multiple people in that role? How do we create more of our work in teams?

Relief teams and mechanisms can be created at the group or organizational level, around particular organizing tasks or roles, or at the personal level, when an organizer stretched thin needs help with basic life tasks, like cooking, childcare, or picking up groceries. Organizing work can be done in shifts so that people have time to take breaks and take care of themselves and those they care for. These mechanisms and formations will vary in shape across communities and between organizing models, but their core function is essential: to treat organizers as human beings whose lives will sometimes interrupt their labor, rather than as batteries to be drained.

"How do we create more of our work with the idea that any of us may need to take a pause at any point in time?" Dixon asked. Rather than grounding self-care in individualism, "it's really about building structures for collective and collaborative care that also don't leave anyone behind."

To create sustainable movements, we must view relief structures, mechanisms, and agreements as essential to the architecture of our movement work.

We Don't Just Need Rest, We Also Need Rejuvenation

Organizing never felt like a choice to Morning Star Gali. "I was raised within it," she told us. "I was born at the AIM for Freedom Survival School. I didn't have a choice to say no, and I'm OK with that."

Gali, the longtime Native organizer and a member of the Ajumawi band of the Pit River Nation, has coordinated annual "Thanks-taking" gatherings at Alcatraz for over twelve years. Gali was born at a time when Native people were rising up. The commitment and sacrifice of the organizers helped her understand that in matters of justice, "we all have a responsibility individually and collectively." But as an organizer who has navigated environmental devastation, the impacts of the opioid crisis, MMIW and MMIR work, and more, Gali is no stranger to burnout.

She told us that balance and reciprocity are crucial to sustainable organizing. To understand what we owe to the Earth and what we owe each other, we must recognize our place within a larger webwork of interdependent life.

We all have a responsibility to care for our communities and care for the Earth. And again, it is that reciprocal relationship, and it's part of how we're in balance with ourselves, in balance with our communities, in balance with our tribal communities, and that's how it was historically. We all had a place, and we all had a role within our tribal villages. It's just fulfilling that little part that you can do to help take care of one another.

Embracing interdependency and rejecting individualism can help us develop sustainable practices of balance in our organizing.

At the same time, we must take seriously the daily, personal practices that can nurture our well-being—and that can easily become compromised amid a heated struggle or campaign. "I think rest is a big one," Gali told us. "None of us get enough rest." To resist exhaustion, Gali has started going to bed as early as 8:00 p.m. and "just shutting my phone off." She has a daily practice of prayer and meditation and "greeting the sun as soon as I'm up." Gali believes daily rituals are important. "There's a medicine that I'll boil for the day," she told us. "I'll throw in some cedar and some orange, or lemon slices from our trees in the backyard, some wormwood, not only for our internal respiratory health, but also to clear the air and try to reset in that sense."

However, rest alone will not sustain us or our movements. "Not only do we need rest, we also need rejuvenation," Gali said. In her own pursuit of rejuvenation, Gali turns to the wisdom of movement elders. "Our elders talk a lot about, in our fight to protect sacred places, in our fight for clean water, for clean air for the land—we need to go to it. We need to go to those places. I think we don't make it down as often as we'd like to of course, but when I was living back home under tribal lands, it was an everyday practice of just being at the creek, or being at the water. Just putting my feet in the creek." Sometimes Gali would make her way to the creek on her lunch break. "Just that little bit of rejuvenation and being back in touch with the land and water" was enough to sustain her, she told us.

Gali acknowledged that our responsibilities and life circumstances can get in the way of such excursions, but she emphasized the need to find rejuvenation when and where we can. She no longer lives near the creek she used to dip her feet in daily, but when she can, she packs up her family and heads for the water. "I bring our family dog and bring the kids and go down to the water and just make some offerings there, put our prayers down, to give whatever heaviness that we're carrying from that day, just being able to give it away in that sense, and not hold on to it."

Is there a place that makes you feel whole or revived in some way? How often are you able to inhabit that space? If that place is inaccessible, what ritual or experience brings you closest to it? What practices or experiences help you experience a sense of renewal? Are these practices an ongoing part of your life?

Enjoy Life

Aly Wane remembers the days when he would feel guilty about missing any meeting or rally, as though his presence were always essential and any failure to show up was a failure of solidarity. Looking back, he realizes, "There's actually something slightly egotistical about thinking that you have to be at that rally, like you are the one person [whose presence] is going to make the difference." Aly said that when organizers start to understand movements in terms of roles and labor that can be shared among people who cycle in and out they can develop a more sustainable flow.

After so many years in the work, Aly is unapologetic about taking the time he needs to rest and be well. "If I decide, 'You know what? I'm going to take two or three months to just relax,' I'm going to do that. And if, one day, I decided, 'You know what? From this day on Aly Wane is going to focus his life on interpretive dance, I'll do that. I'm serious. . . . I know based on my life's trajectory that abolitionist work is probably going to be part of my life for as long as I can think. But if I have some kind of epiphany, and I decide to do something else, I don't have to be an activist."

Wane emphasized the importance of living fully and making time for the people and activities we enjoy outside of organizing. "I want to spend some of my time creating community and transforming society and all of those things, but I also want to spend some time just hanging out with friends, watching TV, playing guitar," he says. "I've been playing guitar more these days. Just enjoying the process. And I think I didn't give myself as much permission to do that when I was younger. And that's the number one thing I would tell my younger self is just, 'It's OK. Enjoy yourself, and enjoy life as well, because we're here for a very short time.'"

Respect Your Season

Organizers are not machines. We are living beings who experience stages of energetic growth, periods of exhaustion, and various stages of healing, reconfiguration, and renewal. The same is true of movements and communities.

However, under capitalism, our value is measured in terms of our productivity. When our capacity wanes due to illness, exhaustion, or duress, workers are largely expected to remain productive anyway and to continue to contribute to the economy. When we fail to do so, we are viewed as less valuable and made to feel inadequate or even burdensome, and we are at risk of disposal. It is unsurprising that this mentality manifests itself in our movement work, but the idea that we must remain "productive" at all costs leads to frustration, resentment, burnout, and collapse.

The Ayni Institute, which offers political education grounded in Indigenous principles of reciprocity, reminds us that movements, organizations, and organizers all experience seasons. As Ayni Institute organizer Carlos Saavedra told Kelly on *Movement Memos*,

I think sometimes what is missing from this leadership conversation is that leadership has, in some ways, ebbs and flows. There are times where you can respond, and there's times where you cannot respond as much. And we believe that actually at the institute I'm part of, at Ayni, that leadership in some ways goes through cycles. . . . A good metaphor, I think, that could ground us in that is a metaphor of seasons, or seasonality, meaning that there's a time where a leadership is going through a winter period, meaning it's going through a period of hibernation where you are trying to rejuvenate yourself, rejuvenate your body, your emotions, your capacity—and also have a breakthrough, an insight that could allow you to then have, maybe, a spring in your leadership, where you're maybe opening up, you're doing more things. You feel very energetic, and potentially maybe going through a summer in your leadership where it's "go, go, go" energy—"let's go, let's move around as quick as we can." There's so much energy. And then, hopefully, a time of fall where we're reaping the rewards of the work that we've done and preparing for another cycle of winter.[3]

The metaphorical spring is a time of growth: the capacity to educate and organize new people is ramped up, relationships are expanded, and new coalitions are built. Summer, in this metaphor, is a time of consistent action, when energy is high and victories are potentially claimed. Fall is a time of harvest, when movements have achieved victories or endured losses. In fall, projects and coalitions may break down or sunset as the pace of work slows, allowing organizers time to reflect, share stories, and uplift the labor of the previous season. The metaphorical winter is the most difficult season for many organizers, because we have been conditioned to view less energetic periods of organizing as times of failure.

"I believe that individuals, organizations, and social movements go through seasons through this metaphor of seasonality," Saavedra told Kelly. "I believe one of the main reasons why it's so difficult for us to be in a rhythm of seasons nowadays is because of the nature of the global system that we're in, that is highly, extremely productivist, which is capitalism." Saavedra explained that capitalism "creates this expectation of what we call the eternal summer and this expectation that everyone should be in the eternal summer all the time."[4]

Saavedra also pointed out that we have been conditioned to zero in on people's productivity as a point of interest by asking what they do or what they are working on. "There is even a stigma to burning out or not having that capacity to keep producing," he added, noting that "this is exacerbated by not taking a long-view perspective that recognizes how social movements operate in cycles of five to fifteen years."[5]

Some activists are averse to slowing down and embracing periods of introspection and renewal. Saavedra refers to this aversion to or fear of taking winters as "winter phobia," explaining that "[some] people are scared of taking winters. They're scared of going within, or maybe to deal with the pain of previous seasons to be able to then regenerate. And so people sometimes are stuck. They know that the eternal summer is bad, but they are afraid of going into a time within."[6]

Rather than operating at a breakneck pace until we crash and burn, respecting our seasons allows us to cultivate and build meaningful connections and projects throughout each cycle. As Saavedra told us, "In order for us to be effective, meaning doing the right thing at the right time, we must recognize which season we are in, honor it, and most importantly, protect it."

While experiencing winter, on a personal level, some organizers may step back from movement work entirely. This can be the result of a major life change, such as an illness, the arrival of a new child, moving to a different city, caring for a loved one, or some other development. It can also be the result of burnout, exhaustion, or simply being fed up with the challenges of social justice work. For whatever reason, many people step back for long stretches but ultimately return to the work of organizing. So if it has been a long time, but you are feeling called to return, perhaps spring has come.

Knowing When to Let Go of a Project

Sometimes when we feel burned out or confused about how to move forward with our group, it may be because our project, container, or organization has simply run its course. It's important to understand that deciding it's time to end something we have created is not a mark of failure. The groups and projects that we have sunsetted or intentionally concluded were meaningful and generative. Due to evolving conditions, those projects were no longer the best container or group for the work participants wanted to do. Sometimes this happens because people's aims or intentions simply outgrow the container they have created. This can be a good thing.

When the two of us organized with the Chicago-based police abolitionist project We Charge Genocide (WCG), a number of working groups were formed within the broader organization. These groups developed efforts that endured long after WCG itself ended. For example, Kelly's collective, Lifted Voices, would not exist without the WCG Radical Ed Working Group, which focused on the kind of abolitionist direct action and movement education work that Lifted Voices would ultimately take up. Multiple founders of the Lifted Voices collective brought the lessons of their projects with the Radical Ed Working Group and WCG to the table as they devised new direct-action curriculums. Lifted Voices would subsequently train thousands of people in direct action in Chicago and around the country.

Sometimes we must release a current project in order to pursue new visions. Many of the people involved with We Charge Genocide have gone on to create projects that have done essential work, such as Assata's Daughters, the grassroots collective of radical Black women and girls whose early founders include Page May, Caira Lee Connor, and other former members of WCG. After doing generative work together, people often grow in a variety of directions. We should appreciate the beauty of that growth.

WCG's original purpose was to send a delegation of Black youth to the United Nations to present a shadow report on the violence of Chicago's police. In addition to successfully challenging the UN to call out the violence of Chicago police, WCG contributed meaningfully to the Reparations NOW campaign, which was seeking reparations for police-perpetrated torture, and played an important role in a historic period of mobilization in Chicago. It launched art projects and research efforts, built relationships, and made new formations possible. Unlike many groups that are now defunct, WCG was not in turmoil due to internal conflict; nor was it suffering from waning participation. But in the months after the delegation went to the UN, we engaged in soul-searching conversations about whether we had done what we had set out to do, within that particular container, and ultimately agreed that we had. For some people, it was hard to say goodbye to what we had built together, but most of us would continue to be part of the same organizing community, and the bonds we built through WCG would stretch across the city and the country as we built and joined new projects.

As Chicago-based healing justice organizer Tanuja Jagernauth told Kelly on *Movement Memos*, it can be helpful to think of the groups and containers we create as having life cycles. "I do think of the things we create as living things," Jagernauth said. She noted that this idea of a life cycle can be important, not only in terms of the care with which we bring our projects into the world but also in terms of how we let them go. "If we do decide to hold on to the idea that our projects and our formations are alive, we can also hold space for the idea that all things that are alive do die," Jagernauth said. "And the most beautiful thing you can do when something is dying is to allow it to pass on with as much dignity and grace as possible, honoring it in all of its complexity."[7]

We have learned that letting go can be a beautiful thing. Honoring what a group or project has accomplished and what it has meant to us while preserving its history and, most importantly, carrying its lessons forward, can be an emotional process, but not everything in organizing is about fighting tooth and nail. Some moments are about recognizing where we have been, what we have learned, how we have grown, and what we now believe the future demands of us.

The end of one project can mean the beginning of new dreams and schemes about how to remake the world. We have said many goodbyes in our work, yet the work goes on, and so do we, building, hoping, and creating in concert with other human beings.

CONCLUSION

Relationships, Reciprocity, and Struggle

Kelly Hayes

At the start of chapter 1, Mariame and I described an action where we showed up outside mayor Rahm Emanuel's house on a freezing winter night, carrying a message in lights. It seems fitting that I should find myself in a similar situation as we complete our work on this book. On the second day of Hanukkah in December 2022, I was outside governor J. B. Pritzker's mansion in Chicago's Gold Coast neighborhood, singing and protesting with a group of about twenty people, some of whom were holding lighted letters that read "Free Bernina." It was around twenty-five degrees out, but on this occasion, we were not rushing to secure an image, because while thought had gone into the protest's imagery, this action held a different intention. I had not organized the event, though I did bring the light boards. Members of Love & Protect, Tzedek Chicago, and others had gathered for a Hanukkah-themed appeal to the governor to grant clemency to Bernina Mata, a fifty-two-year-old criminalized survivor who is the victim of a homophobic, racist prosecution. At first, I intended to exempt myself from singing. I turned down a song sheet because singing with my KN95 mask on in those freezing temperatures would cause my glasses to fog up. But ultimately I could not resist the moment, so I leaned closer to my friend Maya

Schenwar to read from her song sheet. That irresistible urge to join in a collective experience, to embrace a fuller sense of connection and communion with those around you because something beautiful is happening, is not attached to every moment of protest or struggle, but we do need those moments to exist.

While only about two dozen people were in attendance, I considered the event to be a near perfect action. The protest generated an article in *Windy City Times*,[1] and our own social media posts and images helped propel a petition for clemency online. The action also created inspiring imagery that would hearten an imprisoned co-struggler, challenge a government official, and bring community members together in a moment of political communion, where our sense of moral certainty and belonging overwhelmed any impulse to justify, tolerate, or cooperate with the system and made us feel more whole for acting against it together. Our sense of certainty, our sense of connection to each other, to Bernina, and to the cause, were more powerful than the cold or any concern we had about the police vans that were staged nearby.

Maya's four-year-old son, Kai, bopped and sang throughout the event. She had told me at the start of the night that she might have to leave early if Kai felt too cold. I told her I might similarly have to head out early on account of my lower back pain, which often worsens in the cold. But we both stayed the full hour of the event. Like Kai, we were deeply engaged in the moment. I had a feeling that I sometimes get in justice work, one that I am sure some of you can relate to, that I was exactly where I was supposed to be at that moment in time. As I told the participants during my remarks, while we do not all practice the same faith, and some of us have no religious faith at all, we were all bound together in that moment by something sacred. That communion against injustice, that defiant love, that refusal to abandon, our willingness to stand in the cold together, and the ability to find joy in that togetherness, despite our discomfort. I was so grateful in that moment, because in our incredibly fractured world there was a sense of wholeness to be found, out there in the cold, in struggle with other human beings. I thanked the organizers, but the words could not do my gratitude justice. My back would, in fact, cramp up later from the cold, but other needs were met that night—the kind that help keep us in the fight when we are hurting or when we feel the universe has kicked us in the teeth yet again.

As volunteers carried the light boards back to our car, Kai asked his mother, "Why are we leaving?" When she explained that it was time to go, Kai yelled out "Free Bernina!" repeatedly, in a jubilant voice, as they headed for their vehicle. While most of us were probably more eager than Kai to get out of the cold, we were moving with the same spirit, the same sense of empowerment and hope that we might see Bernina freed.

Will Bernina be freed? As of this writing, I do not know. But I know to be hopeful, because I know that when we set out to challenge injustice, we have barely begun to discover what's possible.

As Mariame mentioned in this book's introduction, she and I have engaged in a lot of defense-committee work together. Defense committees or campaigns are grassroots efforts to secure the freedom of a person who has been incarcerated or otherwise targeted for criminalization, through community organizing, political pressure, community education, legal and media advocacy, and other strategies. Defense-committee organizing is a form of mutual aid that embodies a number of the ideas that we have discussed in this book: resisting state violence, refusing to abandon people, and delegitimizing the carceral state's simplistic conclusions about who is worthy of punishment and who is worthy of life. Mariame and I have worked together to help free survivors like Naomi Freeman, Marissa Alexander, Cherelle Baldwin—Black women who were faced with the prospect of having their futures stolen by the carceral system because they were willing to defend their own lives against abusive partners. It is essential, especially in these times, to understand that under this system, some people are simply expected to die rather than disrupt the order of things.

Bresha Meadows was one of those people. In July 2016, fourteen-year-old Bresha Meadows shot and killed her father in an act of self-defense. Bresha's father had been sexually abusing her since she was eight years old. He had brutalized Bresha's mother throughout her life and terrorized the family, at times waving a gun at them— which he kept under his pillow at night. Bresha had attempted to escape the violations and brutality of her household by running away and by confiding in teachers, police, and relatives. She did everything that children are told they should do if they experience abuse, but the system would not help Bresha. When police came to the family's home, they refused to interview Bresha outside the presence of her father. When Bresha's aunt, who was a police officer, tried to keep Bresha in her home for protection, she was told by other police that she must return Bresha to her parents.

In a fair world, there would have been no thought of punishing Bresha. In a just society, people would have hung their heads in shame, asking how we could have allowed this child to arrive at such a choice. How could we have failed an abused child, one who begged to be saved, so horribly that she would have to do the unthinkable? In a just world, a loving community would have rallied to meet the needs of Bresha's family, to ensure she could access healing, and to make whatever changes were necessary to ensure that no child would ever be plunged into a similar hell. But we do not live in that society. In our world, Bresha was charged with murder. The prosecution intended to try her as an adult. Bresha had been robbed of her childhood by her father's cruelty and violence, and now the state was assuming the abuser's role and threatening to steal her future as well.

By the time Bresha was arrested, Mariame and I had worked on a number of defense committees and campaigns, and we had a community of friends and co-strugglers who were familiar with and enthusiastic about this kind of work. So when a friend sent an email to a number of like-minded organizers, asking if we were familiar with the case, an ad hoc defense committee quickly took shape. We connected with Bresha's family and organizers on the ground in Ohio while coordinating decentralized awareness efforts around the country. Groups like Survived & Punished, Project NIA, Love & Protect, Moms United against Violence and Mass Incarceration, and my collective, Lifted Voices, planned teach-ins and staged direct actions and social media storms. We wrote op-eds and held rallies, sometimes gathering people outside the juvenile detention center in Chicago, in order to draw connections between the violence of Bresha's incarceration and the incarceration of children from our own communities. We also rallied people to send postcards and letters to Bresha and circulated a petition demanding that the charges against her be dropped. Thanks largely to our efforts on social media, the campaign drew national and international attention.

Bresha's mental health was deteriorating over the course of her incarceration, and eventually she was placed on suicide watch. We quickly ramped up our efforts, urging supporters to send Bresha notes of love and support. She would later tell me that the letters and postcards people sent helped her carry on, even on days when she could barely read them or remember what she had just read. "I was so confused, and full of so much hurt," she told me. "I went from one situation that seemed like it would never end, and there was no way out, to another situation that felt like it would never end, and there was no way out." Bresha had begun to think of death as the only "way out." But thanks to the postcards and letters, which streamed in so steadily that she was not allowed to access them all, "I knew I wasn't alone, even though I was. There were people fighting for me and waiting for me." No one had intervened to save her from her father, but her new abuser, the carceral state, was being fought. There were people trying to defend her and trying to save her life. It was as though, after years of reaching out for help without anyone grabbing her hand, people were finally reaching back. There were walls and bars and in some cases thousands of miles between Bresha and those people, but their existence and their encouragement gave her strength.

In late 2016, under tremendous national and even international pressure, the prosecutor opted to charge Bresha as a juvenile after all. Bresha accepted a plea that led to a period of incarceration in a mental health facility. The defense committee raised funds so she could spend those months in the facility of her choosing, rather than a state hospital she had heard horror stories about. On February 4,

2018, Bresha was finally freed from confinement. Upon getting out, she began to read some of the articles and op-eds that had been written about her case. She also came across a video of an action that was co-organized by my collective—Lifted Voices—and Circles and Ciphers, which is a Chicago-based hip-hop-infused restorative justice organization led by and for young people impacted by violence. The action was an "abolitionist night of art and action" and included local artwork inspired by Bresha's case, musical performances by Tasha and FM Supreme, and poetry spoken by youth from Circles and Ciphers. Bresha was moved by the video and reached out to thank Lifted Voices for the action.

That thank-you began a conversation between Bresha and me that would go on for years. I was thrilled to hear from this young person who had become such an important part of my life even though we had never met. I had written and cowritten pieces about Bresha's case, organized direct actions, led teach-ins at local high schools, and worked to raise national awareness around the #FreeBresha campaign, but I never actually expected to meet her. After all, I didn't feel that she owed us anything. It was my honor to be part of such an effort, and Bresha having a future outside of a cage was all the reward any of us had dared hope for. But getting to build a relationship with Bresha, to hear her side of things, to laugh at her jokes, to ease her doubts about herself—these were gifts I had not imagined. Eventually, she asked if she could join the Lifted Voices collective.

Since joining Lifted Voices, Bresha has attended Project NIA's Youth Abolitionist Institute for young organizers and has trained to become an abortion doula. She is passionate about reproductive justice and, after the fall of *Roe*, was eager to take action to expand abortion access. As I sat with Bresha and another member of my collective one night, eating ice cream and watching the documentary *The Janes*, I watched Bresha's eyes light up. She was moved and inspired by the story of how these women formed a conspiracy to ensure that pregnant people could access safe abortions, even at the risk of going to prison. "We have to help people get abortions," she told me afterward.

"I know," I told her. "And we will."

I never imagined, when I agreed that we needed to form a defense committee to help Bresha, that she and I would one day meet and become close. And yet, Bresha and I have hiked through the woods, practiced self-defense moves, and touched waterfalls together. We have comforted each other in moments of fear and doubt, and we have also laughed our asses off. My friendship with Bresha is an everyday reminder that the work of fighting for other people and a better world can bring rewards we never imagined, and those rewards will often come in the form of relationships.

In a world that is breaking down our connections, isolating us, and sub-siloing us to death, life-giving relationships are our best hope. The connections that will sustain us will not happen instantly, and some people are heartbroken when a movement space does not provide a sense of family or belonging. But, in my experience, the work of doing justice transforms people, relationships, and the dynamics between people over time. In those transformations, there is a great deal of joy and meaning to be found. I am the person I am today because of the people who chose to build relationships with me along the way. Mentors like Mariame changed my life by inviting me to organize alongside them, valuing my feedback, trusting my creativity, and building with me from a place of mutual care and concern. I know what it's like to go it alone in this brutal world, and today, as a person who has a broad and loving community of activists in my life, I feel deeply for people who are still out there, going it alone, believing they are supposed to make it as individuals and blaming themselves when they falter. We were not meant to survive that way, and it's no surprise when we cannot in a world that is set against us in so many ways.

That is not to say that having a loving community erases all the world's horrors and tragedies. Like many of you, even as I feel called to act against injustice, I also get overwhelmed by the vast terror of it all. But then I look at Bresha and I remember that we can refuse to leave each other behind. We have that power.

❡

I am writing these words on Christmas in 2022, well after most of the words in this book have been written. I am writing to you from a moment when people are needlessly freezing to death as another historic storm batters the country. I am writing to you from a moment when people are being forced to remain pregnant and to give birth in twenty-six states, and where patients are developing sepsis as they wait for doctors to decide their miscarriages have progressed enough for life-saving care to not to be considered an abortion. I am writing to you from a moment when migrants are being shipped between US cities as a form of ideological warfare that the Democrats seem woefully ill-equipped to counter. In this moment, many others are living their lives as though a pandemic is not raging, because while we cannot seem to develop a lasting immunity to COVID, people can become psychologically immune to the impact of death tolls. Many of us are waging acts of care in response to these crises, but far too many people have embraced the status quo. People tend to justify the systems they depend on, or to deem the functions of those systems inevitable.[2] It's a short-term palliative reflex with long-term consequences, and a great many people are navigating these times through justification, rationalization, and attempts to replicate what we have often already lost.

Perhaps this moment from which I'm writing to you sounds familiar. Maybe it's similar to the moment you're living in. It's also possible that, by the time you are reading these words, things will have gotten much worse in terms of environmental destruction, the impacts of COVID, or the fracturing of our shared reality. I also hold hope for a third possibility: that you are reading this book in a moment of transformation that exceeds anything I might imagine right now.

I have hope you might find this book and, in some ways, view it as a relic: a time capsule of words from a moment when we were lost and had not yet truly found each other. I have hope that you, and I, will know a level of solidarity with other human beings that we have yet to experience in my lifetime. I hope you have experienced that level of solidarity with all of the creatures that inhabit this Earth, and with the water and with the air, because I believe that's what survival looks like—that level of connection and understanding, and a true sense of what's sacred. Above all else, I hope you are free, and that this book is an artifact of struggles that no longer need to be waged. I believe that your picking up this book at such a moment in time is possible, and right now I am in love with that possibility, along with so many others.

However, if you are not that lucky student of history, looking back on these words as echoes of a tragic past, then I have hope that you may be battling for the world we want, or that you may be on the cusp of doing that work. I have hope that you will build reciprocal movements, grounded in care and a regard for life on Earth, that will cultivate hope and give life greater meaning in these times.

I have hope that you will rebel against the continued normalization of mass death, human suffering, and annihilation. I have hope that you will choose to keep feeling the things that are hard to feel, even as people around you may surrender their values. I have hope that you will continue to give a damn, even when it's hard, and that you will fight for each other. Perhaps I will even see you in the streets.

I believe in your creativity and in your potential to cast aside the limitations of individualism: the obsession with notoriety, the illusion that our fates are divided. I believe you can fight and continuously build worlds worth fighting for, even as the worlds we have known collapse all around us. I recently read *Rehearsals for Living*, by Robyn Maynard and Leanne Betasamosake Simpson, and I found these words from Simpson especially grounding:

> Imperialism and ongoing colonialism have been ending worlds for as long as they have been in existence, and Indigenous and Black peoples have been building worlds and then rebuilding worlds for as long as we have been in existence. Relentlessly building worlds through unspeakable violence and loss. Building worlds and living in them *anyway*.[3]

The work before us is the work of our ancestors and the work of those who will come after: to relentlessly build new worlds, even on the edge of oblivion, and live in them anyway—together. That work, which sounds epic in scope and scale, begins with human connection, human relationships, and reciprocity in struggle. It begins with care.

CONCLUSION

Beyond Doom, toward Collective Action

Mariame Kaba

I t. Can. Be. So. Terrible. Here.
        Sometimes this must be said to begin.

If you're feeling discouraged, alienated, or scared at this moment, I want you to know that you are not alone. There are many days when it is difficult to muster the energy to continue to struggle for another world. I wake up in the morning and wonder if anyone actually cares about justice, freedom, and liberation. I question whether another world is possible given how selfish and reckless some humans can be. I am overwhelmed by the enormity of the work before us.

We are living in and through calamitous times. We are bombarded twenty-four seven, it seems, by terrible political, public health, economic, and ecological news. We aren't offered space to process collectively or to grieve all that has been lost. We're living through the perpetual frontlash of white supremacy and heteropatriarchy. So we can all be forgiven for not showing up as our best selves. We all need more grace. Many of us are just trying to keep our heads above water.

We're all impacted by the storms in some way. Some of us simply have more resources to weather them. "No time can be easy if one is living through it," said the great writer James Baldwin.[1] This is a reminder that the present looks different from inside of it. So my invitation, as you emerge from reading this book, is that you try to look at the current moment from outside of it—that you try for a little distance from the daily slog.

Yes, there is bad news, but it's not the only news. I agree with poet and writer Elizabeth Alexander, who, in the wake of the 2016 election, reminded us that "there is more than one thing happening at once. So, as bad as this is, it's not the only thing." It's so important to remember this message during difficult times, lest we become despairing. Despair is a thief. It saps your energy, depletes your time, and robs you of your ability to dream. And we need lots of dreamers and doers right now.

There are countless stories around the world that can and should buoy our spirits. Stories of kind people doing generous things for years without expecting anything in return. Stories of people who are practicing restorative and transformative justice, often without using those terms. Stories of communities of people coming together across differences to help one person keep their business alive. Stories that remind us that, in the words of South African antiapartheid writer and organizer Dennis Brutus, "somehow tenderness survives."[2]

This book that you are reading suggests that an antidote to the relentless drumbeat of doom is strategic and persistent collective action. In the West in particular, individualism is prized and often promoted over collectivity and, most importantly, interdependence. Yet we will not accomplish anything transformational alone. We won't.

Archbishop Desmond Tutu, a courageous and profoundly decent man, passed away in late 2021. Tutu helped to popularize the Zulu concept of Ubuntu as the understanding that "'a person is a person through other people.'" He used to say that Ubuntu can best be understood as "me we." I love that term—"me we." He wrote that the "solitary, isolated human being is a contradiction in terms." All humanity is interconnected and interdependent. Tutu wrote that "the only way we can ever be human is together. The only way we can be free is together."[3]

For me, the truth of Tutu's words is made all the clearer by the response to this global COVID pandemic that we have been trying to live through over the past three years. From the start, the question was whether we would embody a "me we" ethos or a "me me" one. I think that we've seen both at play. The outpouring of mutual aid efforts in communities around the world encompasses the "me we," while the hoarding of vaccines by the Global North, for example, epitomizes the "me me." Ask yourself whether the global pandemic has increased or diminished your personal sense of Ubuntu.

Experiencing the incompetence of—and in some cases intentional abandonment by—our governments (including our local ones) during this pandemic has left many of us feeling despondent, increased our fears, and made us feel like passive consumers of news and information. All of these can fuel a sense of helplessness. All can erode our sense of Ubuntu.

If we pay attention, though, we notice that there are people all around us working right now to lessen suffering by taking action in their communities, using the resources that they have gathered. These people have internalized a lesson taught by spiritual teacher Ram Dass: "We are all affecting the world every moment, whether we mean to or not. Our actions and states of mind matter, because we are so deeply interconnected with one another."[4] Alongside stories of war, death-making, cruelty, and inhumanity, there are also ones about compassion, kindness, and people acting selflessly. Indeed, those stories help me to refuel and keep me pushing forward. Perhaps they do for you as well. If you feel alienated from the "me we," a good remedy is to plug into local mutual aid efforts and other collectivist projects.

Aristotle taught us, "We become just by performing just actions, temperate by performing temperate actions, brave by performing brave actions." The key is to take action, however and wherever we can. It is to keep in mind Unitarian Universalist minister Victoria Safford's admonition that "we cannot do this all at once. But every day offers every one of us little invitations for resistance, and you make your own responses."[5] I love the idea of "little invitations for resistance." The question before all of us, I think, is, What will we make of this moment in history? One thing I know for sure is that we need to build our *action* muscles. We need to get outside of ourselves and act, both individually and collectively.

An important thing to do when injustices compound is to resist numbness. In order for change and transformation to occur, we must refuse the current order of the world. What does this mean? It doesn't mean repeating the buzz phrase "this is not normal." It means active refusal to become numb to the horror. The renowned poet, writer, and activist Dionne Brand warns, "If I am peaceful in this discomfort, is not peace, / is getting used to harm."[6]

Of course, turning away from the "news" intermittently is essential for one's well-being. The people I most admire, like organizer Ella Baker, remind us that "the tribe increases. . . . The struggle is eternal. Somebody else carries on."[7] These touchstones are also honest about their disappointments and doubts. I don't wake up every day feeling prepared to confront oppression and looking forward to struggle. Many days I'm annoyed as hell at my fellow human beings and express this to anyone within the sound of one of my rants. Some days I want to ignore what's happening in the world, stay in bed, and watch the Hallmark Channel. So I do. It isn't realistic or sustainable to never take a break from the relentlessness of injustice. The struggle is eternal, but our energies are limited.

Still, it's important to stay interested in the stories of people who are suffering under the current regime. To turn away from that suffering is tacit complicity with current systems of violence. It is getting used to harm. Once again, here we can learn from Desmond Tutu, who said, "When we look squarely at injustice and get involved, we actually feel less pain, not more, because we overcome the gnawing guilt and despair that festers under our numbness. We clean the wound—our own and others'—and it can finally heal."[8]

So how can you—how will you—lessen suffering where you are?

There are times when I feel overwhelmed about what to do, where to start. The problems seem so big and so intractable. In those times, I ask myself a set of questions that serve as guideposts and help to ground me:

1. What resources exist so I can better educate myself?
2. Who's already doing work around this injustice?
3. Do I have the capacity to offer concrete support and help to them?
4. How can I be constructive?

I shared these questions on Twitter a few years ago, and it is still my pinned tweet. I have heard from others that they find them helpful. You are not needed everywhere, but we are all needed somewhere. It's important to find your somewhere and plant yourself there.

There are other things you can do as you answer the question of how you will lessen suffering today. The first step is to refuse to accept that nothing can be done and that nothing will or can change. Don't be cynical. Sincerity is a virtue. I'm a fan of uncynical people who don't justify their inaction by suggesting that nothing will change.

If you are faltering at internalizing the fact that change is constant, find others to remind you. In fact, everything is changing all of the time. We must remember the teachings of visionary world builder Octavia Butler, who wrote in *Parable of the Sower*,

> All that you touch
> You Change.
> All that you Change
> Changes you.
> The only lasting truth
> Is Change.[9]

So, how do we make change happen? You, as an individual, are only a tiny pebble in a vast sea. We can personally make ripples, but it takes collective action to make waves. It may be unfashionable or too earnest to say, but the reality is that each of us bringing our pebbles to the lake, and throwing them in is what it takes to make change. I think the image of an endless line of us throwing our pebbles into the lake is beautiful: a necessary act taken together.

Of course, collective action is not the only ingredient to make transformative change. We also need sound strategy and resources.

And we need radical imagination. Radical imagination is essential to organizing and also important to me because the horizon that I am working toward is a world I have never seen: a world without policing, imprisonment, or surveillance. As my friend writer, artist, and scholar Eve Ewing says, "In order to create pathways toward that which we have never seen, we have to lead with imagination."[10]

All of the most important and impactful social transformations happened because people fought and struggled for things they had never seen.

My comrade and fellow organizer B Loewe posted something on his Facebook page at the end of 2021 that I found to be a useful reminder of what can happen when we combine collective action with radical imagination:

> As we prepare for more waves of bad news, I'm remembering that there is always a next right thing to do, that I am never alone in my despair, and that when we come together, we can create new worlds that are kinder and more of what we all deserve.
>
> After such a long year filled with so many different forms of loss, I'm remembering Organizing is always an option, and it works.[11]

We all have a role to play in building those new worlds. Determine what the next right step is for you. There is always something that is worth doing. Find your lane and push ahead. Make connections with others. Refuse to acquiesce to despair. Imagine your way forward. There are many ways that things can be different in the world, and we don't know how things will turn out, so we might as well fight like hell for the world we want to inhabit.

History teaches us that relatively small groups of people have been responsible for some of the most consequential societal changes. It's usually the minority of the minority that engages in struggle in any historical moment. This is reassuring because it means that we don't have to convince everyone in order to attain critical goals. It leaves room for surprise.

If you are reading this book, then you've been chosen to be a helper. You've been enlisted to take constructive action. As playwright Anna Deveare Smith advises, "Start now, every day, becoming, in your actions, your regular actions, what you would like to become in the bigger scheme of things."[12]

Though we can't stop all suffering, we can each work to lessen suffering for someone else. My attention is focused on looking for and trying to nurture the things that will lessen suffering. Every day I commit to bringing my imperfect and small actions to the pile. What are those concrete actions for you?

Finally, I wake up every single day and decide to practice hope. I do so because this is something that is singularly within my control to do. The social theorist Henry Giroux writes, "Hope expands the space of the possible and becomes a way of recognizing and naming the incomplete nature of the present."[13]

For me, hope is not a metaphor; it's a lived practice. It isn't a thing I possess. Rather, I have to remake it daily. I don't have hope, I do hope. It's an active process that I have to regularly commit to— hope not as an emotion but as a discipline. Hope for me is grounded in the reality that wondrous things happen alongside and parallel to the terrible. Every single day.

To paraphrase Rebecca Solnit, hope isn't a substitute for action; it is a basis for it.[14] In Islam, one of the Hadiths says, "The Messenger of Allah, peace and blessings be upon him, said, 'If the Resurrection were established upon one of you while he has in his hand a sapling, then let him plant it.'"

This, for me, is the embodiment of a hope practice. Even if the end times are upon us, we should still plant trees. This is disciplined hope. This is hope in the doing, hope as action.

How will you practice and cultivate hope today?

Movements Make Life

Harsha Walia

Reading *Let This Radicalize You* on a snowy winter day amid organizing support for migrants affected by the violence of an end-of-year deportation frenzy by Canada Border Services Agency was the balm my heart needed. Mariame frequently reminds us in moments of crisis, "Let this radicalize you rather than lead you to despair." So I tell myself, every deportation, every detention, every moment of despair creates the terrain for continued struggle and the possibility of future victories—a habitable world without borders and cages—if we do not allow immobilization to seep in.

Kelly and Mariame's book is a gem, every page bringing life to Howard Zinn's words,

> To be hopeful in bad times is not just foolishly romantic. It is based on the fact that human history is a history not only of cruelty, but also of compassion, sacrifice, courage, kindness.
>
> What we choose to emphasize in this complex history will determine our lives. If we see only the worst, it destroys our capacity to do something. If we remember those times and places—and there are so many—where people

233

have behaved magnificently, this gives us the energy to act, and at least the possibility of sending this spinning top of a world in a different direction.

And if we do act, in however small a way, we don't have to wait for some grand utopian future. The future is an infinite succession of presents, and to live *now* as we think human beings should live, in defiance of all that is bad around us, is itself a marvelous victory.[1]

Kelly and Mariame have been movement touchstones for many of us, generously modeling what it means to behave magnificently in service to transforming this world. They have been at the center of a dizzying number of crucial projects: leveraging social networks and fundraising resources, freeing people from the clutches of police and prisons, imparting movement lessons, making visible the often unglamorous parts of organizing such as administrative labor, doing political education and practicing mutual aid to grow our imaginations about other ways of living, and nurturing the conditions for organizers to learn and act. Their careful and caring labor enacting the vocabulary of abolition, as well as this book—itself a constellation of wisdom gleaned through their many coconspirators—are reminders that movements do not happen: *movements are made.* And in the spirit of Ella Baker, movements are not made through singular heroes; movements are made through our many hearts and hands.

This compelling, humbling, essential, and brilliant book by Kelly and Mariame distills three key points for me:

1. Organizing Is the Antidote to Despair

Community organizing requires us to move beyond our own circles to bring in and work alongside those who may not share our life experience or analysis. This is not a simple call for unity; rather, it is working despite and through difference. Artist and organizer Lila Watson famously declared, "If you have come here to help me, you are wasting your time. But if you have come because your liberation is bound up with mine, then let us work together." Or as Kelly and Mariame put it, "make connections, not comparisons." Organizing is deeply transformative: it subverts and transforms dominant systems of power, it transforms our imaginations in prefiguring a future beyond our present-day apocalyptic deathscape, it transforms our collective processes by nurturing relationality, and it transforms us as people as we realize our own capacities. Organizing thus not only changes the material and social conditions around us; it also changes *us* in the process.

Collective work also encourages abundant leadership. Abundant leadership is about sharing space and power, as opposed to capitalist competition over space and power. Instead of assuming that only some people are capable of being leaders, or adhering to the notion that no one should be a leader, valuing abundance shifts us toward a different framework: we are all leaders in different ways, and we can all become even more skilled leaders. This necessitates proactive steps to share skills and knowledge. Leadership comes from sustained practices that Kelly and Mariame's book makes visible: facilitating meetings, producing education materials, creating banners and agitprop, preparing meals, public speaking, organizing childcare—all vital skills that might be our strengths or new skills that we can sharpen. Sharing tasks and skills decentralizes knowledge, ensures a more sustainable division of labor, encourages learning, and strengthens interpersonal bonds as we work on projects together. We are all needed in the ecosystem of struggle.

2. Collective Liberation Necessitates Collective Care

While many of us have our own self-care rituals, few have collective-care and conflict-resolution skills. Frankly, it is often easier to be dangerous to the state systems that we confront than it is to be tender with each other. Working collectively to nurture care and healing within liberation work is not easy; it challenges us to bring voice to those unnamed hurts and complicated edges that stem from our deepest cracks and interpersonal dynamics that traverse often-contradictory layers of power and marginalization.

"To resist the erosion of empathy" that Kelly and Mariame warn about, it behooves us to build movements where we are emancipated rather than alienated or burned out, where we feel supported rather than abandoned as we move through our traumas, and where we generatively challenge each other's behaviors but learn to do so without hurling daggers or punishing one another. Fostering the spiritual, physical, and mental well-being needed to create community requires intentional space to discuss and practice—a deliberate learning of how to manifest and align ourselves with our abolitionist, decolonial, and anticapitalist visions (*plural*) for the world.

3. We Need Each Other

Interdependence and reciprocity are not optional. One of the contradictions of capitalism is that while we are dependent on intricate production processes for our basic needs, we are increasingly atomized and isolated from one another. The COVID pandemic has exposed how ingrained individualism is and how human worth is based on a racist, gendered, and ableist system of commodification and productivity. In the face of such cruel and callous disposability, it is a radical act to admit that we are made and undone by each other.

Connection is the antithesis of commodification. Those of us who experience an avalanche of violences and cannot rely on the state or market for relief know how much we need and depend on one another to survive and stay safe. Life-affirming communities can rarely be sustained based only on shared political analysis or critique; we need genuine, empathetic, and mutual social relations. Communing and kinship make movements *and make life*.

"We write the meaning of life as we live it," Kelly writes. Ruth Wilson Gilmore similarly tells us, "Abolition is presence, which means abolition is life in rehearsal, not a recitation of rules, much less a relentless lament."[2] The world-building teachings weaved throughout this book are a compass for a life in rehearsal. The rest is up to us, together.

Navigating Police Use
of Chemical Weapons

Given that this book discusses protest situations in which police deploy chemical weapons, we want to provide some basic information about how to navigate and respond to such onslaughts. The following information and advice is reprinted with permission from Vision Change Win's resource Get in Formation: A Community Safety Toolkit, *written by YaliniDream, Ejeris Dixon, Che Johnson-Long, Krystal Portalatin, and Ang Hadwin, with contributions by Lindsey Charles. The full tool kit can be found at https://www.visionchangewin.com/wp-content/uploads/2020/07/VCW-Safety-Toolkit-Final.pdf.*

Navigating Tear Gas, Pepper Spray, and Other RCAs

During Uprisings, it is common for police to use chemical weapons, also known as RCAs (Rebellion Containment Agents)* as a form of control and repression. The next section discusses some common forms of RCAs and how to address them should your team come into contact with any. It should be noted that in recent times, it can be difficult to predict when and how cops will use RCAs and we recommend that your team prepare for their potential use at any action during an uprising.

What Are RCAs?

We define RCAs as Rebellion Containment Agents, though they are referred to by the police as Riot Control Agents. They include tear gas, pepper spray, flash bangs, other chemical agents, and nerve agents.

Tear gases, counter-intuitively, are not actually gases, but solid particles dispersed through the air via aerosol. They are nerve agents that can contain various chemicals that specifically activate pain-sensing neurons. Pepper spray, also known as OC spray, is an oil-based derivative of capsaicin, the active ingredient in chili peppers.

For some people, the effects of RCAs are temporary. For others, the effects can be long-lasting and life-threatening.

Despite being used by law enforcement, border patrol agents, and correctional officers within US prisons, tear gas and other RCAs are chemical weapons outlawed for use during wartime.

Within the conditions of the COVID-19 pandemic, RCAs such as tear gas, pepper spray, and other chemical agents increase the spread of COVID-19 by causing people to cough and causing inflammation in the airways.

How to Respond to RCA Attacks

- Do not panic: Rapid breathing and increased heart rate can quicken the reaction and increase the pain of tear gas exposure.
- Protect your airways and lungs: If you do not have a respirator mask, protesters have used an acidified cloth to temporarily (meaning for a few minutes) mitigate the effects of chemical weapons. Carry a bandana or mask soaked with cider vinegar or lemon juice in a zip-top bag. As soon as there is indication that tear gas will be fired, cover your mouth with the soaked material. If you have no protection, cover your mouth and nose with a cloth or some clothing—but keep in mind the outside of your clothes might be contaminated with chemical irritants and/or infectious droplets. Hold your breath if possible. Moderate your breath, breathe slowly, avoid deep inhalations, and focus on longer

and stronger exhalations. Some people are able to breathe through the acidified cloth for several minutes, which can buy you some time to get to an area with no chemical exposure. While acidified cloth may temporarily mitigate the effects of RCAs, it will not filter or prevent against dioxins, cyanide, and some other chemicals found in tear gas.

- Move with clarity: Do not run before assessing which direction is the safest for you to move. Tear gas (also called CS gas) is a chemical weapon used to disperse crowds and cause chaos. If security is present, follow their directions. Running without clarity causes falls, collisions, and trampling.

- Assess direction: Tear gas is often discharged in the form of a grenade, fitted on the end of a gas gun and fired with a blank shotgun cartridge. When you hear the shot, try to identify the direction of the grenade and get out of its path. Assess the direction of the wind and move upwind so the chemical agent is blowing away from you.

- Do not crouch: Try getting to higher ground—most tear gases are heavier than air, so the highest concentrations tend to sit nearer to the ground. If the route is known ahead of time, it is helpful to identify areas of higher ground.

- Redirecting a canister: After the grenade explodes, it delivers a metal canister that emits the chemical agent(s). The canister will become very hot. If a canister lands near you, kick it away from you (assuming you are wearing sturdy footwear), and kick it away from other people. Do not pick up an unexploded canister, as it may cause serious injury. Only pick up a canister emitting chemical agents if you are wearing thick, heat-resistant gloves and safety goggles. If you are wearing heat-resistant gloves, you can pick up the canister and move it away from where protesters are gathered.

- Do not touch or rub your eyes or face: This will reactivate crystals and cause more irritation.

- Do not touch exposed clothing: Chemicals will infuse clothing for many months. Flapping outstretched arms and legs will help some CS gas to come off your clothing. Carefully shake out your hair. Any clothing that may have been contaminated should be discarded. Carry an extra set of clothes (loose, like sweats) so that clothes that were contaminated can be removed and discarded. If you must keep your clothes, wash them several times in cold water, separate from any other clothes. Run the empty washer a few times afterwards, as the chemicals can remain in the washer.

Chemical Exposure Aftercare

There are different kinds of tear gas and pepper spray, with different chemical properties, concentrations, and reactions. Some RCAs use a combination of chemicals. For example, Clearout is a brand of aerosol grenade containing chemicals that are in both tear gas and pepper spray.

Different kinds of chemical weapons require different treatments. For example, flushing eyes and skin with large amounts of water can help with decontamination after CS tear gas exposure. On the other hand, water can exacerbate the irritation caused by CR tear gas and some other types of chemical agents.

People react differently to various remedies, and as a result there's a range of sometimes conflicting information. You may have heard about using milk and diluted baby shampoo. Some people report that this helps, but studies show it is no better than water alone. Which remedy should you use? It can be difficult to know, so pay attention to each person's needs, responses, and reactions in the moment.

When possible, and if necessary, seek medical support after an exposure. Look for medic stations at protests and try to locate them ahead of time. The following are remedies, treatments, and tips that have been used in various movements to address RCA exposure. In addition to these guidelines, we recommend you talk to your medic team for their advice.

- Blow your nose, rinse your mouth, cough, and spit. Try not to swallow. When coughing, contain infectious droplets by coughing into a tissue, and move away from others.

If a tissue isn't available, cough into your elbow or the inside of your shirt to minimize transmission of COVID-19.

- Fan and blow onto eyes and face before rinsing or flushing eyes. Carry a battery-operated portable hand fan if possible. Carefully shake one's head and hair. Tear gases are composed of solid particles, many of which can be blown or shaken away when dry.
- Stretch out and wave limbs after RCA exposure, before rinsing or wiping skin.
- Use large amounts of water. Many of these chemical agents come in the form of crystals, which react with water. Using small amounts of water (such as a wet towel or shirt) immediately after exposure to CS gas is likely to reactivate these crystals and may prolong the effects. In response to a CS exposure, skin should be washed with soap and large amounts of water. Shower first in water that is as cold as possible (to keep pores closed), and then in warm water. Do not take a bath.
- Always irrigate from the inside corner of the eye towards the outside, with head tilted back and slightly towards the side being rinsed.
- Do not wear contacts if you are at risk of being exposed to chemical weapons. Contact lenses have been known to trap the chemicals against your eyes, which could damage the cornea. You must remove the lenses or get someone to remove them for you, with CLEAN, uncontaminated fingers. Destroy the lenses after exposure.
- When using an inhaler after an exposure, do not contaminate the inhaler. Carry an inhaler in a zip-top plastic bag to minimize possible contamination, and use it with a clean uncontaminated hand.

Additional Solutions and RCA Remedies

Antacid solution: Protesters commonly recommend solutions of 50 percent water and 50 percent aluminum hydroxide or magnesium hydroxide based antacids, such as Maalox, for immediate relief from chemical exposure. People have used it to rinse their eyes, their skin, their mouths. The solution must be spit out after rinsing one's mouth.

Saline: Other people have found it very helpful to flush their eyes with large amounts of saline.

Canola oil: Some protesters recommend using canola oil and a cloth to vigorously wipe chemical agents off of exposed skin. After wiping with canola oil, wipe skin off again with rubbing alcohol.

Milk and cola: Milk and cola is a remedy that some protesters have used to rinse eyes and soothe skin. However, milk can spoil when unrefrigerated. Both milk and cola can contain sugar and preservatives and can be irritants for some people's eyes and skin.

APPENDIX B

Attorney's Note

Given that this book includes discussion of the police raid on the Chicago Freedom School, we want to include a note from a trusted attorney about what organizers should know and do in a similar situation. Our thanks to Joey Mogul for crafting the following advice.

What to Do if the Police Come to Your Not-for-Profit or Organizing Space

- You do not have to let police/agents into your space unless they produce a search warrant.
  - A search warrant is a written court order that allows the police to conduct a specified search.
  - A valid search warrant should specify in detail the places to be searched and the things to be taken away.
- Ask police/agents to slide the search warrant under the door, or step outside and close the door behind you to read the search warrant.
- Do not consent to their searching your space. State that "I do not consent" to search of the space or person. This is to warn them about searching areas outside those specified in the search warrant.
- Ask if you are allowed to watch the search. If so, take notes and include the names, badge numbers, and departments

243

of the police/agents. Describe where they searched, what
they photographed, and all items they seized.

- If police/agents ask you to give them anything, look to
see if the item is listed in the warrant. If it is not, do not
consent to their taking it.
- Everyone, regardless of citizenship, has a right to remain
silent and not answer any questions. Anything you say
may later be used against you. State that you do not want
to speak with them and you want to speak with a lawyer.
- If the agents have an arrest warrant, they may perform
only a cursory visual search of your space to find the person in the named warrant.
- If police/agents do not have a search warrant, they should
not come in.
- If you physically resist or physically obstruct an officer (even if
they do not have a warrant), you can be charged with a crime.
- You have the right to verbally argue with police/agents.
- In many states, you are allowed to record police/agents
visually and audibly.
- Lying to police/agents can be a crime.
- If you are arrested, it may be best to give your name, date
of birth, and address, otherwise it will delay the length of
your detention.
- Each state is different. Best to look up Know Your Rights
materials in your location.
- Here are some resources:
  - Law for Black Lives: http://www.law4blacklives.org/
  tool-kits-tip-sheets
  - National Lawyers Guild: https://www.nlg.org/know-
  your-rights

While these are your rights, they mean little outside courts of
law. A person's race, gender, gender identity, disability, sexual orientation, class, and outward political affiliation will affect how the officers treat you in any given encounter, and Black and brown people
are routinely treated with violence, hostility, and disrespect.

Acknowledgments

This book sprang out of a much smaller idea. We wanted to create a pamphlet for young organizers that would include various lessons and tips we've learned along the way. From our friends who reviewed the first draft of that pamphlet in 2018 to the people we interviewed over the last few years, many people have helped coax this book into being. You will see some of their names in these pages. People like Aly Wane, Ruth Wilson Gilmore, Barbara Ransby, Lisa Fithian, Page May, Jenni Martinez-Lorenzo, Ejeris Dixon, Harsha Walia, Sharon Lungo, Marissa Fenley, Dan Orsini, Lea Kayali, Shane Burley, Halle Quezada, Tony Alvarado-Rivera, Juliana Pino, Asha AE, Morning Star Gali, Carlos Saavedra, Freddy Martinez, and Anoa Changa helped give this book life. We not only had the honor of sharing their stories and insights with you, but we also had the good fortune to learn from these people during some dark and difficult times. We are grateful for those lessons and for their time. We are also grateful to our friends who shared stories, wisdom, and insights that are not directly quoted in this book but that helped shape its creation.

We are grateful to friends like Adam Heenan, who made time to talk; to Micah Herskind, for his help creating the book's glossary; to Joey Mogul, for authoring our attorney's note; to Jacqui Shine, for early valuable feedback; and to Carolyn Chernoff, for working on the footnotes. We would also like to thank Vision Change Win for allowing us to include an excerpt from *Get in Formation: A Community Safety Toolkit* as an appendix so that our readers will have instructions about how to treat exposure to pepper spray and tear gas. We are also grateful to Lifted Voices and Project NIA for supporting the creation of this book.

We are grateful to our loved ones, including Kelly's partner Charlie, and to our friends Delia Galindo, Megan Groves, and Bresha Meadows for their support, and also to Mariame's family, friends, and co-conspirators. We are deeply appreciative of Maya Schenwar, our dear friend and co-struggler, whose editing helped this book find its form. We are also grateful to Michael Trudeau for copyediting this book.

We would also like to thank *Truthout* for allowing us to reprint material from Kelly's *Movement Memos* podcast and for the publication's support of this book. Kelly's colleagues Anton Woronczuk, Melody Ng, Jocelyn Martinez-Rosales, Alana Yu-lan Price, Samantha Borek, Ayo Walker, and Ziggy West Jeffery all helped to make this book possible.

Mariame has often noted that everything worthwhile is done with others, and the creation of this book was no exception. To everyone else who played a role in making this book possible—as it would be impossible to list everyone whose work helped usher this project into being—we thank you for your love, for your labor, and for all that you do to create more justice and some peace.

Glossary

Ableism: A system, according to Talila "TL" Lewis, that assigns "value on people's bodies and minds based on societally constructed ideas of normality, intelligence, excellence, desirability, and productivity. These constructed ideas are deeply rooted in eugenics, anti-Blackness, misogyny, colonialism, imperialism, and capitalism. This systemic oppression leads to people and society determining who is valuable and worthy based on a person's language, appearance, religion, and/or their ability to satisfactorily re/produce, excel and 'behave.'"[1] See, for example, *Decarcerating Disability: Deinstitutionalization and Prison Abolition* (Liat Ben-Moshe, 2020).

Abolition: A broad-ranging movement to both eradicate the prison-industrial complex and its foundations of racial capitalism, settler colonialism, and cis-hetero-patriarchy and to create new systems in its place that focus on meeting people's needs, preventing and transforming harm, and building true community safety and well-being. See, for example, *No More Police: A Case for Abolition* (Mariame Kaba and Andrea Ritchie, 2022) and *Becoming Abolitionists: Police, Protests, and the Pursuit of Freedom* (Derecka Purnell, 2021).

Activism: The many ways that people fight for justice, including through advocacy, research, canvassing, fundraising, attending marches or meetings regularly, and using other skills in service of a cause or campaign.

Capital: Money that is used to accumulate more money. Those with capital have the power to accumulate more capital due to the social relations under capitalism in which workers are compelled to labor and produce value for the capitalists.

Capitalism: An economic system under which private actors control and own the means of production (tools and materials necessary for production such as land, factories, office buildings, machinery, IT infrastructure, and so on) and pay workers a wage while keeping the surplus value of workers' labor (profit). Capitalism relies on the exploitation of the working class to maintain concentrated power and profit for a small group. See, for example, *A People's Guide to Capitalism: An Introduction to Marxist Economics* (Hadas Thier, 2020).

Capitalist class: A class of people made up of those who control the means of production, have political power, dictate the terms of others' working conditions, or own capital that can be invested in production.

Colonialism: The practice of violently taking and maintaining political, physical, and social control of another country or territory and either expelling or subjugating the prior inhabitants in order to extract resources and concentrate power. See, for example, *The Wretched of the Earth* (Frantz Fanon, 1961).

Direct action: Tactics often used in social movements such as protests, civil disobedience, sit-ins, blockades, strikes, walkouts, dearrests, banner drops, and sabotage that are meant to disrupt the system and achieve a political goal outside of the formal channels of civic engagement. Direct action tactics are used for a wide range of purposes, such as to prevent evictions, defend the environment, highlight systemic contradictions, bring awareness to a problem, stop harmful proposals, and express community outrage. See, for example, *Shut It Down: Stories from a Fierce, Loving Resistance* (Lisa Fithian, 2019).

Healing justice: A framework, according to healer and organizer Cara Page, that "identifies how we can holistically respond to and intervene on generational trauma and violence and to bring collective practices that can impact and transform the consequences of oppression on our bodies, hearts, and minds. Through this framework we continue to build political and philosophical convergences of healing inside of liberation movements and organizations." See, for example, *Care Work: Dreaming Disability Justice* (Leah Lakshmi Piepzna-Samarasinha, 2018) and *Healing Justice Lineages: Dreaming at the Crossroads of Liberation, Collective Care, and Safety* (Cara Page and Erica Woodland, 2023).[2]

Migrant justice: A movement for dignity, freedom, housing, self-determination, medical care, and freedom of movement for migrant communities and workers. Like all movements, the migrant justice movement has varying aims, but it generally works against deportations, immigrant detention, and the criminalization of migrants and in favor of open borders or a world without borders. See, for example, *Border and Rule: Global Migration, Capitalism, and the Rise of Racist Nationalism* (Harsha Walia, 2021).

Mutual aid: Collective and community-based practices and efforts to meet people's needs, independent of state systems and other hierarchical, oppressive arrangements. Mutual aid is grounded in reciprocity and solidarity rather than charity, and builds shared understandings of the systemic failures that make community care for survival necessary. Mutual aid is a form of political participation that allows us to build relationships and formations that make the conditions we face more survivable and strengthen our ability to take collective action. See, for example, *Mutual Aid: Building Solidarity between This Crisis (and the Next)* (Dean Spade, 2020).

Neoliberalism: A political-economic dynamic generally beginning in the 1970s and 1980s that is characterized by prioritization of "free"-market capitalism, deregulation, hyper-individualism, government austerity, and cuts to social welfare spending, manufactured scarcity, and upward redistribution of resources. See, for example, *Neoliberalism's Demons: On the Political Theology of Late Capital* (Adam Kotsko, 2018).

Nonreformist reforms: Reforms that get at the root of a problem and don't maintain the status quo. The idea of nonreformist reforms has been taken up by prison-industrial complex (PIC) abolitionists and include changes to the criminal legal system that remove power, authority, equipment, legitimacy, and resources from the PIC, reducing the system's capacity for violence and social control. Nonreformist reform is a common framework in PIC abolition movements, dedicated to the principle that we should not support reforms that we will later have to dismantle (such as building "mental health" jails or supporting electronic monitoring and other forms of community control). See, for example, *Prison by Any Other Name: The Harmful Consequences of Popular Reforms* (Maya Schenwar and Victoria Law, 2020).

Organizing: The process of building collective power as a group and using this power to create positive change in people's lives and shift existing power relations. Organizing involves building people power, constantly bringing new people into the struggle, challenging systemic injustice and inequity, and giving people who are directly impacted by injustice a sense of their own power and a way to exercise it.

Prison-industrial complex (PIC): The vast web of government and private interests that create, sustain, and reproduce the criminal punishment system. According to the organization Critical Resistance, the PIC is a term used "to describe the overlapping interests of government and industry that use surveillance, policing, and imprisonment as solutions to economic, social, and political problems."[3] See, for example, *Abolition Now! Ten Years of Strategy and Struggle against the Prison Industrial Complex* (CR10 Publications Collective, 2008).

Safety: The ability, according to the organization API Chaya, "to bring, be, and move through the world as your full self." See, for example, *Beyond Survival: Strategies and Stories from the Transformative Justice Movement* (ed. Leah Lakshmi Piepzna-Samarasinha and Ejeris Dixon, 2020).

Working class: A class of people made up of anyone who must sell their labor in order to survive and has no access to the means of production themselves.

NOTES

Foreword: Radicalization Is Vital

1. Angela Y. Davis, "Let Us All Rise Together: Radical Perspectives on Empowerment for Afro-American Women," in *Women, Culture, and Politics* (New York: Random House, 1990), 14.

2. Kelly Hayes, "On the Cusp of Change," *Transformative Spaces,* December 18, 2014, https://transformativespaces.org/2014/12/18/on-the-cusp-of-change.

3. *Oxford English Dictionary,* 3rd. ed., s.v. "Radical," https://www.oed.com/viewdictionaryentry/Entry/157251.

4. Joanna Macy, "Entering the Bardo," *Emergence Magazine,* July 20, 2020, https://emergencemagazine.org/op_ed/entering-the-bardo.

Introduction: Remaking the World

1. Krista Franklin, "Call," in *Too Much Midnight* (Chicago: Haymarket Books, 2020), 89.

2. Robin D. G. Kelley, *Freedom Dreams: The Black Radical Imagination* (Boston: Beacon Press, 2003), 9–10.

3. Diane di Prima, "Rant," in *Pieces of a Song: Selected Poems* (San Francisco: City Lights, 1990).

4. Di Prima, "Rant."

5. Di Prima, "Rant."

6. Di Prima, "Rant."

7. Di Prima, "Rant."

8. Di Prima, "Rant."

9. Di Prima, "Rant."

Introduction: We Can Only Survive Together

1. Hazel Henderson, *The Politics of the Solar Age: Alternatives to Economics* (Garden City, NY: Anchor Press/Doubleday, 1981), 411.
2. See Kelly's conclusion to read more about Bresha Meadows's story.
3. Mary-Wynne Ashford, "Staying the Course," in *The Impossible Will Take a Little While: A Citizen's Guide to Hope in a Time of Fear*, ed. Paul Rogat Loeb (New York: Basic Books, 2004), 385.

Chapter 1: Beyond Alarm, toward Action

1. Paulo Freire, *Pedagogy of the Oppressed* (New York: Herder and Herder, 1970), 34.
2. Kelly Hayes, "Chicago Police Torture: Explained," *Appeal*, December 5, 2019, https://theappeal.org/the-lab/explainers/chicago-police-torture-explained.
3. Chris Hayes (@chrislhayes), "Almost without exception. every single time we've covered it's been a palpable ratings killer. so the incentives are not great," Twitter, July 24, 2018, 10:08 a.m., https://twitter.com/chrislhayes/status/1021759145425489920.
4. Organized abandonment refers to the dismantling of and divestment from private, capitalist structures and public structures that communities depend on, such as schools, public health-care systems, and safe infrastructure, in favor of heavy investments in law enforcement, which is deployed as the lone remedy for all problems that arise from the deficits disinvestment creates. See Chenjerai Kumanyika, "Ruth Wilson Gilmore Makes the Case for Abolition," *Intercept*, June 10, 2020, https://theintercept.com/2020/06/10/ruth-wilson-gilmore-makes-the-case-for-abolition.
5. Doyle Canning and Patrick Reinsborough, *Re:Imagining Change: How to Use Story-Based Strategy to Win Campaigns, Build Movements, and Change the World* (Oakland, CA: PM Press, 2010), 20–21.
6. The preceding quotations and this statement and are from Taylor, *The Psychology of Pandemics* (Cambridge, UK: Cambridge Scholars, 2019), 53, 53, 54, and 88, respectively.
7. Taylor, *Psychology of Pandemics*, 30.
8. Big Door Brigade, "What Is 'Mutual Aid'?" n.d., https://bigdoorbrigade.com/what-is-mutual-aid.
9. Nita Lelyveld, "How Sewing Masks for the Vulnerable Stitched

Together an Empowering Facebook Community," *LA Times*, April 3, 2021, https://www.latimes.com/california/story/2021-04-03/facebook-group-united-sewing-covid-masks-vulnerable.

10. Dahr Jamail, "Learning to See in the Dark amid Catastrophe: An Interview with Deep Ecologist Joanna Macy," *Truthout*, February 13, 2017, https://truthout.org/articles/learning-to-see-in-the-dark-amid-catastrophe-an-interview-with-deep-ecologist-joanna-macy.

11. Kelly Hayes, "Dean Spade Is Asking Activists, How Much Bolder Could You Be?" *Truthout*, March 17, 2022, https://truthout.org/audio/dean-spade-is-asking-activists-how-much-bolder-could-you-be.

12. Prashanth U. Nyer and Mahesh Gopinath, "The Effect of Public Commitment on Resistance to Persuasion: Preliminary Findings," in *LA—Latin American Advances in Consumer Research*, vol. 1, ed. Silvia Gonzalez and David Luna (Duluth, MN: Association for Consumer Research, 2006), 52–53.

13. Radha Agarwal, *Belong: Find Your People, Create Community, and Live a More Connected Life* (New York: Workman Publishing, 2018), 17.

Chapter 2: Refusing to Abandon

1. Kelly Hayes, "People in Prison Organize Collectively for Survival. We All Need to Learn How," *Truthout*, December 9, 2021, https://truthout.org/audio/people-in-prison-organize-collectively-for-survival-we-all-need-to-learn-how.

2. Kelly Hayes, "Incarceration Is Killing Us," *Truthout*, April 27, 2020, https://truthout.org/audio/incarceration-is-killing-us.

3. Laura Wernick, John Krinsky, and Paul Getsos, *WEP: Work Experience Program . . . New York City's Public Sector Sweat Shop Economy* (New York: Community Voices Heard), August 2000.

4. Ayni Institute: ayni.institute/about.

5. Dahr Jamail, "Hurricane Harvey Shows What Climate Disruption–Amplified Flooding Can Do," *Truthout*, August 29, 2017, https://truthout.org/articles/hurricane-harvey-shows-what-climate-disruption-amplified-flooding-can-do.

6. Jamail, "Hurricane Harvey."

7. Jamail, "Hurricane Harvey."

8. Chris Begley, "We're Preparing for the Wrong Apocalypse," *Men's Journal*, June/July 2022, https://www.mensjournal.com/entertain-

ment/were-preparing-for-the-wrong-apocalypse-says-chris-begley.

9. Chris Begley, *The Next Apocalypse: The Art and Science of Surviv-al* (New York: Basic Books, 2021), 202.

10. Begley, *Next Apocalypse*, 206.

11. *Next Apocalypse*, 220.

12. *Next Apocalypse*, 220.

13. *Next Apocalypse*, 224.

Chapter 3: Care Is Fundamental

1. Jorge Díaz Ortiz, "Organizing Mutual Solidarity Projects as an Act of Resistance in Puerto Rico," *A Blade of Grass* 4 ("Governance Re-imagined," 2020), https://abladeofgrass.org/articles/organizing-mu-tual-solidarity-projects-act-resistance-puerto-rico.

2. According to Cara Page, one of the architects of the healing justice framework, "Healing Justice is a framework that identifies how we can holistically respond to and intervene on intergenerational trauma and violence, and to bring collective practices that can impact and transform the consequences of oppression on our collective bodies, hearts and minds." "Reflections from Detroit: Transforming Wellness and Whole-ness," *INCITE!*, August 5, 2010, https://incite-national.org/2010/08/05/reflections-from-detroit-transforming-wellness-wholeness.

3. Joel Rose, "A 'War' for Medical Supplies: States Say FEMA Wins by Poaching Orders," *All Things Considered*, NPR, April 15, 2020, https://www.npr.org/2020/04/15/835308133/governors-say-fe-ma-is-outbidding-redirecting-or-poaching-their-medical-supply-or.

4. Kelly Hayes, "How to Fight Fascism While Surviving a Plague," *Truthout*, March 30, 2020, https://truthout.org/audio/how-to-fight-fascism-while-surviving-a-plague.

5. Mallory Simon, "Over 1,000 Health Professionals Sign a Letter Saying, Don't Shut Down Protests Using Coronavirus Con-cerns as an Excuse," CNN.com, June 5, 2020, https://www.cnn.com/2020/06/05/health/health-care-open-letter-protests-coronavi-rus-trnd/index.html.

6. Dhaval M. Dave et al., "Black Lives Matter Protests, Social Dis-tancing, and COVID-19," IZA Discussion Paper Series, no. 13388, IZA—Institute of Labor Economics (June 2020): abstract, 2, https://docs.iza.org/dp13388.pdf.

7. For an in-depth discussion of how "rioting" relates to social move-

ments, see chapter 6, "'Violence' in Social Movements."

8. Cops out CPS is a campaign to get police out of Chicago Public Schools. Defund CPD is a campaign aimed at defunding the Chicago Police Department.

9. María Inés Zamudio, "City Drops Cease-and-Desist Order against Chicago Freedom School for Feeding Protestors," WBEZ Chicago, July 3, 2020, https://www.wbez.org/stories/cease-and-desist-order-dropped-against-chicago-freedom-school/87e68cf9-94d5-44a2-81eb-23d7f0e451f3.

10. PDX Community Jail Support (@PDXJail_Support), "Hello, we are back up and running! But also very broke," Twitter, May 9, 2022, 6:57 p.m., https://twitter.com/PDXJail_Support/status/1523799381471731712?s=20&t=RJQuRq22jI_MB1qKH-OonQ.

11. *Global Trends 2040: A More Contested World* (National Intelligence Council, March 2021), https://www.dni.gov/files/ODNI/documents/assessments/GlobalTrends_2040.pdf.

12. *Global Trends 2040.*

13. *Global Trends 2040.*

14. *Global Trends 2040.*

Chapter 4: Think Like a Geographer

1. Kelly Hayes, "Ruth Wilson Gilmore on Abolition, the Climate Crisis, and What Must Be Done," *Truthout*, April 14, 2022, https://truthout.org/audio/ruth-wilson-gilmore-on-abolition-the-climate-crisis-and-what-must-be-done.

2. Hayes, "Ruth Wilson Gilmore."

3. Jesse Hagopian, "A People's History of the Chicago Teachers Union," *International Socialist Review* 86 (November 2012), https://isreview.org/issue/86/peoples-history-chicago-teachers-union/index.html.

4. Luis Feliz Leon, "Amazon Workers on Staten Island Clinch a Historic Victory," *Labor Notes*, April 1, 2022, https://labornotes.org/2022/04/amazon-workers-staten-island-clinch-historic-victory.

5. Ian Alexander, "Study Groups and Moving Together: An Interview with Stephen Wilson," *AbolitionistStudy*, February 3, 2021, https://abolitioniststudy.wordpress.com/2021/02/03/study-groups-moving-together-an-interview-with-stephen-wilson.

6. Rustbelt Abolition Radio, "Abolitionist Study with Stevie Wilson," November 20, 2019, https://rustbeltradio.org/2019/11/20/ep33.

7. "Abolitionist Study with Stevie Wilson."

8. Jon Schwarz, "The Origin of Student Debt," *Intercept*, August 15, 2022, https://theintercept.com/2022/08/25/student-loans-debt-reagan.

9. Diane di Prima, "Rant," in *Pieces of a Song: Selected Poems* (San Francisco: City Lights Books, 1990).

10. Kelly Hayes, "Abolitionists Are Fighting against the Surveillance State in Their Neighborhoods," *Truthout*, December 2, 2021, https://truthout.org/audio/abolitionists-are-fighting-against-the-surveillance-state-in-their-neighborhoods.

Chapter 5: Rejecting Cynicism and Building Broader Movements

1. Eitan Hersh, "College-Educated Voters Are Ruining American Politics," *Atlantic*, January 20, 2020, https://www.theatlantic.com/ideas/archive/2020/01/political-hobbyists-are-ruining-politics/605212.

2. Dorothy Roberts, *Torn Apart: How the Child Welfare System Destroys Black Families—and How Abolition Can Build a Safer World* (New York: Basic Books, 2022), 48.

3. Staci K. Haines, *The Politics of Trauma: Somatics, Healing, and Social Justice* (Berkeley, CA: North Atlantic Books, 2019), 75, 102, 108, 112.

Chapter 6: "Violence" in Social Movements

1. Olúfẹ́mi O. Táíwò, *Elite Capture: How the Powerful Took Over Identity Politics (and Everything Else)* (Chicago: Haymarket Books, 2022), 5.

2. Táíwò, *Elite Capture*, 5.

3. Liza H. Gold, "Domestic Violence, Firearms, and Mass Shootings," *Journal of the American Academy of Psychiatry and Law* 48, no. 1 (February 2020): abstract, https://jaapl.org/content/jaapl/early/2020/02/05/JAAPL.003929-20.full.pdf.

4. See, for example, https://www.usatoday.com/story/news/factcheck/2020/10/17/fact-check-trump-quote-very-fine-people-charlottesville/5943239002.

5. Grace Hauck, "Cars Have Hit Demonstrators 104 Times since George Floyd Protests Began," *USA Today*, July 9, 2020, https://www.usatoday.com/story/news/nation/2020/07/08/vehicle-ramming-attacks-66-us-since-may-27/5397700002/.

6. US Protest Law Tracker, International Center for Not-for-Profit Law, https://www.icnl.org/usprotestlawtracker/?location=&status=&is-

sue=&date=custom&date_from=2021-01-20&date_to=2022-01-20.

7. Kelly Hayes, "Ruth Wilson Gilmore on Abolition, the Climate Crisis, and What Must Be Done," *Truthout*, April 14, 2022, https://truthout.org/audio/ruth-wilson-gilmore-on-abolition-the-climate-crisis-and-what-must-be-done.

8. Kelly Hayes, "A New Wave of Jim Crow Laws Is Here. Here's What You Need to Know," *Truthout*, May 5, 2021, https://truthout.org/audio/a-new-wave-of-jim-crow-laws-is-here-heres-what-you-need-to-know.

9. Dara Kam, "Judge Clears Way for Challenge to Florida Protest Law," WLRN, August 11, 2021, https://www.wlrn.org/news/2021-08-11/judge-clears-way-for-challenge-to-florida-protest-law.

10. Barbara Ransby, "Mass Protests Led to Chauvin's Conviction. Now They're Being Criminalized," *Truthout*, April 21, 2021, https://truthout.org/articles/mass-protests-led-to-chauvins-conviction-now-theyre-being-criminalized.

11. Kaylana Mueller-Hsia, "Anti-Protest Laws Threaten Indigenous and Climate Movements," Brennan Center for Justice, March 17, 2021, https://www.brennancenter.org/our-work/analysis-opinion/anti-protest-laws-threaten-indigenous-and-climate-movements.

12. Philip Joens, "Iowa Climate Activist Sentenced to Eight Years in Federal Prison for Dakota Access Pipeline Sabotage," *Des Moines Register*, June 30, 2021, https://www.desmoinesregister.com/story/news/crime-and-courts/2021/06/30/iowa-activist-jessica-reznicek-sentenced-dakota-access-pipeline-sabotage-catholic-workers/7808907002.

13. Kelly Hayes, "Line 3 Resisters Light the Way in a Battle for Life on Earth," *Truthout*, September 9, 2021, https://truthout.org/articles/line-3-resisters-light-the-way-in-a-battle-for-life-on-earth.

14. "Water Protectors Arrested Resisting Line 3 Pipeline Call on State Officials to 'Drop the Charges,'" press release, November 11, 2021, https://www.stopline3.org/drop-the-charges.

15. Ruth Wilson Gilmore, *Abolition Geography: Essays Towards Liberation* (London: Verso, 2022), 474.

16. Kelly Hayes, "Enough Colonial Pageantry. Let's Rally behind Criminalized Water Protectors," *Truthout*, November 25, 2021, https://truthout.org/audio/enough-colonial-pageantry-lets-rally-behind-criminalized-water-protectors.

17. Stop Cop City website, https://stopcop.city.

18. Evan Bush and Denise Chow, "Environmental Protests Have a Long

History in the U.S. Police Had Never Killed an Activist—Until Now." CBS News, February 5, 2023, https://www.nbcnews.com/science/environment/environmental-protests-long-history-us-police-never-killed-activist-no-rcna68255.

19. BBC News, "What Is the Police and Crime Bill and How Will It Change Protests?" April 28, 2022, https://www.bbc.com/news/uk-56400751.

20. CBC Radio, "Captain Charged after Saving Migrants in Mediterranean Says People Are Still Drowning," March 5, 2021, https://www.cbc.ca/radio/asithappens/as-it-happens-friday-edition-1.5938509/captain-charged-after-saving-migrants-in-mediterranean-says-people-are-still-drowning-1.5938557.

21. Harsha Walia, *Border and Rule* (Chicago: Haymarket Books, 2021), 94.

22. Pia Klemp, "The City of Paris Is Awarding Pia Klemp the Medaille Grand Vermeil," Facebook, August 20, 2019, available at https://web.archive.org/web/20191005000346/https://www.facebook.com/pia.klemp/posts/10156318059491611; see also Sasha Ingber and Vanessa Romo, "Captain Who Rescued Migrants at Sea Refuses Paris Medal, Calling It Hypocritical," NPR, August 21, 2019, https://www.npr.org/2019/08/21/753107888/captain-who-rescued-migrants-at-sea-refuses-paris-medal-calling-it-hypocritical.

23. "Israel Convicts Palestinian Poet for Incitement to Violence," *Middle East Monitor,* May 4, 2018, https://www.middleeastmonitor.com/20180504-israel-convicts-palestinian-poet-for-incitement-to-violence.

24. Israel Shahak, "Banning the 'Terrible' White, Black, Green, and Red," *Christian Science Monitor,* March 3, 1981, https://www.csmonitor.com/1981/0303/030324.html.

25. Kelly Hayes, "What the Mainstream Media Never Told You about Palestine," *Truthout,* May 20, 2021, https://truthout.org/audio/what-the-mainstream-media-never-told-you-about-palestine.

26. "What Is BDS?" Palestinian BDS National Committee website, https://bdsmovement.net.

Chapter 7: Don't Pedestal Organizers

1. Charles M. Payne, *I've Got the Light of Freedom: The Organizing Tradition and the Mississippi Freedom Struggle* (Berkeley: University of California Press, 2007), 440.

2. Harsha Walia (@HarshaWalia), "I wasn't dismissed; I did resign on my own terms. But through the days, my leadership was undermined, my hiring was questioned, and there was no consideration for my safety. The board leadership acknowledged this all 'served to push her out in any event,'" Twitter, July 26, 2021, 12:28 a.m., https://twitter.com/HarshaWalia/status/1419514942164668420?s=20&t=xUBk7kwdPMJcda-1P3cxoQ.

3. UBCIC (@UBCIC), "UBCIC stands in strong solidarity with @HarshaWalia in condemning the brutally gruesome genocide of residential 'school' system by Canada and Church while crown stole FN land. She is a highly respected and valued ally; we are grateful for her ongoing support and leadership @bccla," Twitter, July 4, 2021, 7:16 p.m., https://twitter.com/UBCIC/status/1411826236364529674.

4. Harsha Walia (@HarshaWalia), "But everyone's support means so very much—a reminder that struggle, kinship and grounded relationships is home. That when oppressive power structures come for you, there are so many who show up with generosity and ferocity and reciprocity to co-create resistance and care," Twitter, July 26, 2021, 12:28 a.m., https://twitter.com/HarshaWalia/status/1419514959461949447?s=20&t=xUBk7kwdPMJcda-1P3cxoQ.

5. Electronic Frontier Foundation, "Surveillance Self-Defense: Tips, Tools and How-Tos for Safer Online Communications," https://ssd.eff.org/en.

6. Robert Elliott Smith, "My Social Media Feeds Look Different from Yours and It's Driving Political Polarization," *USA Today*, September 2, 2019, https://www.usatoday.com/story/opinion/voices/2019/09/02/social-media-election-bias-algorithms-diversity-column/2121233001.

7. Smith, "Social Media Feeds."

8. Brandy Zadrozny, "'Carol's Journey': What Facebook Knew about How It Radicalized Users," October 22, 2021, https://www.nbcnews.com/tech/tech-news/facebook-knew-radicalized-users-rcna3581.

9. Shoshana Zuboff, *The Age of Surveillance Capitalism: The Fight for a Human Future at the New Frontier of Power* (New York: Hachette, 2019).

10. Jeff Horwitz and Deepa Seetharaman, "Facebook Executives Shut Down Efforts to Make the Site Less Divisive," *Wall Street Journal*, May 26, 2020, https://www.wsj.com/articles/facebook-knows-it-encourages-division-top-executives-nixed-solutions-11590507499.

Chapter 8: Hope and Grief Can Coexist

1. Katie Farris, "Why Write Love Poetry in a Burning World," in *A Net to Catch My Body in Its Weaving* (Beloit, WI: Beloit Poetry Journal, 2021).

2. *Let This Radicalize You: A COVID Memorial Mixtape*, Transformative Spaces, October 7, 2020, https://transformativespaces. org/2020/10/07/let-this-radicalize-you-a-covid-memorial-mixtape.

3. Valerie Masson-Delmotte et al., ed., "Summary for Policymakers," in IPCC, 2021, *Climate Change 2021: The Physical Science Basis; Contribution of Working Group I to the Sixth Assessment Report of the Intergovernmental Panel on Climate Change* (Cambridge, UK, and New York: Cambridge University Press, 2021), 3–32, doi:10.1017/9781009157896.001.

4. Cindy Milstein, ed., *Rebellious Mourning: The Collective Work of Grief* (Chico, CA: AK Press, 2017), 4.

5. Kelly Hayes, "Indigenous Abolitionists Are Organizing for Healing and Survival," *Truthout*, April 28, 2022, https://truthout.org/audio/ indigenous-abolitionists-are-organizing-for-healing-and-survival.

6. Audre Lorde, *The Cancer Journals* (San Francisco: Aunt Lute, 1980).

7. Audre Lorde, *The Cancer Journals* (New York: Penguin, 2020), 8.

8. "With Chicago's Little Village Hardest Hit by COVID-19, Residents Are Urged to Stay Home," CBS News Chicago, May 5, 2020, https://www.cbsnews.com/chicago/news/with-chicagos-little-village-hardest-hit-by-covid-19-residents-are-urged-to-stay-home.

9. For case rates, see Feliciano Ocegueda and Brenda Santoyo, *Little Village Economic and Public Health Analysis*, Little Village Environmental Justice Organization, January 2020, http://www. lvejo.org/wp-content/uploads/2022/04/LV-Report-FINAL.pdf. For death rates, see Yukare Nakayama, "Little Village Woman Shares How COVID-19 Deaths Have Impacted Her Life, as Well as Her Community," WLS-TV, February 24, 2021, https://abc7chicago. com/chicago-covid-deaths-little-village-vaccine/10365390.

10. Timothy Williams and Danielle Ivory, "Chicago's Jail Is Top U.S. Hot Spot as Virus Spreads behind Bars," *New York Times*, April 8, 2020, https://www.nytimes.com/2020/04/08/us/coronavirus-cook-county-jail-chicago.html.

11. Eric Reinhart and Daniel L. Chen, "Incarceration and Its Disseminations: COVID-19 Pandemic Lessons from Chicago's Cook Coun-

ty Jail," *Health Affairs* 39, no. 8 (August 2020): 1412–18, https://www.healthaffairs.org/doi/pdf/10.1377/hlthaff.2020.00652.

12. Andres Malm, "The Walls of the Tank: On Palestinian Resistance," *Salvage Zone*, May 1, 2017, https://salvage.zone/the-walls-of-the-tank-on-palestinian-resistance.

13. Kelly Hayes, "What the Mainstream Media Never Told You about Palestine," *Truthout*, May 20, 2021, https://truthout.org/audio/what-the-mainstream-media-never-told-you-about-palestine.

14. Linda Ereikat, "Carrying Palestine's Grief," *Electronic Intifada*, June 30, 2021, https://electronicintifada.net/content/carrying-palestines-grief/33501.

15. Ereikat, "Carrying Palestine's Grief."

16. "The Dignity and Hope Manifesto," *Mondoweiss*, May 18, 2021, https://mondoweiss.net/2021/05/the-manifesto-of-dignity-and-hope.

17. "Dignity and Hope Manifesto."

18. "Dignity and Hope Manifesto."

19. "Dignity and Hope Manifesto."

20. Ereikat, "Carrying Palestine's Grief."

21. Ereikat, "Carrying Palestine's Grief."

22. Malkia Devich-Cyril, "Grief Belongs in Social Movements. Can We Embrace It?" *In These Times*, July 28, 2021, https://inthesetimes.com/article/freedom-grief-healing-death-liberation-movements, excerpted in *Holding Change: The Way of Emergent Strategy Facilitation and Mediation*, by adrienne maree brown (Chico, CA: AK Press, 2021).

23. Joanna Macy and Chris Johnstone, *Active Hope: How to Face the Mess We're in with Unexpected Resilience and Creative Power* (Novato, CA: New World Library, 2022), 203.

24. Lee Sandusky, "Dust of the Desert," in *Rebellious Mourning: The Collective Work of Grief*, ed. Cindy Milstein (Oakland, CA: AK Press, 2017), 23.

25. Sandusky, "Dust of the Desert," 29.

26. Richard Avedon and James Baldwin, *Nothing Personal* (Cologne, Germany: Taschen, 2017), 49–50.

Chapter 9: Organizing Isn't Matchmaking

1. Kelly Hayes and Ejeris Dixon, "'We Surrender Nothing and No One': A Playbook for Solidarity amid Fascist Terror," *Truthout*, June 5, 2020, https://truthout.org/audio/we-surrender-nothing-and-no-one-a-

playbook-for-solidarity-amid-fascist-terror.

2. Freire, *Pedagogy of the Oppressed*, 24.

3. Freire, *Pedagogy of the Oppressed*, 62.

4. Freire, *Pedagogy of the Oppressed*, 68.

5. Project NIA, *"Giving Name to the Nameless": Using Poetry as an Anti-Violence Intervention with Girls*, https://givingname.wordpress.com.

Chapter 10: Avoiding Burnout and Going the Distance

1. Kelly Hayes, "Dean Spade Is Asking Activists, 'How Much Bolder Could You Be?'" *Truthout, March 17, 2022, https://truthout.org/audio/dean-spade-is-asking-activists-how-much-bolder-could-you-be*.

2. See Leah Lakshmi Piepzna-Samarasinha, *Care Work: Dreaming Disability Justice* (Vancouver, British Columbia: Arsenal Pulp Press, 2018).

3. Kelly Hayes, "From Burnout to Breakthroughs, Weary Organizers Can Come Back Stronger," *Truthout,* October 14, 2021, https://truthout.org/audio/from-burnout-to-breakthroughs-weary-organizers-can-come-back-stronger.

4. Hayes, "Burnout to Breakthroughs."

5. Hayes, "Burnout to Breakthroughs."

6. Hayes, "Burnout to Breakthroughs."

7. Kelly Hayes, "Hope Is Not a Given. We Must Cultivate It Together," *Truthout,* May 26, 2022, https://truthout.org/audio/hope-is-not-a-given-we-must-cultivate-it-together.

Conclusion: Relationships, Reciprocity, and Struggle

1. Carrie Maxwell, "Activists Gather outside Pritzker's Home, Call for Lesbian Prisoner Bernina Mata's Release," *Windy City Times,* December 12, 2022, https://www.windycitytimes.com/lgbt/Activists-gather-outside-Pritzkers-home-call-for-lesbian-prisoner-Bernina-Matas-release-/74493.html.

2. John Jost, *A Theory of System Justification* (Cambridge, MA: Harvard University Press, 2020), 2, 8, 62.

3. Robyn Maynard and Leanne Betasamosake Simpson, *Rehearsals for Living*, Abolitionist Papers (Chicago: Haymarket Books, 2022), 44.

Conclusion: Beyond Doom, toward Collective Action

1. James Baldwin, "Why I Stopped Hating Shakespeare," excerpt from *The Cross of Redemption*, ed. Randall Kenan (New York: Penguin Random House, 2010), originally reprinted in the *Observer*, April 19, 1964, available at https://www.penguinrandomhouse.ca/books/7754/the-cross-of-redemption-by-james-baldwin-edited-with-an-introduction-by-randall-kenan/9780307275967/excerpt.

2. Dennis Brutus, "Untitled Poem from a South African Writer in Exile," *Christian Science Monitor*, November 9, 1987, https://www.csmonitor.com/1987/1109/ubrut.html, from Dennis Brutus, *A Simple Lust: Collected Poems of South African Jail and Exile* (London: Heinemann, 1973), reprinted by permission.

3. Desmond Tutu, *Believe: The Words and Inspiration of Desmond Tutu* (Boulder, CO: Blue Mountain Press, 2007), 3, 5.

4. Ram Dass, "Being Love," n.d., https://www.ramdass.org/being-love.

5. Mark Ward, "Sermon: Waking to the Work," Unitarian Universalist Congregation of Asheville, November 14, 2016, https://uuasheville.org/sermon-waking-to-the-work.

6. Dionne Brand, "I Have Been Losing Roads," in *Nomenclature: New and Collected Poems* (Durham, NC: Duke University Press, 2022), 271.

7. See Ellen Cantarow, *Moving the Mountain: Women Working for Social Change* (New York: Feminist Press, 1980), 93.

8. Desmond Tutu, *God Has a Dream: A Vision of Hope for Our Time*, repr. ed. (New York: Image, 2005), 68.

9. Octavia Butler, *Parable of the Sower* (New York: Four Walls Eight Windows, 1993), 3.

10. Julian Randal, "True Story: Eve L. Ewing Revisits the Deadly Riots of 1919," *Poetry Foundation*, June 17, 2019, https://www.poetryfoundation.org/articles/150310/true-story.

11. B Loewe, "I'm ending the year remembering that Organizing works," Facebook, December 31, 2021, https://www.facebook.com/bjustb.loewe/posts/10159692833789621.

12. Maria Popoca, "Anna Deveare Smith on Discipline and Learning to Stop Letting Others Define You," *Marginalian*, June 16, 2014, https://www.themarginalian.org/2014/06/16/anna-deveare-smith-discipline.

13. Henry A. Giroux, "Amid Apocalyptic Cynicism, Let's Embrace

Radical Hope in the New Year," *Truthout*, January 5, 2022, https://truthout.org/articles/amid-apocalyptic-cynicism-lets-embrace-radical-hope-in-the-new-year.

14. Rebecca Solnit, *Hope in the Dark: Untold Histories, Wild Possibilities* (Chicago: Haymarket Books, 2016), xviii.

Afterword: Movements Make Life

1. Howard Zinn, *You Can't Be Neutral on a Moving Train: A Personal History of Our Times* (Boston: Beacon Press, 1994), 208.
2. Ruth Wilson Gilmore, "Abolition on Stolen Land" (lecture, UCLA Luskin Institute on Inequality and Democracy, via videoconference, October 9, 2020).

Glossary

1. Talila Lewis, "Working Definition of Ableism—January 2022 Update," January 1, 2022, https://www.talilalewis.com/blog.
2. Cara Page, "Reflections from Detroit: Transforming Wellness and Wholeness," INCITE!, August 5, 2010, https://incite-national.org/2010/08/05/reflections-from-detroit-transforming-wellness-wholeness.
3. Critical Resistance, "What Is the PIC? What Is Abolition?" https://criticalresistance.org/mission-vision/not-so-common-language.

INDEX

ABOUT HAYMARKET BOOKS

Haymarket Books is a radical, independent, nonprofit book publisher based in Chicago. Our mission is to publish books that contribute to struggles for social and economic justice. We strive to make our books a vibrant and organic part of social movements and the education and development of a critical, engaged, and internationalist Left.

We take inspiration and courage from our namesakes, the Haymarket Martyrs, who gave their lives fighting for a better world. Their 1886 struggle for the eight-hour day—which gave us May Day, the international workers' holiday—reminds workers around the world that ordinary people can organize and struggle for their own liberation. These struggles—against oppression, exploitation, environmental devastation, and war—continue today across the globe.

Since our founding in 2001, Haymarket has published more than nine hundred titles. Radically independent, we seek to drive a wedge into the risk-averse world of corporate book publishing. Our authors include Angela Y. Davis, Arundhati Roy, Keeanga-Yamahtta Taylor, Eve L. Ewing, Aja Monet, Mariame Kaba, Naomi Klein, Rebecca Solnit, Olúfẹ́mi O. Táíwò, Mohammed El-Kurd, José Olivarez, Noam Chomsky, Winona LaDuke, Robyn Maynard, Leanne Betasamosake Simpson, Howard Zinn, Mike Davis, Marc Lamont Hill, Dave Zirin, Astra Taylor, and Amy Goodman, among many other leading writers of our time. We are also the trade publishers of the acclaimed Historical Materialism Book Series.

Haymarket also manages a vibrant community organizing and event space in Chicago, Haymarket House, the popular Haymarket Books Live event series and podcast, and the annual Socialism Conference.

ALSO AVAILABLE FROM HAYMARKET BOOKS

Abolition Feminisms Vol. 1
Organizing, Survival, and Transformative Practice
Edited by Alisa Bierria, Jakeya Caruthers, and Brooke Lober
Foreword by Dean Spade

Abolition Feminisms Vol. 2
Feminist Ruptures against the Carceral State
Edited by Alisa Bierria, Jakeya Caruthers, and Brooke Lober

Border and Rule
Global Migration, Capitalism, and the Rise of Racist Nationalism
Harsha Walia
Foreword by Robin D. G. Kelley, afterword by Nick Estes

Elite Capture: How the Powerful Took Over Identity Politics
(And Everything Else)
by Olúfẹ́mi O. Táíwò

Lifting As They Climbed
Mapping a History of Trailblazing Black Women in Chicago
Mariame Kaba and Essence McDowell

Missing Daddy
Mariame Kaba, illustrated by bria royal

Saving Our Own Lives: A Liberatory Practice of Harm Reduction
Shira Hassan
Foreword by adrienne maree brown, introduction by Tourmaline

See You Soon
Mariame Kaba, illustrated by Bianca Diaz

ABOUT THE AUTHORS

Mariame Kaba is an organizer, educator, curator, and prison-industrial-complex abolitionist who is active in movements for racial, gender, and transformative justice. Kaba is the founder and director of Project NIA, a grassroots abolitionist organization with a vision to end youth incarceration. Mariame is a researcher at Interrupting Criminalization, a project she cofounded with Andrea Ritchie in 2018.

Kaba is the author of the *New York Times* bestseller *We Do This 'Til We Free Us: Abolitionist Organizing and Transforming Justice* (Haymarket Books, 2021); *Missing Daddy* (Haymarket Books, 2019); *Fumbling Towards Repair: A Workbook for Community Accountability Faciltators* coauthored with Shira Hassan (Project NIA, 2019); *See You Soon* (Haymarket Books, 2022); and *No More Police: A Case for Abolition* coauthored with Andrea Ritchie (New Press, 2022).

Kelly Hayes is a Menominee author, organizer, movement educator, and photographer. She is also the host of *Truthout*'s podcast *Movement Memos*. Hayes is a cofounder of the Lifted Voices collective and the Chicago Light Brigade. Her written work is featured in numerous publications and multiple anthologies, including *Who Do You Serve, Who Do You Protect? Police Violence and Resistance in the United States* (Haymarket Books, 2016), *Education in Movement Spaces: Standing Rock to Chicago Freedom Square* (Routledge, 2020), and *The Solidarity Struggle: How People of Color Succeed and Fail at Showing Up for Each Other in the Fight for Freedom* (BGD Press, 2016). Hayes also coauthored an essay with Mariame Kaba in Kaba's book *We Do This 'Til We Free Us: Abolitionist Organizing and Transforming Justice* (Haymarket Books, 2021). Hayes's movement photography is featured in the *Freedom and Resistance* exhibit of the DuSable Museum of African American History.